When the Music Stopped

Discovering My Mother

THOMAS J. COTTLE

STATE UNIVERSITY OF NEW YORK PRESS

Published by
State University of New York Press, Albany

© 2004 State University of New York

Printed in the United States of America

For information, address State University of New York Press,
90 State Street, Suite 700, Albany, NY 12207

Production by Judith Block
Marketing by Fran Keneston

Library of Congress Cataloging-in-Publication Data

Cottle, Thomas J.
  When the music stopped : discovering my mother / Thomas J. Cottle.
    p. cm.
  Includes bibliographical references.
  ISBN 0-7914-5997 (hardcover : alk. paper)—ISBN 0-7914-5998-5 (pbk. : alk. paper)
  1. Gradova, Gitta, 1904–1985. 2. Pianists—Biography. I. Title.

ML417.G69C67   2004
786.2'092—dc22
[B]
                                                                2003066186

10 9 8 7 6 5 4 3

Music resembles poetry; in each
Are nameless graces, which no methods teach,
And which a master hand alone may reach.
　　　　　　　　—Alexander Pope, 1709

. . . the true nature of music: is it a sensual joy on the same
order as gastronomy, or in essence a veiled art, born of a dream,
a reminiscence of the great unconscious universe?
　　　　　　　—Marc Pincherle, *The World of the Virtuoso*

The hand reaches and extends, receives and welcomes–and not
just things: the hand extends itself, and receives its own welcome
in the hands of others. The hand holds. The hand carries. The
hand designs and signs, presumably because man is a sign . . . the
hand's gestures run everywhere through language, in their most
perfect purity precisely when man speaks by being silent . . .
Every motion of the hand in everyone of its works carries itself
through the element of thinking, every bearing of the hand bears
itself in that element.

　　　　　　　　　　　　　—Martin Heidegger

Love thinks only in sweet sound
For ideas are too far;
All that love cares to reveal
Only music may surround
　　　　　　　—Tieck

Most people use music as a couch; they want to be pillowed on
it, relaxed and consoled for the stress of daily living. But serious
music was never meant to be a soporific.
　　　　　　　—Aaron Copland, *In Praise of Music*

When I but hear her sing, I fare
Like one that, raised, holds his ear
To some bright star in the supremest round;
Through which, besides the light that's seen,
There may be heard, from heaven within,
The rest of the anthems that the angels sound.
—Owen Felltham, "Upon a Rare Voice," *In Praise of Music*

To Gitta Gradova Cottle
and Maurice H. Cottle,
my parents

Contents

Preface

―――――――⟨≈⟩―――――――

Anyone who has written biographies and memoirs knows the pitfalls of what James Boswell called this "presumptuous task." To begin, it almost cannot be done without a willingness to pry into the lives of our subjects, not to mention our own. Katherine Powers is right when she says "nothing can be done about this trampling of privacy." Perhaps the most precarious ledge in enterprises of this sort, however, is the age-old theme of the child of a significant figure, a celebrity perhaps, deciding it is time to kiss and tell the inside story of someone many admire, or lament the insignificance of one's own life growing up in the shadow of a giant, either idealized, as in the case of some memoirs, or despised, as in the case of a few others.

Mercifully, my mother's name was not a household word, like Philco, as she would have quipped, which liberates me; whatever gossip I could unearth would be of interest to no one. Besides, there wasn't much gossip. The story of her life is far more substantial than any compilation of items of gossip. More intriguing was the task of not only telling her story—or is it our story?—but at the same time gaining some appreciation for the life of the child prodigy, a pianist in my mother's case, whose career was launched practically before she even entered formal schooling, and who ascended to the top of her profession at the very hour most of us are attending high school or commencing our first jobs. In the end, this is a woman's story set in the first half of the last century, in a culture that transmitted powerful values regarding the role of women performing artists, especially those whose careers, by necessity, took them away from their families.

Because she was a renowned concert pianist, there was in fact a rather large amount of public information about my mother to be culled from a variety of sources, her own memorabilia among them.[1] Unfortunately, as many of the people of her generation, mainly her professional colleagues, had passed away, an invaluable realm of information was lost to me. There are, of course, an infinite number of books about music, and specifically on pianoforte, which offered all sorts of perspectives and insights. Most of the citations from the musical literature found in this volume are taken from books once housed in my mother's own library. In some cases, I can only assume she read what I read. In other cases, however, I have cited passages that she had either underlined, or on which she had commented in the margins.

All biographers, I am certain, long to interview the subject of their work, and many, of course, are fortunate enough to be studying someone still alive. In my own case, this particular project came a tad too late; the critical interview was never conducted. As someone who has essentially based his entire sociological and psychological research, not to mention his clinical practice, on interviews and conversations, it is ironic that the one person whom I should have interviewed slipped away before I was ready. Charles M. Olin and Steven Heliotes, however, in fact were prepared to converse with her. Therefore, portions of their tape-recorded interviews appear throughout the book. I am deeply grateful to both men, not to mention envious of them as well.

Yet another dangerous ledge for biographers is the temptation to reduce someone's life, someone's entire psychological world, to one theory or ideology. But documenting preconceptions is not what the biographical endeavor must be about. The ultimate challenge is to develop an appreciation for another person's interior world, and then understand how this interior world has been shaped by a culture and the significant figures and events in that person's life. How easy it would be to develop a single reason, a single, linear explanation for a woman's entire life, replete as it was in my mother's case, with utter joy and consummate anguish. Conversely, how difficult it is to conclude that in the end, one can barely approximate what philosophers call "otherness," the form and substance of another's self, that part of their selves they give to us, or we, impertinently, imagine that we take from them.

I think it fair to say that much of my self is constituted of the self of my mother. Martin Heidegger was right, I believe: we don't *have* relationships as much as we *are* relationships. People literally live within us not only in the form of our recollections and memories, but also as the stuff of our selves, and our souls. For years I have scoffed at the notion that my mother, in the words of some, would always "be there for me." Sitting at my desk one morning several weeks after her death, a blue jay commenced building its nest in the yew tree outside my office window. In almost fifteen years of living in our house, no bird had ever selected this site. How tempting to imagine that this was my mother, transfigured, returning to the earth if only to look out for all of us, or, perhaps, spy on me.

But no magical thinking is required if one subscribes to the Heideggerian dictum: for good or bad, our parents form much of our selves, and the constructions for which they are responsible never leave us. Granted, other people, too, construct scaffolds for our selves, just as we ourselves construct scaffolds. Yet the original ones, what I jokingly call "(m)otherness," never disappear. They are only transcended, if in fact we wish to undertake the work that this brand of transcendence requires. Not so incidentally, one bird or another has continued to return to the bushy yew tree every year since my mother's death, but I have concluded that those counselors who spoke about parents "always being there" were correct. She's here, not in the nest, but in my self, and hopefully too, in these pages.

A word of explanation. According to family therapists, the youngest child is normally the one who becomes the family's informant and chonicler. I am the youngest of two children, and my sister, thankfully, is still alive. I have checked many facts and recollections with her, and she has been profoundly helpful and supportive. In projects of this sort, one cannot predict how a sibling might respond. Judy may well have disparaged the work, claiming it was no one's business to talk about our family. But she never said this. Equally significant, acknowledging that my story is necessarily colored by the lenses developed in childhood, I have felt from the outset that Judy's story is not mine to tell. How she remembers and feels about our parents could not be a part of this personal reflection. Which means that my sister, a genuinely substantial figure, plays only a minor role in these pages.

The origin of this book lies, actually, in the words of two dear friends. Almost as a dare, the psychiatrist Salvador Minuchin informed me that he was writing an autobiography and suggested that I write one as well, but I demurred. Then again, I said, my mother's life may well be worthy of such an exploration. Upon hearing of the proposed book, the educator Sara Lawrence-Lightfoot at once replied, "It's about time!" Sara was referring to the fact that as long as she has known me, she has recognized how important, yet complex, the figure of my mother is in my own life, a woman she had met, actually, on several occasions.

There is no way that I could possibly list all the people who should be acknowledged for their help in writing this book, Salvador and Patricia Minuchin and Sara Lawrence-Lightfoot being the literary parents, my sister, Judith Kreston Lahm and my wife, Kay Cottle, my primary counselors. Several other individuals must be singled out for their support. Robert and Gail Melson, Richard and Anne Rosenfeld, Gerald Platt, Jeffrey Berman, David Cohn, Judith Tick, Don Kaplan, Jack Jackson, Patricia Coan, H. George Mann, Anthony Shafton, Gary and Naomi Graffman, and my colleagues at Boston University, most notably in this one instance, Michael Shavelson, Victor Kestenbaum, Alan Gaynor, David Steiner, Gerald Fain, Roselmina Indrisano, Donna Lehr, Sandra DiIeso, Leadie Wales, Steven Ellenwood, Arthur Beane, and Bruce Fraser, plus a host of good people who were willing merely to listen to me talk about my mother. At the State University of New York Press, special thanks must go to my editor Jane Bunker, an earlier reader, Lenore Langsdorf, Katy Leonard, Judith Block, and Fran Keneston.

The volume's "co-authors" are the people who appear in these pages, notably those family members who played a direct role in raising me, and the professional colleagues and friends of my parents who were the actors in the drama I have sought to describe. I wouldn't begin to know how to thank all of these people, some of whom never knew how much they meant to me. One of them, the late Isaac Stern, my adopted godfather, although he does appear in the book, must be mentioned in this section of acknowledgments. Like many of the others, he, too, saved lives.

Finally, there is my family: my wife Kay, our three children, Claudia, Jason, and Sonya, our number two son, Tony Hinz (my mother never liked the in-law label), and our grandchildren, Luke Thomas Hinz, Nicole Kate Hinz, and Anna Carey Hinz. And finally, there is my mother, Gitta Gradova Cottle, my father, Maurice H. Cottle, my brother David Lahm, my niece Elizabeth Shankin, my cousins Howard L. Wilder, Raymond Sawyer, William Cottle, and Richard W. Cottle, and the one aunt I always mention, Miss Leah Weinstock, because she loved and protected me.

I believe that Leah would like this book, and I think my father would too. As I say, Judy approves, which leaves just one person. I truthfully don't know how my mother would have reacted to these reflections and interpretations. I imagine her dressed in black flannel slacks and a baby blue sweater. She is lying on her bed, her head propped up on pillows, a small blanket thrown over her feet. I am sitting in the easy chair at the end of the bed when at last she puts the book down and removes her tortoise shell glasses. For an instant she looks at me with an expression I cannot discern, and then she begins to speak, as only she could speak.

"Well, Tommy, this is quite something, isn't it? This is . . ."

Then, before she can utter another word I say the words I never spoke aloud to her: "I love you, Mom."

It is about time.

Hawthorne Place

For more than forty years they remained together, touching, each incomplete without the other, together forming something beautiful that neither alone could achieve. Now, for almost two decades, they have sat apart in a basement "junk" room, collecting dirt and anything else that might be strewn upon them: A sleeping bag, several milk cartons, an old print that needs reframing, a pair of shriveled brown panty hose, a mildewed shower curtain, a small hand vacuum cleaner, and a black canvas overnight bag. So much stuff one can barely see them, much less sit upon them, the two sections of my mother's couch.

Ironically, as I think about the symbolism of the couch being something I can't live with or without, I fear that it actually may now be impossible to remove it from the junk room. Two doors lead into this space. The door from the body of the house is conspicuously narrow; there is no way the couch could get through this portal. The other door leads into what used to be a garage, but during a remodeling of that space, the door frame through which the couch originally entered the house was narrowed, and hence, it, too, may not be able to accommodate the couch's removal.

From time to time, I think what my mother might say if she saw her once treasured piece of furniture sitting so ignobly. She would say, and she would mean it: "You have made such a loving, beautiful home for yourselves and your children. What do you need an old war-horse like that for anyway? Get rid of it! Get rid of everything you don't need. It's only going to be a burden for you and your children someday. Make yourself happy. You deserve it." She would definitely have used the term "war-horse," the same term she used for describing the giant piano concertos of Beethoven, Brahms, Saint-Saëns, Dvorak, Liszt, Tchaikovsky, and Rachmaninoff.

They were meant to stand end to end, ten full feet of sofa, the one section with the arm curved to the right, the other with the arm curved to the left, yielding an impressive sweep that stood at the end of our living room in the house on Hawthorne Place, a street on Chicago's north side, just off Lake Shore Drive. Dramatically, the sofa rested in the front bay window which practically embraced it and provided a bench on which stood a carved wooden Chinese figure of a bodhisattva, almost five feet high; the statue served to protect, I always imagined, anyone fortunate enough to sit upon the couch. What a vantage point a seat on the couch offered: From here one could peer across the expanse of the living room to the music room, a space separated from the living room by tall mahogany Doric columns.

At the ends of the couch were matching mahogany tables on which stood lamps with bases of slender wooden Japanese maidens. In front of the couch was a coffee table, its surface covered with a tan leather-like material. A wood-turned structure, the table's legs were actually its surface now curled under itself. Ash trays and a candy dish always sat on the coffee table. Given its design and surface covering, one knew this was not a place to park one's legs. Matching armchairs were positioned to face one another at the ends of the table.

The interior of the brown brick house was truly handsome. Even as a small child I recognized this. The high-decorated ceilings and tall doorways added to the elegance of the rooms. Much of the decor was the work of a man by the name of Harold Walsh, a fit man with horned-rimmed glasses, his dark hair always combed straight back to reveal a smooth, curved forehead. Mr. Walsh, who always appeared to be sporting a tan, was the first person I ever saw wear light tan and khaki colored suits with sky-blue shirts, colorful ties, and saddle-brown loafers with tassels. He was also the first man I ever heard use the word "swatch." In fact, he brought a lot of swatches for my parents to inspect. Every chair fabric was selected by Harold Walsh, as was the fabric that covered my mother's couch. Mr. Walsh also selected the colors for walls, ceilings, and alcoves. At the proposal stage, I couldn't for the life of me see how he narrowed down his choices. *That* blue was to be the ceiling of the living room? And *that* lavender was going in the dining room? What was wrong with white? And yet, when the rooms were completed, the colors proved surprisingly perfect. And Mr. Walsh would ask me, "Do you like it, Tommy?" I'm sure I nodded yes.

I rarely sat on my mother's couch, the magnificent view notwithstanding. When, as a child, I sat in the living room, an occurrence that normally meant important guests had arrived and my sister and I were expected to spend time with them, I sat in one of the striped matching chairs facing each other down the length of the coffee table. More specifically, I sat on the chair nearest the entrance hall as if unconsciously I wished to be near the exit. From this location, I could look out the window facing east toward the Johnson's house, a pink brick home with cream-colored window trim that essentially blocked our view of Lake Michigan. All of this, of course, was before houses like the Johnson's were razed and giant apartment buildings constructed. On second thought, it probably wasn't an unconscious decision to sit in the chair nearest the entrance hall.

Actually, there was one spot on the couch where, on occasion, I would sit if only to enjoy a particularly silly experience. Ideally, the places to sit were at the two ends where the curve of the arms commenced. Where the couches met, and they narrowed slightly at this juncture, was the least ideal position, as invariably one felt the joint beneath them. I never sat on the joint when I didn't experience the image of being on a toilet. I imagine everyone conjured this sensation, just as they probably imagined that the couches could suddenly separate and they would fall through.

Everything about the couch makes me think of my mother. Even the reference to sitting on "the crack," as I called it, reminds me of her telling us that when sitting on a toilet she always feared a rat was going to rise up out of the sewer and bite her tushy. She told this and other tales as well to children and adults alike, many of whom sat on that very couch. If there were a party of three hundred and fifty people, ranging in age from two to a hundred, the one person everyone would remember would be my mother, Gitta Gradova, a concert pianist and an artist capable of expressing the deepest emotions and moods, both in her language and through her fingers. My mother was the last of seven surviving children, and the most gifted, and complex. All the members of her family believed this to be true. James Francis Cooke's remark about magnetism being "one of the most enviable possessions of the successful pianist,"[1] surely applied to my mother.

Idealization or not, no one for me ever possessed her charm, her dazzling talent for storytelling, her compelling style and wit, and her unique intensity when it came to attitudes and judgments. A

Boston critic writing in 1924 had no idea how accurately he described my mother, both on and off the concert platform: "Miss Gradova gave ample evidence that she is a brilliant technician with a gift for eloquent expression, via the piano. . . . Sensuous and introspective, she scales the heights and plumbs the depths of emotional expression. There is no middle ground for her. The emphasis of understatement is a virtue alien to her spirit . . ."[2] And from *The Musical Leader:* "In order to do justice to this brilliant young woman and to know how varied are her gifts it was necessary to hear the program in its entirety, for she is a creature of moods . . ." Not so incidentally, this author goes on to say: ". . . she now takes her place with the best of the young coterie of brilliant artists."

In another context, but applicable to my mother as well, Cecil Smith, wrote: "Extreme individualism is the source of nearly every artist's inner compulsion."[3] Life and death, seemingly, hung in the balance of every decision, every utterance made by my mother. When my mother was downcast she was intensely downcast, when she was angry, she was intensely angry, and when she was disappointed, she appeared intensely disappointed. This also meant that when she was happy, especially when guests filled the living room and sat upon her couch, she was not only intensely happy, but magically so.

No one offered insights with humor and acuity like my mother. On judging others, she often intoned: "People who live in glass houses shouldn't take baths." Regarding a room that suffocated her: "It was so small you had to go outside to change your mind." On couples who seemed a trifle too intimate: "Beware of people who hold hands all the time. If they ever let go, they'll kill each other." On teaching a piano student the subtlety of successive trills she advised: "The first says life is terribly sad. The second one says, I told you so." Her Yiddish transposition of Kipling's famous line, "You're a better man than I am Gunga Din," became "You're a better man than I am, Jake Levin." Then there was her advice to people ambivalent about unexpected guests: Always wear a coat and a hat in the house. That way, if you like who just arrived, you can announce: "Oh, great, I was just coming in." And if you don't like them you can say: "Sorry, I was just on my way out." For reasons of safety, my mother often claimed she answered the door while simultaneously attempting to quiet our three ferocious German shepherd watchdogs; it was enough to scare off any stranger or delivery boy. So what if in reality the family's pet was a docile dalmatian who slept all day beneath the pantry sink rarely rising at the sound of the doorbell? And, of course, her spontaneous reactions and quips: If, for example, a guest, while admiring one of her photographs set on the piano, accidentally knocked it over she would say, "Don't bother, I only live here." "Gitta, darling," she might have been asked, "what year were the Horowitzes married?" "Too soon!" And her musing about a famous conductor, "I thought Fritz was born in Hungary—then why does he speak with an accent if he was born in America? He even conducts with an accent!"

No one could tell stories like my mother. You could hear the same story a hundred times and still be enthralled. As her child I would groan, "Not again," but inside I knew these dramatic moments were delectable. It was said that in the 1940s and 1950s, the greatest storyteller in Chicago was a man by the name of Mort Cooper who owned a downtown Chicago men's clothing store. In fact, there was an occasion when I heard Mr. Cooper at his best. He was sensational, his stories hysterical, his gift for recounting fantastic. But Mort Cooper couldn't hold a candle to my mother. Her accents and subtleties of presentation, the incongruity of an elegantly dressed and coifed woman telling barely off-color stories with several dialects was sublime. With deadpan face, she begins:

A couple is having their house painted. One night the husband comes home and puts his hand on the wall which, of course, is still wet with fresh paint.

"*Oi, Guttenu,*" the woman groans.

Of course she has a Yiddish accent.

"You couldn't keep the hand in the pants?"

"What's the big deal?" comes the husband's response in a distinctly different dialect. "Tomorrow, the painter he'll come, he'll touch up. That's what painters do, they touch up."

The guests in the living room are already coughing from all the laughing. My mother is still in character.

Nu, the next day the painter comes.

"Paintner," the woman greets him, "you'll come with me because I want you should see where last night mine husband put his hand."

"Lady," says the painter, "I'm an old man. I'll settle for a cup of coffee."

How many times did I hear that joke and feel the same sensations: slight embarrassment and utter amusement. I heard Peter Ustinov at a party at the home of our family's dear friends, Edward and Ruth Weiss, who lived across the street on Hawthorne Place. Ustinov regaled the guests with a convoluted story I can no longer recall about a one-legged, one-eyed Egyptian conductor. Until hearing Ustinov, I had never heard a storyteller as good as my mother.

No one, moreover, enjoyed hearing stories as much as my mother. Best of all were the true accounts of people laced with humor, or the hilarious idioms and malapropisms that friends displayed, or that she merely overheard, like the woman in the lobby swooning over the Third Piano Concerto not of Sergei Prokofiev, but of Serge Prokafyoo. And what was tastier than a friend, having just returned from Italy, raving about the food?

"Where did you eat?" my mother only naturally wanted to know.

"I can't remember the names," she was told, "but they were all in the Italian district."

Mrs. Wingerhoff, Ruth Weiss's mother, regularly put forth the sort of verbal errors my mother adored. "It was raining so hard," Mrs. Wingerhoff once told her daughter, "the woman was strangled in the doorway." There was the occasion that a woman got dressed up to the nines and "looked absolutely gorgeous from her heels to her toes." But the best was Mrs. Wingerhoff asking Ruth for a "Kleenec."

"You mean Kleenex, mother."

"No, Ruthie," Mrs. Wingerhoff replied, "I only need one."

Then there were the impressions of people. Given my mother's musical ear, it wasn't surprising that she could capture voices, inflections, and idiosyncrasies that would escape the eye and ear of the average person. One of her many "targets" was the violinist Mischa Elman, a pleasant man who reminded me of Santa Claus; he spoke with a distinctive high-pitched, crackling voice, and a Russian accent to boot. Elman, a man thirteen years my mother's senior, was the most famous prodigy of his generation; he was known internationally by the time he was sixteen. My mother had him to a tee, an act that brought tears to the eyes of family friends who had heard Elman speak.

Then one night, Mischa Elman, who was dining in our home, announced that he understood my mother could do an impression of him.

"No, no," she demurred, "not true."

"Come on, Gitta," he persisted.

"No, really," she refused him again, and once again he pursued her.

Suddenly, she protested in his high-pitched voice. The transition had been so seamless, Elman himself hadn't recognized it. So for an instant the two voices of Mischa Elman were having an argument at our dinner table. When he realized what she was doing, he was flabbergasted but enthralled. He loved it. He loved her. He even informed my father that Gitta was really a great talent, as if my father didn't know.

"Mischa," my mother told him, still in his voice, "*everyone does you!*"

Her stories and impressions invariably left their mark on others, for this was an extremely clever and insightful woman with a rare comedic sense.

Emil Horween, another dear friend of the family, is sitting at the dining room table late one evening enthralled by a dream he is recounting. Indeed, as the narrative of the dream unfolds, it appears that he is within a reverie reliving the events as if they were taking place in the moment.

An amateur violinist and member of my father's chamber music group, Emil has dreamed that he has not only played one violin concerto at Carnegie Hall, but he has played two concertos. Dear, sweet Emil is immersed in the description of the applause, the standing ovation, the clamoring for his autograph in the green room, and the unbelievable reviews. One can see that really he is "there," experiencing it all, when I hear my mother say quietly, and respectfully, "Did you get our flowers?"

My mother was a child prodigy, a pianist of extraordinary talent and strength; a great number of reviews pointed to that strength. In an age when feminism had not quite caught the public consciousness, no one batted an eye when reading words like, "Gitta Gradova plays like a man." When she died, almost nineteen years ago, I remember the words of the obituary writer of one of Chicago's prestigious newspapers. "Do you have any idea who your mother was? How famous she was? How accomplished she was?" the man with a youngish voice asked, clearly stunned that his daily mundane chore of rounding up information about the "recently departed" had suddenly turned into a glorious assignment. "Of course," I responded.

"But whatever you write," I admonished him, with a peculiar sense of anger, dare I say intensity, "there is to be nothing like, 'she played like a man.'"

She did play with amazing force, however, along with great technique, something she always dismissed, for she taught that the technique was merely the obvious means to an end, namely, the creation of something beautiful. Listening to her one would have to agree with Carl Engel's poetic remark: "It would seem that instinct leads the hand, and that the hand awakens the ear."[4] As her friend and colleague, the pianist Josef Hofmann wrote:

> . . . a technic without a musical will is a faculty without a purpose, and when it becomes a purpose in itself it can never serve art. . . . To transform the purely technical and material processes into a thing that lives, of course, rests with those many and complex qualities which are usually summarized (*sic*) by the term "talent," but this must be presupposed with a player who aspires to artistic work.[5]

Technique for my mother was a given in the sense that one worked on it again and again. Yet, she understood, as John Redfield wrote, that it was "little more than the alphabet of interpretive musical art."[6] In Adolph Kullak's *The Aesthetics of Pianoforte-Playing*, published in 1893, my mother underlined this passage:

> Mechanical training is the primary and indispensable condition of pianoforte playing. To the spirit of the same it stands in just the same relation, as the form to the substance, i.e., it is in itself, precisely like the substance, the Whole and differs from it only from the point of view of another mode of contemplation, with which the observant understanding confronts the work of art.[7]

"The piano," according to Michelle Krisel, "that nearly ubiquitous symbol of middle-class aspirations, is second only perhaps to the bed, the most symbolic piece of furniture in the home. It is not only noisy with music, but even when it lays silent, it sings of our dreams and disappointments. . . . To open the door and see the piano in the living room is to come home."[8] Technically speaking, in my mother's case, two Steinway pianos sat, not in the living room but in the music room curve to curve, as two pianos often do so that the pianists may look at one another. A bay window in the music area provided a bench for hundreds of pieces of sheet music.

Never conceiving of her playing as noisy or invasive, but as comforting, actually, I have vivid recollections of her commencing her daily practice sessions. Having first adjusted the height of the piano stool by turning the smooth black knobs on the ends, she then carefully removed her two slim gold wedding bands, placing them on the shelf of the piano. Then the familiar finger exercises commenced and gradually a series of warm-up exercises that were constituted by her composing a rhapsodic, lyrical, and always romantic piece of music that came from heaven only knows where. A phrase would be repeated only if her fingers betrayed her, or she might momentarily return to some elemental finger dexterity exercise. Evidently, she agreed with James Francis Cooke: "To one whose individuality is marred by carelessness, let me recommend very slow playing, with the most minute attention to detail. Technically speaking, Czerny and Bach are of great value in correcting carelessness."[9] Czerny and Bach were indeed in evidence during the dexterity portions of the practice sessions, as my mother believed, along with Daniel Gregory Mason, that Bach was forever modern: ". . . and perhaps most of all it is modern in its inexorable logic, its subtlety and variety, and in its poignant, deeply emotional expressiveness, which is always held within the bounds necessary to supreme architectural beauty."[10] Bach's music, Neville Cardus observed, "was persistently seeking to inflame our imaginations with dramatic and pictorial suggestions . . ."[11] In my mother's own words: "Each concert I give stands out as a big event in my life; I imagine that it is a great religous rite I am about to perform—to take the silent pages of the great Bach and recreate them."[12] Speaking with the critic Eugene Stinson, my mother, twenty at the time, reported:

> But the greatest of all is Bach. He dwells on the heights. His subtle intellectual analysis exceeds anything other writers have achieved. He is not purely emotional, neither is he wholly cold and concise as so many pianists have portrayed him. I shall play his "Italian" Concerto next season. It will be a new interpretation, I believe. It will be a softer Bach, not a composer who seems to say, "See, here is my cold logic," for me that is not the way his music appeals to me. But at least it will show the public that I am not a "one-composer artist."[13]

After minutes of being inflamed by Bach, however, she returned to the mystical concerto.

I often listened to her practice, but I never wanted to communicate to her that I enjoyed listening. Realizing that I did, however, she played my favorite Scriabin, Chopin, Liszt, and Scarlatti pieces, or she would sing foolish ditties she knew would make me laugh. To one of the orchestral melodies of Rachmaninoff's Third Piano Concerto she would sing: "I used to practice ten hours a day / it used to scare the neighbors away." She even sang a song that forever emblazoned Schubert's Unfinished Symphony in my brain: "This is . . . the symphony . . . that Schuuuuubert never finished." Then there was the perfectly ludicrous, "Sarah won't you come for a walk / Sarah won't you come for a talk / Sarah won't you come for a walk, for a talk, for a schmooze / *Aye, Gadalia* / What kind of fruit do you like? / What kind of fruit do you like? / It starts with a 'K' and it ends with an 'Ach,' KREPLACH!"

None of this, however, was as impressive to my sister and me as her inborn and somewhat freakish gift of perfect pitch. Periodically, probably when sensing she was in a particularly good mood, we tested her. One of us would poke at a key: "What's this?" "B-flat," she would answer from her seat at the far end of the dining room table. "And this?" "There's a C and an A-sharp." Now we used two hands. "This?" "In the left hand there's a D, B-flat, A-sharp, E, and in the right hand there's an A, C, F-sharp, G and, what is that, another B-flat?" She was always right. She could even hear the individual notes when I sat on the keyboard, for which I was admonished by my father, but not my mother who was too busy concentrating on discerning the individual notes beneath my tushy. "Schoenberg!" she would yell out to anyone who was around. "My son's a Schoenberg proponent."

Occupying our home on Hawthorne Place was a rather lengthy list of relatives and maids, a cast of people that changed from time to time but surely constituted the essence of an extended family. There is no calculating the benefits my sister Judy, older than I by three years, and I derived from these good and kind individuals. My father, the patriarch of Hawthorne Place, was a man given to assuming the paternal role, with all its nuances and obligations. A noted physician, he was knowledgeable in a variety of fields, ambitious, and a person totally devoted to Asian art and chamber music, which he played religiously once a week in the music room. Although he spent long hours most every week of the year practicing medicine in several hospitals and his downtown office, which meant that he was away a great deal of the time, Hawthorne Place was also the site of his medical research.

My mother's two brothers, Jack and Mark, were handsome, gentle men who, from my mother's standpoint, married strong women. I know she always worried about them. Her sisters, Fanny, Annie, Rosie, and Leah were, in their youth, exquisite beauties. "Especially Annie," my mother would say. "My God, she was such a beauty!" As a boy, I couldn't see it. My Aunt Annie gorgeous? Now, however, when I look at the aging photographs of these women, I see precisely what my mother saw. Annie's claim to fame was that she not only appeared in many of the Yiddish theater productions staged by my grandfather, but on one occasion, when her dress hem got caught on a curtain hook, she actually went up with the curtain, much to the delight of the audience, and the chagrin of my grandfather.

Annie was married to Harry LeVine. A sailor in World War I, Uncle Harry served as a grandfather figure to me. Called Herschel by my mother, Uncle Harry ate every single food doctors claimed would kill a person by the time he was forty; however, Uncle Harry lived longer than anyone else in the family. While my father was served egg beaters, Uncle Harry ate his daily eggs, the white and the yellow, and claimed that long life was all a state of mind. Harry was living proof of what my parents' friend Harry Lackritz used to call "happy tissue."

Uncle Harry played baseball with me because my father rarely had time. Endlessly he threw me grounders and pop flies all the while offering radio-like commentary; he never seemed to tire of the activity. By this point in his life, the once red-haired man was bald, but when we played, he often shook his head as if he were throwing back waves of hair that had fallen over his eyes. Together we watched on television our beloved Chicago Cubs lose most of their games, "Come on Cavaretta, Cav it out there," Uncle Harry would implore the screen. And often he reminded me, "If at first you don't succeed, suck lemons!"

A traveling salesman, Uncle Harry proudly drove his Chevrolets hundreds of thousands of miles with his samples stored in the "back end," for he never used the word "trunk." He sent me postcards from almost every state of the Union. I kept every one, even cataloging them alphabetically by state. Perhaps I was the son he never had. Perhaps there was something else, something having to do with the utter simplicity of love.

Aunt Annie and Uncle Harry lived with us for a time at Hawthorne Place. They occupied the guest bedroom in the middle of the second floor, its bay windows directly over the bay windows of the music room. My Aunt Fanny and her husband, Joe Hornstein, lived for years in the two-bedroom apartment on the third floor, its small kitchen owning the home's best view of Lake Michigan. The third-floor apartment was reached in two ways. One either ascended the stairs to the second floor and then passed through a door opposite the guest room to reach a second set of stairs leading to the apartment, or one could enter the house from a side door that opened onto the driveway and ride an elevator first to the main floor, a distance of some ten feet, and then to the second floor where one emerged at the base of the stairway to the third-floor apartment. The previous owner of the house, apparently, was disabled, and so his family had the elevator installed. My friends loved the elevator, but it regularly got stuck with someone in it, which meant that one had to push the red alarm bell button. Rescuers then retrieved a crank from a cabinet at the top of the elevator shaft and literally cranked up the elevator inch by inch.

I spent some happy minutes riding the barely two-person elevator, but far happier hours on the third floor with Aunt Fanny, a registered nurse, who, when I got sick, gave me what she called A.M./P.M. care. Mostly, I spent time with her son Howard, a cousin whom I have always considered to be a brother, and a man of extraordinary talents. Howard remains a magnificent jeweler, potter, woodworker, watercolorist, tennis player, and golfer. Before retiring, he was an eye surgeon specializing in retinal detachments. With me watching, and occasionally holding the glue or some pins, Howard, whom my mother loved as a son, the perfect one at that—she called him "How"—made gorgeous model planes, cars, and boats. I shall never forget sitting alongside him in his little bedroom under the eaves watching him bend pale white balsa wood which he had soaked in a bucket of water into the shape of a sailboat's prow. It was safe with Howard on the third floor. I missed him deeply when, as a young military physician, he went off to serve in Japan following World War II.

Howard was also an accomplished clarinetist. I recall one evening when he sat in with my father and his chamber music colleagues to play the Mozart clarinet quintet. No one loved the performance more than my mother. I remember thinking it was sensational, and I had recently played the recording that Benny Goodman, no less, had made. To a child, Howard was better than Benny. He was even better than the legendary Reginald Kell. The only thing better would have been that I could have played some instrument well enough to compete with, that is, have the opportunity to play with the quartet, and my mother.

Fanny, Annie, a series of maids, one of them a short, rotund woman, named Emma, with the most perfect disposition, were part of a cast of women who shared in raising me. Emma always sought to calm my mother and make the home serene. She was someone with the skill to put my mother in her place; my father was the other one. I had only the courage, or was it the temerity? God only knows what Emma thought of my mother's dark moods or, during my adolescence, our endless arguing. A woman of constant good cheer who traveled for hours everyday to take care of us, and who lived her life with facial scars left from a severe burn, Emma never complained, never sighed, never grimaced, as my mother often did, and as I now do as well. Never did I catch Emma sitting at the kitchen table looking disheveled with her head in her hands, as so often my mother did.

Unlike most mothers, my mother didn't have to prepare breakfast, lunch, or dinner. She didn't have to do laundry, she didn't have to go shopping, clean a bathroom, make a bed, pick up a stitch of clothing left on the floor by a thoughtless son, because there was always Aunt Fanny, or Aunt Annie, or Emma, or most importantly, Aunt Leah, the final member of the ensemble.

Leah Weinstock was what they called in those days an "old maid." Thin, frail, with a weak but persistent cough, Leah was always cold. Sometimes she wore two sweaters over a long-sleeved blouse. In retrospect, she might have been diagnosed anorexic. Leah lived in our home all of my life, sleeping in the smallest of the second-floor bedrooms, a room probably intended as a laundry room; my sister and I occupied far larger spaces. There was barely space for Leah's bed and a small dresser; there wasn't even room for a chair. My cousin Raymond, who knew our family well, was twenty years old when he learned that Leah was not our maid.

Leah was painfully self-effacing; she practically made herself invisible. Like a cat, she walked without sound. No one knew when she entered or departed a room. She ate dinner with us every night, picking at the food she herself had prepared. She joined us at the table as well when guests visited, but she hated to be seen by what she called "visiting royalty," for she never imagined herself properly dressed, sufficiently handsome, or significant. She always sat in the kitchen at the small table in front of the radiator on the north wall, sitting sideways on her chair as if at any moment she were about to rise. Her entire demeanor bespoke a desire to occupy as little space and consume as little oxygen as possible. She never once acted in a self-interested manner; she never once intruded on anyone's life. I never remember Leah using the bathroom which she shared with my sister and me, and Uncle Harry and Aunt Annie as well when they lived in the house. She bathed when we weren't home so that she would not be in our way, but there was never a trace of water anywhere to indicate she had utilized the room.

Leah was totally devoted to my parents who, after all, provided her with food, clothing, housing, medical care, a nursing home when she grew too ill and infirm to remain in our home, and even a cemetery plot. My parents cared for her, but breakfast times, especially, became scenes of insufferable verbal abuse thrown at her by my mother whose dark moods were intensified in the morning. Leah absorbed it all, and, at some level, understood it all. She never fought back; she always defended my mother: "She's just not herself this morning," she would say. "She didn't get enough sleep. She's in a bad mood. Go ahead, Tommy, eat your breakfast."

I did my best to protect Leah. "Everything to help and nothing to hinder," I facetiously would shout at my mother, citing my school's motto as I turned my back on her and stomped out of the kitchen. My words only fueled the fires and protected Leah not one bit. The two sisters loved and needed each other. Leah surely admired my mother's talent and the career she had constructed. Whether she unconsciously symbolized for my mother their own mother, Grandmother Sonya, or even their father, Grandpa Joseph, I shall never know, just as I shall never know whether Leah received the childish rage my mother could never direct toward her father for sending her off alone as a child to New York to study the piano, or her mother for allowing it to happen. Perhaps she resented Leah because, by fiat, or instructions from her parents, she was designated her older sister's custodian. Perhaps my mother longed to occupy the role of care receiver rather than care giver, child rather than parent. Whatever the reason for my mother's irrational verbal attacks and at times utter disapproval of Leah, and often just seeing her sister in the kitchen every morning was enough to cause my mother to explode, their dance together was wholly disturbing; it was as though she was saying: "Are you still here?"

Several times a month Leah visited the west side home of one of her sister Rosie's sons, Al Rosenfeld and his wife Frances, and their three children, as well as the home of her brother, Mark Weinstock, his wife Jeanette, and their three children; six cousins who, for some reason, I rarely saw. It was evident these visits made Leah happy. The Rosenfelds and Weinstocks constituted her family, along with my sister and me. Significantly, photographs of these two families sat upon the small chest of drawers in her bedroom. There were no pictures of my sister and me.

Born in Budapest where her itinerant actor parents were performing at the time, Leah traveled nowhere in her adult life but to Michigan with us in the summers, and to those two west side apartments, the visits providing periodic reprieves for her. I worried often that she would never return. Leah cooked for us, and did chores around the house that I should have done, like walk our dalmatian, Patsy. Had I been faithful at least in this task, I could have prevented one of the most dreadful events of my childhood. Leah, holding the dog's leash, headed down the back steps from the small enclosed porch leading from the kitchen. At the top of the stairs, Patsy spied an animal and bolted. Instinctively clinging tightly to the leash, Leah was yanked down the steps; her face smashed against the concrete pavement. Fortunately no facial bones were broken, but the lacerations were extensive and deep. I was horrified, but as was my habit, I wouldn't let myself cry. I went to my room, busied myself with one thing or another, and felt the force of guilt in the same way I did after the battles with my mother, which reached a ferocious crecendo during my adolescence.

Upon returning from school the next day, there in the kitchen was Leah, the bruises appearing even worse, but milk and graham crackers laid out on the table for me as always, for I loved nothing better than mushing the crackers into the milk until they reached the texture of soft mortar. My mother always joked that if "the concoction," as it was called, wasn't particularly tasty, I could always tuckpoint the brick work on the outside of the house. I ate my scrumptious graham crackers and milk very slowly, savoring every mushy mouthful. Sometimes when my mother was around, I took the glass and spoon to my room. When she wasn't, I sat with Leah. This description is as accurate as it is simple. We just sat. I don't remember more than a few words ever being spoken. It was quiet in the kitchen with Leah, and in those moments, the kitchen, actually, wasn't all that ugly.

There were relatives on my father's side as well who looked out for me, although none of them ever lived at Hawthorne Place. My Uncle Charley, the manager of several Balaban and Katz movie theaters in downtown Chicago, always let my sister and me into the glitzy stage shows on Saturday afternoons. My Uncle Philly hosted me in his Milwaukee home on several occasions. And then there was Bess Sawyer, Auntie Bessie, as we called her, who never failed to bake an apple pie for me when I visited her which was often, especially during the summers when I went to play with her son, Raymond. Auntie Bessie always gave me the first slice, even before her husband Herbie. Knowing full well I could eat the entire pie, Bessie, in the little ritual that eventually formed, would then offer me a second piece.

"Oh, no, Auntie Bessie," I would demure disingenuously. "I couldn't."

Bessie would smile down at me. "Force yourself," she would say, pronouncing the words with an exaggerated New York accent: "Go ahead, try, Dolly, fawce youself."

Finally, there was my Uncle Jack Weinstock, my mother's brother, but someone my father considered a brother as well. The term brother-in-law wasn't close enough to describe their involvement. J. J. to his children, Yankel to my mother, Jackson to my father, his golfing partner, and Uncle Jack to Judy and me, he was a wondrous character. A man with dark wavy hair and the appearance of always needing a shave, my mother's spirit rose palpably when he visited us which was just about every summer; he brought his two children, Frankie and Sally Ann who were almost the same ages as my sister and I, to our lake house in Union Pier, Michigan. Aunt Sally, typically, remained behind in their Salt Lake City, Utah home. The Michigan life, apparently, was a bit too rustic for this woman who preferred the social world of country clubs and fancy eateries. Union Pier in those days was shorts and jeens country, no-mascara country. There wasn't a fabulous restaurant for miles. There was, however, a bowling alley and a penny arcade, the Palladium, filled with pinball machines and a jukebox.

Anyone familiar with baseball can recognize at once whether a child can throw a ball within the first couple of tosses. One either has that naturally graceful motion or one hasn't. Jack had it. I loved playing catch with him on the beach, which we would do day in and day out, because with Jack, you were in the presence of a genuine ball player. Better yet, the man had stories, like breaking the bank at the blackjack table at Monte Carlo. In his wallet, he carried a well-worn article from the *New York Times* in which his financial bonanza was recounted in scrupulous detail. There was, however, no article recounting the following night's loss of the entire amount. I personally think people would have bought anything Jack tried to sell them because he was so engaging, so entertaining. It is hardly surprising that he established a highly successful insurance business in Salt Lake City.

Several times each summer, Jack, accompanied on the piano, of course, by his sister, whom he called "Geets," did his Eddie Cantor and Al Jolson impressions. They were so good his own children weren't embarrassed by them. I shall never forget this athletic man who grew even more handsome over the weeks as his skin turned brown from the sun, strutting about our Union Pier living room, clapping his hands together in front of his face, and singing in a voice you would swear was Jolie himself: "I've been away from you a long time . . . I never knew I'd miss you so . . ." These were the opening lines to "Swanee." His Jolson impression was sheer rapture. The more we laughed and cheered, the more he enjoyed what he was able to do for us. In fact, this was his manner and all the rest of my extended family offering love. There were no "I love you's," no talks with me, unless I had gotten into trouble, no long embraces nor arms around shoulders, no pats on hands, except the ones from Leah, no genuine affirmations or expressions of pride that I recall. Love came mostly in the form of happiness, amusement, and performance. It came in the form of seeing my mother happy.

Sitting across the dinner table from Jack in the screened in porch, he to my father's right, me, as always, to my father's left, I knew some routine was about to occur. He may have looked serious during the first course, but somewhere down the line he was going to pull off some caper. There. There it was. Oh, my God, Jack was starting to pull out his upper teeth. Look at my mother's expression! Look at Leah and Annie and Fanny! Oh, my God, how disgusting, his teeth are actually rattling into an empty glass. Oh, my God! Look at this!

It was, of course, all a trick, the teeth a handful of coins that earlier he had hidden. At the end of the routine, he fished the coins out of the glass and gave them to the children. And if we laughed with relief at the spectacle that had just taken place, he laughed with us, which made *us* laugh even more. I laughed so much at and *with* my Uncle Jack, a man I loved so dearly that my wife, Kay, and I named our son after him, I never bothered to consider that he, like my mother, struggled with some degree of depression. As I reflect back on him, I can easily see the sadness. I don't know that he was unhappy in his marriage and that the summer trips were meant to nourish him. Although in my darker moments, I have to laugh at the thought that a man feeling blue would travel two thousand miles to be bolstered emotionally by my mother. Still, the visits together were good for all of them, my mother, moreover, having publicly proclaimed in 1937 that she intended "to learn about Utah and the music the pioneers brought with them from the east—it's so different!"[14]

My parents mourned for months when Uncle Jack died. His death crushed my mother. There was a story that, because it was a weekend, this humble man refused to trouble a doctor on his days off at the first signs of intense cardiac pain. I know my parents refused to believe anything but that his death was preventable. Jack's son, who at the time was working with him in the insurance company, decided to leave J. J.'s office exactly as it had been when Jack was alive. Nobody used the room, nobody even thought of moving the smallest object on his desk. I've always wished there was a room somewhere belonging to my parents that remained intact as if magically one clock in the universe had been permanently stopped, even if entering this imagined room might evoke a shiver of sadness.

I was six or seven when the four of us—Leah remained home—traveled to Salt Lake City for a Christmas vacation visit with my Uncle Jack and his family. What is better than train travel, especially in a cozy berth at night, one's head propped up on several pillows, peering out the window as the train speeds through little towns, their lights twinkling in the darkness, the sound of the clanging alarm at the railway crossings, and the steady click clack of the wheels on the tracks? Then the train slows and comes to a stop and one attempts to find any name that might offer a clue as to where one is. This description could well have been written by my mother, these are essentially her words, for she, too, loved train travel, but only when she was surrounded by her family. If a train took her away from loved ones, the charm of it all disappeared. I can't imagine what she felt as a child when all alone she left by train that first time for New York.

We traveled to Salt Lake City in luxury, two adjoining bedrooms, almost every available space filled with suitcases, briefcases containing my father's research, and shopping bags brimming over with colorfully wrapped presents for the Weinstocks. And of course my father's violin case. Late one morning, we arrived in Cheyenne, Wyoming. Snow covered the ground and a chilled wind whipped across the station platform. After inquiring of the conductor regarding the length of the Cheyenne stopover, my father took my sister and me into the station to buy some food and magazines. I felt a trifle nervous. What if the train left before we returned? My father assured me there was plenty of time.

I was just reaching the main lobby of the terminal when I saw our train pulling out. Already starting to cry, I yelled for my father and sister and raced toward the open platform, but it was too late. The train was slowly picking up speed. Then, as if it were a movie, I saw my mother, still in her white night-gown, at the window of our bedroom compartment. Helplessly, she looked out at us. It was horrible. Again and again I cried, "I'll never see my mother again. I'll never see my mother again."

I have no recollection of how my sister reacted to what turned out to be a rather inconveniencing fiasco, but I do remember my father's main concern was his fiddle. Whatever plans might be made, would my mother remember to take it off the train? The reunion came early that evening, for it took us a full day to reach Laramie. My mother had received a telegram instructing her to get off the train with all the baggage and wait for us. Whenever I wish, I conjure up those moments of exiting the train in Cheyenne. I feel the tension that there might not be enough time to enter the station, and then the scene of my mother passes before my eyes, and I collapse in tears. "I'll never see my mother again." I have no recollection whatsoever of our Laramie reunion with her.

I was never happier than when I conspicuously spied on my mother's practice sessions. At these times, I never sat on the couch. Nor would I sit in the high-backed easy chair behind the piano bench opposite the bay window. Instead, I crawled under the piano and lay down pretending to be bored and appearing as if I wanted to nap. From there, of course, I heard the sound of a piano as no one ever does, and watched her pedal, always fascinated by the way her foot lifted just in time to keep a note from lingering too long in the air, thereby making it impossible for the next notes to find their proper home.

I jump ahead many years, for I was a little boy when I went to my bunker beneath the piano, to the occasion of my first visit to Rome. Like all tourists, our family, one morning, visited the Vatican, making our entrance into the fabled St. Peter's Basilica. We turned immediately to the right to view Michelangelo's *Pietà* but gradually I was drawn to the great golden canopy constituting the central altar. Those who have seen it recall how it soars toward the ceiling of the cathedral, its ornate columns appearing to revolve as a result of the carvings and designs. Suddenly, I felt I had been to this altar before. I knew this golden structure from somewhere. In fact, the altar put me in mind of the gold leaf paint on the underside of a piano, my own personal childhood altar. It is not a stretch to say that music was the religion of my childhood, and Hawthorne Place was my inspirational temple.

But my childhood was never about religion and institutions. Inevitably it was about the central figures of my family, the caretakers and providers, and in some instances, the care witholders and deprivers. It was about neither music nor musicians, merely mommies and daddies, daughters and sons, aunts and uncles. And in this one instance, in this one life anyway, it is mostly about mommies.

The Pianist

"The sensational young Russian-American pianist, Gitta Gradova, will play a most unusual program at her first Boston recital at Jordan Hall." These are the words that begin the 1923 A. H. Handley office press release. The announcement concludes: "Born in Russia (one newspaper had listed her birthplace as Odessa) nineteen years ago, coming to America seventeen years ago, her entire training has been received here—although of course she has inherited the musical spirit and traditions of her birthland."[1] The description is intriguing, exotic even, but not wholly accurate.

My mother, as Key's 1926 review of music correctly indicates, was born Gertrude Weinstock in Chicago, Illinois, the last child of Joseph and Sophie (Sonya) Weinstock in 1904. She grew up in relative poverty in a tenement on Avers Avenue on Chicago's southwest side, where at one point her parents hosted young Luther Adler who, along with his sister Stella, would become renowned actors and acting teachers. Luther eventually had a son, Jodie, with the actress Sylvia Sydney, a young boy I once played with but whom I have no memory of meeting. (I actually once met Miss Sydney who expressed anger at me for not letting Jodie play with a toy soldier the afternoon we spent together, more than forty years before!) My mother's neighborhood was home as well to the Wiessenfreund family whose son, Muni, would grow up to become the actor, Paul Muni.

Since my mother's parents were born in Russia, her father in Odessa, her mother in Kiev, the part about inheriting "the musical spirit and traditions of her birthland" is in fact true. "Russian art-music," Montagu Nathan wrote, "is clearly seen to have its root in national and political history. . . . Russian musical history resolves itself into a chronicle in which we see the alternate rise and fall of native folk-melody."[2] Surely my mother identified as much with this history and these folk-melodies as with America's political history and indigenous melodies. More perhaps.

She took a stage name, Gitta Gradova, Gitta pronounced with a hard *g*, as in give. "Gitta, Gitta, for whom there's no one sweeta," she often sang. Gradova, usually pronounced Gra-*doe*-va, but by her Russian colleagues *Gra*-doe-va, was the feminine version of Gradovosky, the name her father assumed when, after leaving the rabbinate in Russia, he toured Europe and Asia, and eventually came to the United States as founder and actor of a Yiddish theater company in Chicago that once listed among its members: Beryl Bernardi, Molly Pecan, Molly Goldberg, and the young Muni Weisenfreund. All of her siblings were born in European cities where their father's troop was appearing. My mother was called Gitta by most everyone— *Gittel*, Yiddish for Gertrude by some family members, "Geets" by her brother Jack, but never in her adult life was she called Gertrude. The best pronunciation of her name came from the Russians: "Geeeeetah!"

She began her formal musical training at age six with Louise Robyn at the American Conservatory in Chicago. At seven, she studied with Maurice Aronson and Esther Harris at the Chicago College of Music, where eventually she graduated with honors.[3] Her graduation photograph revealed her in full academic regalia and no less than ten handsome medals pinned to the front of her gown. Before this, Gertrude Weinstock played concerts throughout Chicago performing with "little" symphonies under the direction of Arthur Dunham and Martin Ballman. The repertoire of this child, still not thirteen years old, included works of Chopin, Liszt, Beethoven, and Moszkowski. Even then the reviewers praised her talent. From one reviewer: "It is seldom that a rare talent attains important recognition without the asset of a personality that is pleasing and attractive. This little artist has, for she leaves a lasting effect upon her audience."[4] And from another reviewer: ". . . the nonchalance of her bearing impresses one as not the least of her assets, and apparently nothing can feaze her. Her playing has a clarity and clean-cut effectiveness that with the dash of her interpretations result in brilliant effects."[5]

At age fourteen, in response to a recent concert, the reviewer complimented her: "Miss Weinstock plays the piano and deports herself in general like a seasoned artist. She displays daintiness of touch, beauty and artistry in tone production, rhythmic sense and interpretive gifts in unusual degree."[6]

Still as a child, she became a student of the prominent Chicago teacher of piano, Djane Lavoie-Herz, pronounced Hairtz. "[Madame Herz's] approach to piano teaching," according to the composer Ruth Crawford, "has been described as being somewhat informal—students are permitted to listen to all lessons, and they may ask questions; there is no following of the clock and after lessons they discuss music, books, or other interesting subjects."[7]

Herz was a disciple and friend of the Russian composer and pianist Aleksandr Scriabin, labeled by Ernest Hutcheson as the "apostle of mysticism,"[8] and by Hugo Leichtentritt as an "exaggerated romantic."[9] Scriabin would eventually become one of my mother's favorite composers. According to the November 1929 issue of *Étude*, she "introduced the Scriabin piano concerto in America"— despite the difficulties imposed on the pianist by his compositions. Influenced by the piano style of Frédéric Chopin and the orchestration of Richard Wagner, "Scriabin's late music," Harold Schonberg wrote, "is a black mass of accidentals, fearsome-looking chords, and murderously difficult piano configurations. . . . To the very end his harmonies . . . have a sensuous quality. Scriabin's music can be called erotic . . . in his mysticism he can be all but incomprehensible."[10] Simply stated, Scriabin probably caught my mother's fancy because of his ability, as George Upton and Felix Borowski noted, "to express . . . something of the emotional (and therefore musically communicable) side of his philosophy of life."[11] Hutcheson suggests, however: "If we ignore Scriabin's philosophy completely, we can enjoy his music better."[12] At age twenty, my mother, too, offered words about the composer:

> Scriabin is beyond modernism. When you speak of modern writers, whom do you mention that has accomplished as huge a task as he? Anyone who can play Scriabin can also play Chopin, although the two are widely separated in matters of technic. Yet how many who are fitted to play Chopin find themselves equipped to play Scriabin?
>
> Scriabin's is really a three-handed technic. The exotic and complicated rhythms, the remarkable consistency with which he develops his ideas, his symphonic structure, even in piano music, the curious problems of tone and nuance, these all require an independence in execution which amounts to a third division of autonomy at the keyboard.

The orchestral effects which are contained in his piano music impose special problems upon the performer. So dependent on tone is the proper interpretation of his music that I intend eventually to use two pianos in my recitals. Upon one I shall play the bitter, the ironic, the brilliant music; on the other I will play the softer, the poetic pieces. This plan might serve also in the interpretation of other composers, but in Scriabin's music it is an absolute necessity.[13]

Although ". . . having been hailed for her playing of Bach and acclaimed as the greatest interpreter of Scriabin,"[14] she concluded this one interview with a warning of the dangers of any pianist focusing her work strictly on one composer, although later in life she would admire Glenn Gould's wholesale commitment to Bach.

It is not enough to play well the works of one composer. It would be fine craftsmanship but it would not be art, for in art one must have the whole scope, the vision of the entire subject and be able to express himself in any phase of it.[15]

For the introduction to Scriabin she remained forever grateful to "Madame Herz," as her pupils called her. Herz's piano studio, located on Grand Boulevard, which would become Bellevue Place, was "the scene of musical soirées where the famous and talented mingled."[16] Clearly it became a school of the arts for my mother:

I was fortunate enough to have my training under conditions which made me appreciate every expression in art, and not only musical art. But where is there another artist like Djane Lavoie-Herz, who accomplishes such a complete artistic education and appreciation of the best in everything?[17]

Madame Herz was also responsible for introducing at least three other modern composers to my mother, for as H. Miller wrote in 1925, she was already "an earnest lover of modern music."[18] She herself, however, was quick to point out: "I am not so ultra-modern that I crane my neck looking for composers not yet in sight."[19]

On December 12, 1925, my mother performed Ruth Crawford's Prelude no. 2 in New York City's Town Hall for a League of Composers concert. It was the first time the piece had ever been heard outside of Chicago. Ruth Crawford, who later married the father of folk artist Pete Seeger, was clearly enamored of, if not intimated by, my mother. She wrote in a 1927 diary entry:

> I go out to Madame Herz' home to hear Gitta's lesson. She plays as I have never heard anyone play. Such masses of sound; she is tremendous. Her fourth sonata of Scriabin brings tears to my eyes. I feel a poetry, a bigness of soul, when listening to her, that comes to me very seldom. She speaks of universes.[20]

On another occasion, however, Ruth Crawford explains, "I seem to have no originality when I am [at Herz's studio]; no ability to get out of my coat of steel. I have an exaggerated feeling of inferiority when I am with Madame Herz or Gradova."[21]

My mother also performed pieces by Dane Rudhyar and Henry Cowell, whose coat sleeves constantly brushed against the keyboard when he played, prompting my mother to describe him as a proponent of the Hart, Schaeffner and Marx School of playing. (Hart, Schaeffner and Marx was a prominent men's clothing store chain.)[22]

At age twenty, my mother had much to say about modern composers and audiences' reactions to them:

> You see . . . I believe that a new language of music is being created by those "terrible" ultramodernists. They are leaving aside the old tonal system which was the basis of European music and to which the youngest European modernists are returning after their attempt at being revolutionary, and they are building not only a new style, but a new musical substance. . . . The more I play them, the deeper I go into them. They are difficult to penetrate, because they lead one so far from the ordinary world. When I play them it is something deeper than my conscious self that is playing.
>
> But perhaps that is the test of real music and true introspection. It is so easy to put pathos and personal vibrato into superficial and sentimental works. Modern music of the real kind is far from sentimentality. It goes deeper. Therefore it is more difficult to get at. But that is why it gives me so much joy to play it . . .
>
> Music being the youngest of all the arts, has the advantage; that which is called the "classic" period is only a hundred years removed from us, and I am inclined to say that

there is no such thing as classic and modern music. For me there is only one differentiation—good and bad music. The word "modern" is only an expression of a certain type of music, the latest classical music. . . . Is not Nietzsche's (sic) *Zarathustra* already a classic, although created only forty years ago? . . . We try to measure a new form with a medium altogether foreign to its origin. Think of Rembrandt, who today is counted as one of the very greatest of all painters, and who at the period when he created his greatest works was "measured" by old standards; therefore his works were not considered masterpieces, and thus the greatest of the Dutch masters died in poverty and obscurity.[23]

This particular involvement with modern composers, however, was never central to my mother's budding musical tastes. She saw herself more aligned with European musical culture than modern American musical culture, although she would later fall in love with composers George Gershwin, Jerome Kern, Richard Rodgers, and Cole Porter, and American jazz pianists Fats Waller, Art Tatum, and Oscar Peterson.[24] Joined by her dear friend, Vladimir Horowitz, they regularly listened to Waller and Tatum in New York clubs, raving to everyone about these extraordinary performers. On occasion, Horowitz and my mother even played double piano, replicating the Waller and Tatum styles and mannerisms. Whenever possible, they also tended to hang out where Eddie Duchin was performing.

Late in her life, when my sister was established as a cabaret singer, my mother listened to popular music as well. On one occasion, she recommended that Judy perform a Stephen Goldstein song she had heard sung by Dionne Warwick. But these were hardly her only forays into popular music. Along with my father, she loved Judy Garland, Barbra Streisand, Ella Fitzgerald, Sarah Vaughn, Mel Tormé, Ray Charles, the music of Marvin Hamlisch, especially the score of the movie, *The Way We Were*, and a host of rock hits, especially the more lyrical compositions of The Beatles. Although she could abide the gyrations and theatrics of rock groups like The Rolling Stones and Kiss, she could not tolerate the smashing of guitars on stage. Musical instruments, no matter what their financial value, were sacred.

If critics such as Cecil Smith are to be believed, my mother's European identifications and heritage stood her in good stead, or at least allowed her to more than merely keep up with her colleagues.

Indeed, this identification was, for a time, the source of some controversy: Could an American artist compete with her European colleagues? "Generally speaking," Smith wrote, "the best American artists are not the equal interpretively of the best European artists."[25] Perhaps the Handley office press release contained an intentional error. If women of that era were held as second-class players, how would audiences take to a *girl* from Chicago! Nationality became a matter of some importance to my mother, as often one finds her later in life making references not merely to artists, but to American artists.

As for her own career, however, any sense of American inferiority was seriously challenged when one New York critic wrote: "Such a pianist is evidence of what can be done by an American in America." In an article entitled "Gradova—An example of American Training," another author wrote the following words about the young "Russian-born" pianist:

> In this day, when all of the great pianists of the world are in America during the musical season, it becomes increasingly difficult for a newcomer to win recognition, but an unusual genius nevertheless has not long to wait for a following. Although Miss Gradova is one of the younger pianists, she is already accorded a place with the most interesting artists of the time. . . . Completely equipped, not only technically but musically, Gitta Gradova is as vital an artist as has appeared before the American public in many a year. . . . This account of Gitta Gradova's American training and sensational debut in New York is an irrefutable proof that a European "polishing up" has become an antiquated idea, an unnecessary asset for American artists to "come back" to their country to achieve success.[26]

By 1941, the nationality issue, presumably, was irrelevant. From *Chicago Daily Tribune* critic Edward Barry:

> If a pianist of the quality of Gitta Gradova were suddenly to burst upon us from some such exotic place as Sofia or Kiev we would be limp with excitement. But she was born in Chicago and still lives here, so despite all the record of her successes in other towns we tend to take her for granted much as we take Lake Michigan for granted.[27]

In the main, my mother's philosophy, such as it was, could be described as theosophical aesthetic. Spiritual insight, for my mother, was at least as significant as empirical knowledge. Music for her was almost supernatural, an experience of the soul, or more precisely, as Romain Rolland wrote, "the most intimate utterance of the soul."[28] According to the musicologist Judith Tick, she described some music as being "of the astral body."[29] In less radical terms, my mother would have subscribed to Josef Hofmann's notion that "the duty of the interpretive artist is to extract from these material things the spiritual essence and to transmit it to his hearers."[30] My mother knew instinctively the way into various composers and their unique styles and visions "calls for wide poetic perception."[31] She may well have subscribed to the words that would be spoken decades later by her older colleague, Igor Stravinsky, when he claimed that "the profound meaning of music and its essential aim . . . is to promote a communion, a union of man with his fellow man, and with the Supreme Being."[32]

Through Madam Herz's husband, Siegfried, my mother eventually met Arthur Judson, who in time would represent her. Known in his day as the most powerful classical musical agent, Judson's clients included pianists Vladimir Horowitz and Sophie Breslau, the New York Philharmonic and Philadelphia Symphony Orchestras, and the violinist Efrem Zimbalist, Sr., whom my mother referred to as "Zimmy." At one point, she and Zimbalist gave a joint recital at Philadelphia's Academy of music:

> Zimmy opened the program which was nice, usually the pianist has to, and he had such an ovation, and so I said to him, "Y'know, Zimmy, how do I follow that act?" He was very decent and he said, "Listen to me, you know why they applaud so much for me? Because I teach at Curtis and half of that hall is all my pupils."[33]

It would seem that the association with Madam Herz was beneficial for a variety of reasons. Yet it was also evident, as my mother revealed in an interview with Judith Tick in 1984, that sometime after their coaching commenced, my mother began to believe that Madame Herz, whom she later called "Madam *Schmerz*" (the German word for pain) was impeding the development of her technique. (Adolph Kullak's book on pianoforte playing was actually a gift to her from Madame Herz.) Nonetheless, by the time she was twelve, my mother had made several public appearances, some with orchestras, and all of them providing evidence of the colossal talent of this young prodigy.

Recognizing her special gifts and believing she required the sort of high powered teachers and coaches that Chicago could not provide, Madam Herz included, my grandfather sent her to New York City when she was thirteen. By all accounts, her mother seems to have owned only a small voice in this significant decision. Her father had arranged for her to become a student of Sigismund Stojowski, a stiff disciplinarian whose style never appealed to my mother. After four weeks, she arrived at her lesson one day with the man she called "the great Stojowski."

> "Why are you bringing back the same lesson?" I said, "You know, Mr. Stojowski," I'm such a liar though. "I have a feeling that I don't really know this lesson so well and I thought perhaps it would be . . ." I'll never forget. [He said] "Take your coat and go!" You didn't fool him. He kicked me out. He's (sic) very strict."[34]

Not so incidentally, my grandfather also assumed that his friend, the composer Sergei Prokofiev, might be of value to my mother, both musically and careerwise. In addition, Prokofiev had been asked by my grandfather to look out for the health and well being of the young prodigy, who actually lived for a time in Prokofiev's New York City home. Prokofiev and my grandfather, apparently, had met on one of the composer's trips to Chicago where a group, headed up by the industrialist Cyrus McCormick, raised money to help the composer and pianist get settled in the United States. Before that he had lived for a period of time in South America. At the same time, Prokofiev had begun making contacts with both the Chicago Symphony and its conductor Frederick Stock, with whom he performed in 1918. In a few years, Dr. Stock would become my mother's dear friend and colleague as well.[35]

In my mother's words, when her father first introduced her to Prokofiev in Chicago, he asked her,

> "What will you play for me?"
> And I said, "Who the hell are you? I don't want to play for you."

He said, "Are you working on anything now?" I said, "the Grieg Concerto," naturally.

I was playing it with the Chicago Symphony. After all, I was thirteen years old.

So he said, "Well, play a little bit."

So, I don't know whether he liked it or not but he came and said to my father, "When does she get to New York?"

"In three weeks," my father replied.

So [Prokofiev] said, "Young lady, I will give you my address and my phone number. . . I would like to hear you maybe once in two weeks, if I'm not on tour, maybe once in three weeks."

So I had to report to him, and I was bored to death.[36]

My mother recalled spending a fair amount of time during her early teenage years with Prokofiev, a man making his own Carnegie Hall and Aeolian Hall debuts during this period. She also grabbed every opportunity to inspect the progress he was making on his opera *The Love of Three Oranges* to be delivered to the Chicago Opera in the autumn of 1919, although it would not be performed until 1921. At one point, in order to study the score more closely, she actually snatched it off Prokofiev's piano music stand and took it home with her. Prokofiev, naturally, was incensed by this and, according to my mother:

> [He] had a warrant out for my arrest. He was going to kill me. I saw him at the hotel and ran the other way . . . but I didn't return the score, and he said to somebody, "If I ever see that girl I'll kill her on the street." . . . No, but he was a wonderful man, and you know what I did one day? I brought Stella Adler [Luther's sister] to him. And she must have been the woman that Debussy had in mind [when he composed] "The Girl with the Flaxen Hair." She was breathtakingly gorgeous . . . that came in very handy for me. . . . He fell madly in love with her. . . . So when they had a big conversation there I went into Prokofiev's bedroom and called my mother long distance. [I] had a lovely conversation with my mother. [I] told Prokofiev I had a fine afternoon, and they had a nice romance. I mean, what the hell.[37]

It was also at this time that my mother developed a reverence for the physical act of composing, the setting down of every dot and line of every instrument, page after page. For some reason, this seems to have affected her almost as much as the actual sounds that these dots and lines created. She marveled at the ability of composers to hold all the themes and individual instrument parts in their minds at once, all of which they could hear. I recall her teaching me that the composer even had to mark down every hit of the kettle drums. Equally impressive, I thought, was that when she practiced a piano concerto, she sang the orchestral parts out loud, be they the oboes, violins, or horns. It was also at this time that she formally adopted her Russian name, Gitta Gradova.

As wondrous a figure as Prokofiev was for my mother, and as much as she might have feared him, or more likely his intellect, she was eternally grateful to him for introducing her to Sergei Rachmaninoff. In the end, however, Prokofiev's association with her own father may have kept her from becoming truly close with him. She did, however, continue to use her visits to Prokofiev's home to telephone long distance to Chicago in order to speak with her mother. A loyal letter writer as a mature woman, she apparently wrote very few letters home during that period when, I imagine, she was not at all happy, and perhaps even resentful of her father for sending her away from home, and her mother for having gone along with the decision.

Interestingly, my maternal grandmother, Sonya, who regularly acted in her husband's theatrical productions, remains a barely visible figure to me. I know my mother was deeply touched, however, when we named our third child after her. I have a dim memory of grandmother Sonya playing a game in which she tickles my fingers while counting in Russian. My mother, obviously, had more substantial memories of her mother, though she spoke more frequently of her father. I know practically nothing about Grandmother Sonya. More significantly, she never rescued her youngest child from the terror inherent in the roles of child prodigy and child traveler that essentially her husband had orchestrated.

Grandmother Sonya lived with my parents from the time my grandfather died in April 1930 when, after acting in a Yiddish Theater production in Milwaukee, he collapsed in a taxi on the way to the railroad station to board the Chicago train. A man dedicated to the theater, he had retired from acting after performing for almost fifty years, but he was never content. He craved one more performance on the stage and, after two years of idleness, got his chance at the Pabst Theater, where, as an article dated Sunday, April 6, 1930, indicates: "He played his last performance and sang his swan song." The obituary goes on to say that "He was happy. He gave a marvelous performance."

Having her mother home with her later in her life as part of what my father called "the royal family" may have brought my mother some peace. Grandmother Sonya died in our Michigan home. At this time, my mother may have felt that the last attachment to any sense of security was now gone, except for her sister, Leah, who always lived with us. I think she sought to resurrect familial bonds by having as many of her sisters live with us, or at least close by. Still, as faithful and indulgent as they were, Leah, by far the most faithful, a certain primitive sense of security was never restored, if, in fact, it existed in the first place.

My father, on the other hand, who never lived alone with my mother but who always shared his home with several members of her family, may have entertained other thoughts on the concept of an extended family. The following brief excerpts come from his letters to my mother around the time of their marriage in 1926 while she was concertizing away from Chicago.

> Anna having been out—without the baby . . . Ma, Pa, Lee, Rose, Ann, Harry, Fan, Joe, Gloria and me are with you always . . .
> February 1927: . . . Mama had given Anna "the devil"— she said that ever since Anna and the baby were in the house no order or cleanliness has been possible—and so forth. . . . The house is fairly well cleaned and is very inviting and [a] comfortable abode. Just a little less noise and fewer people and it would be unbeatable.[38]

My mother's fondest memories of those early years in New York City involved sitting in a window seat in the New York Public Library curled up with her books. Along with studying the piano, she described spending her time reading voraciously, an activity that remained especially significant for her as her concentrated musical studies meant that she attended neither high school nor college. With a melancholy tone, she allowed as to how she had composed her grammar school's class song, but she always felt uneducated, and hence, deficient. The sentiment never left her.

When she wasn't living in Prokofiev's New York home, she reported that she lived with a degenerate pair; she was rotten and he was worse. Sophie Setro, a woman from a foreign land, married to a little guy who drove a car with two big lanterns, an old-fashion[ed] limousine that he turned into a cab on Second Avenue in the *lousiest* neighborhood, and I want to tell you, I had impressions there. . . . I don't know how I lived through that, I don't know how I lived through that.[39]

As horrendous as this one experience must have been for her, it was actually preceded by a far more delightful accommodation presumably arranged by her father, one that yielded a few dividends that no one could have forseen:

When I went to study in New York . . . at the beginning of my stay, I was alone and [had] no place to live in the city. I was sent to live at the Adler home in exchange for Luther coming to our house [in Chicago]. . . . The [Adler] daughters were living there and they ordered eggs for breakfast and they didn't say, "I'll have two . . . I would like two eggs *rahther* well done." I wasn't used to *that*. I said, "What the hell is this? *Rahther* difficult to manage with a fork, you know . . ."

Luther was two years older than I, sixteen years old, blond hair, blue eyes, a young Greek god. When I left our home there never was a girl [friend coming] there because I was never allowed to play with anybody. When I came back after one year in New York, we had a harem . . . there were girls hanging around the beds and around the couches and our house became like a brothel. I didn't know I lived there. He had a passion for girls that was far worse than his father, and God knows that his father was impossible. When I lived in that [New York Adler] apartment, I came by the bedroom, I expected to see old-lady Adler but he had another lady in bed with him

So I'll never forget, we wrote and corresponded, Luther and I. Luther fell in love with me and I was overcome by him. So I thought, how do you live in New York when the best beau you ever went around with lives in Chicago? So he wrote me one day how he was progressing . . . he was at the Lewis Institute where I went for a year after I came back from New York to study . . . I was dying to take up English literature, and he said, "I study Latin now and I can conjugate very well: amo, amas, amat." I got a bang out of that.[40]

Luther Adler, however, wasn't the only Greek God to catch my mother's eye. For on the floor beneath the Adlers lived another Adonis:

A young boy my age who always played for me the *Polonaise* of Chopin, and he would stop, and I would finish. I stopped, and he would play the next part, because his father wouldn't let him talk to me. I was living in the Adler house and that was a house of ill-repute, and you know who he was? [The composer] Alfred Newman. . . . Beautiful young boy. We were dying to get together but we weren't allowed to. . . . And who do you think took me to the concerts? Oh, I love going back in the past, [the pianist] Lorin Mazel's father, Martin . . . I would love to meet Lorin and say, "How are you? I used to go to the movies with your father."[41]

My mother's New York debut at Town Hall took place on the afternoon of November 20, 1923. She was nineteen years old. Her program that afternoon consisted of the Handel *Chaconne and Variations* in G, two works of Brahms, the Liszt sonata, *Fantasia After Dante*, and finally works of Scriabin, the composer she had grown to love through her studies with Madame Herz. Five weeks later on January 8, 1924, she would play her second New York recital.

Although Cecil Smith was probably right when he noted that in the main, a New York recital is "not the quick route to prosperity and fame,"[42] my mother proved the exception. As Smith also remarked, the reviews of the concert, almost unanimously sensational, turned out to be worth their weight in gold; she was an overnight success.

In response to the recital, Frank H. Warren of the *Evening World* claimed my mother had exhibited "Sympathetic intelligent playing."[43] The *New York American* called her: "A player of exceptional gifts, consisting of strongly marked interpretive talent, splendidly virile attack, accurate technical mastery, and a sensitive touch and soulful tone."[44] The *New York Times'* critic wrote: "The young artist, who has a far off resemblance to a Chopin portrait. . . . Her technique is strong and supple, full of grace, and allows free play to an analytical mind and a poetic personality."[45]

From W. J. Henderson in the *New York Herald*:

In many respects one of the best and most talented young pianists heard here in some time. Virility and great power, musical insight, an astonishing command of finger technic, together with feeling and imagination were qualities observed in her style.[46]

Henderson's words are reminiscent of Niccolò Paganini's dictum: "To play with power one must feel deeply."[47]

According to the *New York Staats Zeitung*, my mother "presented with great success a masterful and tremendously difficult program. Her touch and technique are superb. She completely captivated her public."[48]

F. D. Perkins, writing in the *New York Tribune*, described: "Talent far beyond the measure displayed by the average, a combination of technique and expressive power that captured and held the interest . . . technical brilliance . . . expressive ability. . . . It was energy with a purpose. . . . The young pianist should go far."[49]

My favorite review was written by G. W. Gabriel in the *New York Sun and Globe*. I only wish I knew my mother's response to it:

> She brought a picturesque personality and a dramatic and admirably controlled temperament to hold her audience. The occasion was in fact quite portentous. Miss Gradova, looking like a combination of Peter Pan and Lord Byron. . . . There was mystery about her interpretation, complete concentration, variety of color, but a profoundly mature suggestiveness as well. One felt the ghastly silences of the *Inferno* (in Liszt's *Fantasia After Dante*). Miss Gradova rose to take her inflammatory applause with a wan aloofness that might have belonged to Virgil himself. . . . One will look forward eagerly to the next recital of this absorbing young pianist.[50]

Only one review revealed the lack of respect sometime shown by certain critics of women artists, a sentiment that extended into the 1930s when it was alleged by some on the continent that the greatest European pianist was Marie Pleyel. This critic, whose name I cannot discover, wrote of the "young woman with a peculiar name . . . [that] hers was an impressive debut. She is said to be only nineteen years old. If she continues to develop at that same ratio it will only be a year or two before she must be reckoned with in the very front ranks of women pianists."[51]

As is often the case, my mother's success left a wake of people claiming credit. Madame Herz, obviously, believed she was the prime educator of the young prodigy, an assertion that Stojowski too, was eager to make. Back in Chicago, however, an aggrieved Esther Harris felt that she had not received proper acclaim for this wonder child:

> January 17, 1924: *To the Musical Courier:* A former student of mine, Gertrude Weinstock, who made a very big success in New York recently under the name of Gitta Gradova, is reputed in another musical paper to be a student of another piano teacher in Chicago [presumably Madam Herz]. In justice to myself and to the school of which I am president . . . I would like to inform your readers that Gitta Gradova studied with me for seven long years, taking from two to three lessons per week, lasting from one to three hours, which really means ten years of actual study. Her musical foundation was laid by me and with my untiring efforts, she has acquired success in the musical world. . . . In 1919 she gave me her picture on which she wrote, "To Esther Harris, the woman who made me what I am." . . . I do not believe that any teacher can claim any pupil unless they have studied four years, taking two lessons a week.[52]

In fact, tensions were brewing between my parents, on the one hand, and Madame Herz and her husband, on the other. In numerous letters from my father to my mother, one reads of his outright disrespect for Mr. Herz who seems to have failed my mother concerning his managerial responsibilities. But Madame Herz, who had accompanied my mother on several trips to New York, was also the target of his wrath:

> 1924: I talked on the phone to Madam Herz and felt a sort of sour grapes expression in her voice. . . . she was decidedly not over enthusiastic in spirit. She said among other irrelevant things, "Believe me she'll have to work this next year to keep up the high standard of recognition which [my mother] has attained." Is it that she didn't get all she thought she had coming . . . . Stay away from the witch as much as possible . . ."[53]
>
> April 1926: Contrary to what I expected there was no good reason for going to the Herz's on Tuesday. The topic of conversation was chiefly student suicides. . . . His talk was more of the same thing—still the indecision, the deceit, the

probable future, mental illness . . . in all, all selfish delusions. . . . As a parting word to me, Mr. Herz had the audacity to tell me not to call you long distance. His intention was your unbroken rest, but his officious dictatorial attitude appears now in my eyes as a child's presumptuousness; and as such I smilingly and casually tolerated his words to pass by my nose to get lost in the wind. It was of no avail to start a useless harangue with a loose-mouth individual who knows only to soliloquize. . . Mr. Herz is hopeless—He's bugs, daffy, disillusioned, mishuga. Poor soul—Damn fool. . . .

[Madame] Herz had the audacity to believe that you might take more lessons with her if it would help his plans any—and I quickly changed his mind.[54]

On November 26, 1924, Gitta Gradova played a recital in New York's Aeolian Hall in which she performed works of Bach, Scriabin, Mussorgsky, Chopin, Nikolai Medtner, a composer greatly admired by Rachmaninoff, and ended the concert with Liszt's *Mephisto Waltz*, hardly an easy conclusion to a long evening. But the audience wanted more, leading the critic of the *New York Times* to write the next day: "Not content to giving several encores to an arduous program, Miss Gradova had to play additional pieces at the end of the concert to satisfy her admirers."[55] A writer from the *New York Times*, remarking on her "girlish black frock," noted that she "fascinated her hearers with unaffectedly beautiful playing, backed with a rare force of temperament and personality."[56] The Scriabin work chosen for the Aeolian Hall concert was his fifth sonata, a piece that Alfred J. Swan in his book, *Scriabin*, described as having "been likened to a piece of wizardry, a deed of black magic, illumined by the rays of a black sun."[57] Swan inscribed a copy of his book to my mother in January 1924: "To Mlle. Gradova as a souvenir of her fine sensitive playing of the 5th sonata and other works of the hero of this little volume."

Sexist or not, the one critic's allusion to a ratio was not wholly inaccurate. Within a few months the career of Gitta Gradova was soaring. On November 6, 1924, she played at The Women's Musical Club of Toronto where a critic proclaimed that Mlle. Gradova

. . . gives authentic evidence of genius with qualities of emotion and magnetism not easily described. Her personality is youthful and diffident, but her power in the evocation of vast, beautiful, unforced tone is amazing. Though the color and fire of Russian music obviously finds natural expression in her, she is very versatile. . . . As an interpreter of what James G. Huneker called "the larger Chopin," Mlle. Gradova is also extremely gifted and if he had lived to hear her, Huneker probably would have revised his celebrated judgment that women cannot interpret Chopin.[58]

In that same year—my mother was nineteen at the time—the music critic of the *Nation*, Henrietta Straus, wrote the sort of review about which performers can only dream:

> Gitta Gradova is one of those rare musicians in whom the miracle of the artist is repeated in the human being . . . she challenges one's heart and one's brain. For hers is not that wandering genius that comes and goes at will, like a stranger at a hostelry, but that permanent, all-embracing kind, the fine flowering of a race. One feels that back of her dominant musical personality lies another even more powerful—the combined heritage of a supremely intellectual, emotional, philosophical, and mystical ancestry. . . . She does for [Scriabin] what no other pianist has yet been able to do—she pierces those outer wrappings that make their appeal solely to the nerves and reveals the flame that was the man himself. . . . We listen as though we were listening in a cathedral. . . . From the moment when she walks on the platform until she walks back, one realizes that here is an artist of perfect poise who knows exactly what she wants to say and how to say it. Here are no hesitant impulses, no faltering fingers, but a tremendous musical mentality guiding an equally enormous technique and controlling an unsurpassed variety of tonal color.[59]

At the conclusion of the review, Straus declared my mother to be "the foremost woman pianist now before the public." Evidently, women in those days had difficulty moving beyond that one barrier to complete success and acceptance, which only confirms the entrenched power of sexist culture inasmuch as a long list of women pianists had built successful careers, especially in Europe. Historians of the piano know the names of Marie Pleyel, Fannie Bloomfield Zeisler, Annette Essipoff, Teresa Carreño, Sophie Menter, Paula Sealit, Natalie Janotha, Fanny Davies, Arabella Goddard, Ilona Eibenschütz, Adelina de Lara, Marie Krebs-Brenning, Cécile Chaminade, and Helen Hopekirk.[60] The names of Myra Hess, Ania Dorfmann, and Guoimar Novaes are better known to contemporary audiences and students of music.

Examining this period eighty years later, some of the reviews seem almost comical as writers practically fall over themselves attempting to reconcile their admiration for a young woman. Some, of course, like the critic of the *Toronto Saturday Night*, who also labeled Gitta Gradova a genius, or the critic who reviewed her concert at the Stanley Music Club at the Stanley Theater in Philadelphia, and referred to her as a "tempestuous young genius,"[61] or the person at the *Daily Times-Star* of Cincinnati who called her, "a new star," apparently took no notice of her sex. But others did.

There was, for example, Herman Devries who wrote in *Music in Review*, that my mother was "The world's greatest feminine pianiste." In 1928, Mr. Devries intoned: "Today Gradova is a young giantess of the keyboard. . . . Beside all this, she is engagingly simple and modest upon the platform and at the piano."[62] Again from Devries: "Gitta Gradova, always promising from her youth, now has reached maturity. But the maturity of an artist of great distinction and a personality in the pianistic world of today comparable to the Fannie Bloomfield Zeisler and Theresa Carreño of the past generation."[63]

Even in 1939, Mr. Devries could not let go of the qualification:

Gitta Gradova, Chicago's foremost woman pianist and one of the world's best among the feminine exponents, made her re-entry as soloist with the Chicago Symphony last evening. . . . A numerous army of admirers showered volleys of plaudits on the triumphant soloist, whose attitude toward her art has developed into the simplicity of the aristocrat, which further enhances her own personality.[64]

Clearly my mother had read these reviews and thus was totally prepared to tell an interviewer in February 1928—she was twenty-four—that her favorite pianist was [Miss] Guiomar Novaes.[65] In a letter written to my mother by my father about this time, we find these words: "Madam Herz was just telling me that Novaes thinks that you are the only great woman pianist (besides herself) who has anything to say."[66]

My mother first performed with the New York Philharmonic Orchestra at Carnegie Hall on November 11 and 12, 1926, under the baton of William Mengelberg; she played Rachmaninoff's Piano

Concerto no. 2. On January 13 and 14, 1927, she launched what would be years of successful performances with conductors such as Fritz Reiner, Pierre Monteux, and Frederick Stock, the longtime conductor of the Chicago Symphony. In the Chicago Symphony Orchestra program's "Soloist of the Week" section, one reads that on the occasion of my mother's first appearance with the symphony she had already appeared with major American orchestras: New York, Philadelphia, Cincinnati, Los Angeles, Minneapolis, and St. Louis. (Beneath her program biography, it indicates that the next week's guest conductor would be Maurice Ravel.)

Her European career was inaugurated in 1928 with a series of recitals, but she did not play with a major European orchestra until 1934 when she performed with the Warsaw Philharmonic. Not so incidentally, the trip home to America that year embarked from Naples on the ocean liner the *Rex*. Accompanying her on the voyage were the violinist Nathan Milstein and his wife, Rita, pianists Ignaz Friedmann and Josef Hofmann, along with Hofmann's wife, Betty, and the fifty-two-year-old composer, Igor Stravinsky. Two stories from that voyage remained with my mother. The first takes place the afternoon she was asked by Friedmann and Stravinsky to complete a hand of bridge; the game was conducted solely in French. My mother responded that she felt it unfair for her to join a game being played in French when she didn't know how to play it in English.

The second story also involves Friedmann, who wondered how secure my mother felt when she walked onto the concert stage. In many ways it was a telling and prophetic question.

"Sure," my mother said.

"But how sure?" Friedmann pursued her.

"Sure enough," she claimed she answered.

Friedmann, clearly, wished her to ask him the same question which she did, and his answer seems worth hearing: "Two hundred percent sure, because you lose half of it when they knock on the door to tell you to go on stage."[67]

Shortly after her first European tour, she left the management of Paul Bechert. This quickly prompted a letter from the esteemed London musical agent Wilfrid Van Wyck. Van Wyck wrote to her on July 1, 1935: "Does this mean that you are not coming to Europe next season? It would be a thousand pities if you were to stay away after having scored such brilliant successes. Do let me know if I can help you in any way."[68] Although she ultimately would make a business connection with Van Wyck, the decision not to return to Europe that season may have been a harbinger of events to come within six years.

In the meantime, however, success and recognition arrived for my mother. One after another, mountains of reviews were glowing, reverential even; the allusions to female players or feminine performances were quickly disappearing. In fact, critics were amazed that a person so young and slim could be so forceful at the keyboard:

> [The Saint-Saens C Minor Concerto] is ungrateful, in fact almost trite in comparison with other orchestral works, but Miss Gradova with her myriad of color effects and shading, her amazing gift for contrasts and her technical equipment made the work a masterpiece. To see her, a mere slip of a young woman, it seems incredible that she can draw from the piano such an immense tone.[69]

Chicago critic Hans Rosenwald: "Gradova belongs in the first line of interpreters at the keyboard, and I do not mean in the first line of women interpreters."[70]

E. S., *Chicago Daily News*, "Mme. Gradova Wins New Piano Laurels," January 12, 1932: "And both in the pianistic and also in the musical respect, [the Chopin B-flat minor sonata] was of a purity and intensity that place her directly in the line of the great."

And finally from *Music News*, May 8, 1925, p. 27, under the title, "Gradova is Given Ovation":

> Again all critics are unanimous in commenting upon Miss Gradova's unusual power. The *New Orleans States* wrote: Dazzling were the effects she wrought . . . Amazing was the power she exhibited at the instrument; this rather frail girl with the apparent strength of a masculine master. . . . She has tremendous power and brilliancy, together with a manual dexterity and resource that any masculine player might envy her. . . . Unless we greatly err, that young woman's name will soon stand near the top among the world's pianists of her sex, and possibly either sex, for her's is an art that needs no concessions because of sex.

Olin Downes, the music critic of the *New York Times*, remarked that in performing the Beethoven Piano Concerto no. 3 with the Beethoven Symphony Orchestra, my mother "displayed again her indisputable talent and virtuoso blood as a pianist, certain exaggerations and a rather tough orchestral accompaniment to the contrary."[71] Similarly, in a column announcing her forthcoming appearance with the St. Louis Symphony Orchestra in November 1927, an unnamed writer quotes Richard L. Stokes the former music critic of the *St. Louis Post-Dispatch*, writing in the *New York World* on the occasion of her performance of the Rachmaninoff C-minor concerto:

> Miss Gradova swept erect and free of stride upon the platform, bent her athletic form over the piano and plunged with *masculine strength* and decisiveness into the concerto. Its music leapt *rugged and almost savage* from beneath her hands. Yet there was subtle workmanship in the lyric episodes and at moments the strings sang under her touch. The finale was proclaimed with unmistakable brilliance.[72] (emphasis added)

One of the more significant sets of reviews came from Claudia Cassidy, the powerhouse—my mother's term—music critic of the *Chicago Tribune*. Miss Cassidy could be an acerbic writer who seemed to detest everything in music my mother loved, and loved everything in music my mother despised. I can't believe how often totally disparate were their perceptions of a concert, although my mother always admired Miss Cassidy's intelligence. If Claudia Cassidy gave an artist a bad review, the artist might not return to Chicago for years, a fact that troubled my mother. She might well have wished for others for the sort of review she received from Miss Cassidy in the *Chicago Tribune*, when the critic first heard the young pianist on February 10, 1932:

> Yesterday afternoon I heard Gitta Gradova for the first time and I feel like marking the date with asterisks in all the more important colors. This handsome young Chicagoan has something to say and her pianistic equipment knows how to say it. . . . Literally she seemed to hurl herself at the piano as a thoroughbred responds to the gun; actually, she was uncommonly quiet, with an unruffled brow which by no means hid the inner intensity. . . . Miss Gradova's gifts are doubtless news to no one but myself. . . . Nevertheless, it was a great joy to discover this extraordinarily talented girl,

whose fingers can steel hammers as readily as they can coax satin whispers from her instrument.[73]

To my knowledge, Miss Cassidy never sat on my mother's couch, though she often reviewed my mother's concerts in her characteristic style, writing, for example, on February 14, 1936, about a performance of the Moszkowski Concerto:

> To the credit side of the season add the reappearance of Gitta Gradova, who returned to the Chicago Symphony Orchestra after four years' absence and turned the inferior Moszkowski Concerto into the triumph of her hometown career. Always an interesting pianist with an unmistakable flair for symphonic performance, Miss Gradova has developed a fresh brilliance of attack, a broader range of dynamics and, what is more important, a deepening regard for the poetry of the piano. She seems to me to have been listening to Horowitz, and I can think of no better use of a pianist's ears when he is resting them from his own music. . . . Audience eyes have always feasted upon Miss Gradova, who looks like an artist and who understands the platform value of the right clothes.[74]

In 1939, Miss Cassidy would offer up another reference to my mother's appearance on the stage: "At the time of her orchestral debut eleven seasons ago, Miss Gradova looked like an unmistakable success. She had technique, temperament, and the sultry Russian quality that makes box office . . ."[75]

Miss Cassidy's reference to stage appearance was hardly unique. I have only the initials C. E. W. listed as the author of this excerpt from the *Music News*, November 7, 1924:

> Gitta Gradova, besides being, as she always has been, a wonder pianist, is now also an amazing and a very striking personality. She is handsome in a dark, petite way, but she assumes a severity of dress and hair-cutting which make her stand alone among young female figures of the moment, and she accents this plainness of dress by austerity of carriage and a preternatural solemnity of countenance which have never been equaled on the concert stage except by that talented young Russian violinist, Jascha [Heifetz] Something-or-Other . . ."[76]

In fact, quite a few people commented over the years on my mother's stage presence, the word "aloof" appearing more than once in reviews. "Gradova may seem cool and aloof," Albert Cotsworth wrote in 1925, "since she chooses to be chary of the customary approaches that an artist uses to develop comradeship with an audience . . ."[77] December 2, the *Musical Leader:* "The audience, unabashed by her aloofness, clamored until she had added several encores."[78]

From a Chicago society column entitled, "Breezin' Round," January 20, 1941:

> My neighbor at the Chicago Symphony concert wagged to me as Gitta Gradova walked out on stage last Friday toward the great black instrument which awaited her. "Well, she is still the original white-collar girl!" Yes, the same juvenile Buster Brown costume of her prodigy days, which still suits her without seeming to be an affectation of youthfulness but worn as the foremost American woman pianist of our time and a "bank-night wad" to anyone who can produce her rival. Our own Gradova, as poker-faced as [tennis champion] Helen Wills, walk and manner a bit on the Greta Garbo side, and still doesn't know how to bow and look happy about it. A real "trouper," too, for she had a temperature of 101 degrees at the first performance and when Friday came—well, they just "mislaid" the thermometer.[79]

By 1941, she was either so aloof or so totally uninvolved with her audience that critic Robert Pollak was obliged to observe:

> After the intermission, Miss Gradova emerged from the wings chewing a wad of gum, brushed the bugs off the keyboard and went at the Rachmaninoff variations with her characteristic vigor. . . . I doubt if anybody, even the composer, plays this virtuoso affair with any more precision or sonority than she does.[80]

It was the music critic Eugene Stinson who most accurately described what an audience may have taken to be aloofness. The whole point was that my mother was working to effect an association between herself and the composer, not between herself and her audience.

From Stinson, published in *Music Views:*

For she played with a musician's expressiveness and with an exquisitely thought out clarity of style. . . . And this was more a tribute to Miss Gradova since there is no trace of showmanship in her whatever and the gist of her excellence is a polished, extremely facile and most beautiful playing; one of the very finest systems of workmanship to be heard today.[81]

And from a column titled "Chicago Pianist is Soloist": "One of Miss Gradova's most important qualities as a performer is her poise. So great is her sureness of herself that she is able to impart her intentions unmistakably to the orchestra and so achieve greater unity of ensemble.[82]

I can only guess that my mother either was utterly unaffected by this attribution of aloofness, or claimed that critics, using one of her favorite expressions, completely "missed the boat" on this subject. For her, the essence of performance came down not to entertainment of an audience, but to interpretation of a composition, or more precisely, a composer. In her own words:

> Now let us ask ourselves how many musicians enter as deeply into their subject as to succeed in giving a complete analysis of the meaning of every bar the composer wrote and his motive in writing it. If it were the case and the interpreting artist had a clear conception of the masterwork, an audience would feel the unity and harmony of the work and get the poetic message and essence of the composition. . . . It follows, therefore, that an interpretive artist must strive to gain a capacity of understanding and feeling [for] the very depth of creative genius. Only what has entered the soul of the interpreter can emanate from it again and then be transmitted to the audience. The thing which the audience keenly feels when listening to a great artist, commonly called "a thrill," is merely but a glimpse of their experience of the creative genius through the medium of the re-creative artist. Such feeling of the soul experience of genius cannot be taught. It must be inborn in a person. . . . If the composer has used his supreme effort to put a great message into his score and often has done this fighting against terrible odds, under great strain and physical deprivations, what is all this compared with the interpreter who "sacrifices," if such could be the case, a part of the program to help to proclaim this latest message and make it a living force? Indeed, it is no sacrifice

for the interpreter. I would rather call it a privilege to be endowed with a sufficient capacity to do justice to a new work. . . . After all, the aim of a great work is the same no matter from what period. This aim has been very clearly expressed by the Chinese master, Kuo Hsi, in his work on landscape painting, where he says: "The artist must, before all, bring himself into spiritual communion with the hills and brooklets which he wishes to paint." This is a lesson applicable to music as well. The inner composure must be valued higher than the exterior execution, and it is in this spirit I understand the great masterpieces of Scriabin which otherwise would remain unintelligible to me. . . . I will endeavor to convey to my audience the fact that all good music, whether classic or modern, has the same lofty aspirations, although totally different in expression, form and rhythm, alike on one thing only—beauty![83]

Although she played a rich and varied repertoire, there can be no mistake that the compositions of Rachmaninoff occupied a special stature for my mother. It was not uncommon to find the sort of commentary that Stinson offered in describing my mother's performance of Rachmaninoff's *Rhapsody on a Theme of Paganini*, performed at Chicago's Ravinia Park with conductor Nicolai Malko in front of the largest crowd of the season, "with that impeccable perfection which sets her apart from most pianists and with that delicious fluency of finger which sets her apart from all of them."[84] No so incidentally, according to the program notes of the 1940 Carnegie Hall concert, the *Rhapsody* was composed in the writer's Switzerland home on Lake Lucerne between July 3 and August 24, 1934. Which means that my parents were visiting with Rachmaninoff during the precise period he wrote the score.

On the occasion of her performance of Rachmaninoff's *Concerto in C Minor*, Stinson wrote:

It was ensemble work on the noblest level and of the finest discrimination. Yet it was also piano playing of splendid power. . . . Her competence, subdued though it was, retained that genuine distinction which from the beginning marked her as due to rank among the first dozen of her fellow pianists.[85]

In March 1935, a critic observed that "Mme. Gradova had so absorbed the spirit of Rachmaninoff's work that her interpretation had the force of an original creation."[86] And from an uncited source we learn:

> The pessimism that seems prevalent in Mr. Rachmaninoff's playing is apparent in his new [fourth] concerto. . . . But there was no pessimism in Miss Gradova's performance of it. . . . There is in her playing an undeniable germ of individual and assertive musical thought: the creative power of the interpreter. The bent of this thought is primarily pianistic. But it is not coldly pianistic. Rather the warmth and brilliance and imaginativeness of her mind and of her feelings concentrate with perfect balance in her pianism.[87]

Commenting on my mother's performance of Rachmaninoff's Concerto no. 3, Edward Moore wrote:

> She has an accurate ear for dramatic possibilities in a composition, and being also a technician of a highly expert order, she has not the slightest difficulty in sending across to the audience through her fingers what has been previously conceived in her mind. So the profuse, luscious melodies and the thunders and lightnings of virtuoso display were reproduced in a manner that would have pleased Rachmaninoff himself.[88]

From a review of a performance of the Rachmaninoff Piano Concerto no. 2 by a critic whose name does not appear on the photocopy in my possession:

> Miss Gradova played the piano solo with such vitality, with so tense a musical interpretation, with such a dominant command of technical resources and of musical design that she carried her audience away with her performance. The concerto is a brilliant show piece, and it was played in that manner by the soloist.[89]

Rachmaninoff would remain with her, literally, to her dying days. But there were, still, the other great concertos, what she called the "warhorses," that also captivated audiences and critics. Stinson, for example, wrote of her interpretation of the Moszkowsky Piano Concerto with the Chicago Symphony Orchestra on Valentine's Day 1936:

> . . . One of Miss Gradova's highest virtues last night was that she kept it a truly musical scale, making it as much as possible an ensemble piece. . . . It is the most coloratura of all piano concertos, I dare say, and it is mountainous with difficulties. In Miss Gradova's swift and flawless performance a singularly pure and agile workmanship kept the filigree in faultless estate. But there was power besides, in notable dimension.[90]

Chicago Symphony Orchestra, February 29, 1936:

> [Moszkowski's] E-Major Concerto is at the same time exhilarating and obvious, a show piece pure and simple, and Miss Gradova is too witty to make anything else of it. Her valiant and sprightly humor swept the audience into a tumult of applause which called for several encores.[91]

Edward Moore observed that my mother played the Charles-Camille Saint-Saëns Concerto in C Minor "as though it was one of the finest and most brilliant show pieces ever written. As a matter of fact it is, and Miss Gradova is just the sort of brilliant pianist to give it all its values. . . . She is alert, speedy, in control of as many kinds of tone as the piano can produce, from persuasive lyricism to brittle hardness and when she lashes out, tigerlike, at a rapid passage, the Saint-Saëns fireworks glow more brightly."[92]

No longer known simply as "that talented pianist," it was evident that Gitta Gradova was now in the front rank of pianists, female and male alike. The responses to her concerts from Ania Dorfmann, Guiomar Novaes, Myra Hess, Sergei Rachmaninoff, Vladimir Horowitz, Gregor Piatigorsky, Nathan Milstein, and Rudolf Serkin, revealed their assessment of her as being nothing short of sensational, and of this there is some documentation.

On December 5, 6, and 8, 1940, my mother performed Rachmaninoff's *Rhapsody on a Theme of Paganini* with the New York Philharmonic Orchestra. Making these performances especially eventful was that the Sunday, December 8 concert would be broadcast nationwide on radio. Recognizing the significance of the concert, my mother's dear friend, Vladimir Horowitz, telegrammed her on November 26 to report that he had arranged for her to use his own personal orchestral concert grand piano.

For that same Philharmonic concert, my mother was staying with Horowitz and his wife in their Ninety-fourth Street Manhattan home. Horowitz coached her during her visit. On the evening of the performance, during their ride to Carnegie Hall—a description by pianist Gary Graffman,[93] once a student of Horowitz's, perfectly depicts their relationship as I knew it. While Horowitz encouraged and coached her, and presumably supported her with words like "under no circumstances can you stop, for stopping is provincial," he managed to cause himself and my mother to become physically ill.

The reviews of the concert were, as usual, spectacular. According to Francis D. Perkins: "She impressed her hearers as an artist of unusual consequence, not only in thorough technical mastery, but also in her understanding and projection of the differing moods of the variations, her exceptional ability to give each measure its right degree of volume."[94] From a Brooklyn newspaper: ". . . which gave Miss Gradova the full opportunity to display her highly regarded qualities as a mistress of technique and virtuosity, of tonal strength and warm emotion."[95] The *World Telegram* critic felt much the same way: "This is fire and brimstone in music, and Mme. Gradova fanned them into a dazzling blaze of brilliance."[96]

For all I know, millions of people listened to my mother that one evening over sixty years ago. One listener, my sister, later told me that, during those minutes, she finally understood what my mother did when she went away, as she did so often during our childhood.[97] For slightly different reasons, the performance was equally extraordinary for the cellist Emanuel Feurermann, who wrote to my father on the night of the concert: "It was magnificent playing and beautifully phrased and characterized."[98] Before the concert, the pianist Ania Dorfmann telegrammed my mother: "Every minute my affectionate thoughts and wishes are with you darling," and then again immediately after the concert: "Bravo Darling. Absolutely beautiful."[99] Rudolf Serkin had a similar response. He sent this telegram to my mother at the Crescent Hotel on New York's Riverside Drive: "Congratulations on your magnificent performance which I enjoyed immensely."[100] Serkin also commented on the quality of the broadcast when he added: "Splendid transmission."

My mother, of course, kept these loving affirmations, just as she kept the letter she received from her nephew, Howard, who was in his first year at The University of Illinois at the time, and who had done his level best to hear the broadcast. Several days after the concert, Howard wrote: "Dear Aunt Gitta: Just a small note to tell you that I listened to you last Sunday. Of course there was a bit of static in the car which made it impossible to hear, but I know it was swell any how."[101]

Then came the recordings, not as technologically advanced in that era as they presently are, but distinguished nonetheless. My mother recorded music rolls for the corporation Pianola and Duo-Art. In their catalog of July, 1932, one finds recordings of the Arensky *Études*, which the catalog claims is played with "fine spirit and verve," as well as Modest Mussorgsky's *Gopak*, with transcription by Rachmaninoff. Among her other Duo-Art recordings are the Étude in F Minor of Chopin, Moszkowski's Melodie in G, opus 31, and a piece entitled *Polichinelle* composed by Edna Bentz Woods, who dedicated the piece to my mother; she played it in manuscript form before it was published. The Duo-Art catalogue proclaims that Miss Gradova interprets the music ". . . with keen appreciation of its humor and its charm as well as with the technical proficiency it demands."

It was abundantly clear to many that the young Gertrude Weinstock was more than gifted. She was, in fact, a colossal talent, urged on, I can only assume, by a strict, disciplinarian father who made her practice until her fingers ached. She told me that on occasion the intensity of these childhood practice sessions, during which he sat in the corner of the living room, caused blood to appear on her fingertips. It is because of these sessions, perhaps, that she never forced her own children to play an instrument, although I heard my parents speak numerous times about how music instruction should be a nonnegotiable matter for children.

From her own descriptions, it appears as if my mother loved and admired but at times feared her father. My grandfather must have known that the youngest of his seven children carried the family's ticket to fame and grand achievement. I don't think the money aspect of a prospective career for the young virtuoso played as significant a role in his pushing her as much as his desire to see her recognized as a famous talent. I do think that she might have brought some of the same complex feelings she held about him to her relationship with me, the bearer of his name.

And so her career took off, in the United States and Europe as well, her terror of travel and stage fright probably ruining every moment of glory she experienced. But the reviews and articles only confirm her artistic triumphs. It was evident that she was a great performer, a poet, and a wonderful colleague. Over the years, our house was filled with those illustrious colleagues, each of whom sang her praises and raved about her consumate playing. If, as many allege, an artist's happiness rests in great measure on the recognition of her contemporaries, my mother must have been happy indeed.

Alas, a few words from the guests who sat on my mother's couch, a few piano roll recordings from the 1920s, and some recordings made by my father on early recording devices, are all I have, along with my memories, one of which consists of seeing her perform in public. The memory, sadly, is truncated, which implies, I imagine, all sorts of meanings.

My father, my sister, and several other people and I sit in a box overlooking the stage at Chicago's Orchestra Hall. Harry Zelzer and his wife, Sarah, are also in the box. Mr. Zelzer, the impresario who arranged for celebrity artists to perform in Chicago, was also the author, allegedly, of the line: "Good music isn't so nearly as bad as it sounds.[102] I remember Mr. Selzer for years begging my mother to return to the stage. I was very young at the time; she was too, for that matter. Throughout my childhood, standing beside her in stores and elevators, and riding on buses, someone inevitably would come up to her and quietly say, "We still miss you." I imagine she liked those expressions. I'm certain she did. As most artists well know, "to be forgotten by the public who once worshipped you, is an experience sharper than any serpent's tooth."[103] She often told a story of Arturo Toscanini being recognized at the World's Fair grounds by someone who remarked: "Aren't you the world famous Arturo Toscanini?" and Maestro, as he was known, shook his head and muttered, "If only I were." I think she liked this story, apocryphal or not, because it spoke to a modesty that barely masked a desire for recognition and public affirmation.

The lights of the hall dim, and the lights of the stage come up, creating a golden glow around the gleaming black piano. Below me, not that many feet away, my mother strides onto the stage from a door beneath our box.

I can't remember the applause, nor the program she performed on that Sunday afternoon. I remember only her high-heel platform shoes and the large shoulder pads in her dress. From where I sat, they seemed immense and silly looking. I think the piano bench was black and covered with tan, tufted leather. The memory ends with a vision of her holding on to the piano with her left hand and bowing to the audience.

My mother was at her best when music filled her head, and our house. In Tobias Matthay's words, music roused her "to a sense or feeling of *something vital and alive* . . . and are therefore *in harmony* with Nature herself!"[104] (emphasis added). Music, or the discussion of it, the gossiping and *schmoozing*, temporarily pushed away her sadness and anger and all that evil intensity. Martin Luther was right: "The devil does not stay where music is."[105] These were the times I liked her the most, when she was genuinely being herself, especially when she practiced. Well, that of course is an idealized vision. She was all that she was. But it is when the music was flowing that I loved her, even more than when she took me for hot fudge sundaes while my sister sat in a dentist's chair. No audience, no inner demons, no signs of the personal torture that no amount of psychoanalysis ever seemed to diminish. It was just her and her beloved Bach, Chopin, Liszt, Scarlatti, Schubert, Brahms, Scriabin, and Rachmaninoff.

The career that had been officially launched on November 20, 1923, at New York's Town Hall came to an end less than twenty years later in 1941. At thirty-seven-years-of-age, a wife and the mother of two small children, my mother gave it all up, and retired from the concert platform.

———————————

My Mother's Couch

*S*ergei Rachmaninoff was the first official visitor to our house on Hawthorne Place. I have read that he and Prokofiev were frequent visitors to my parents' several Chicago residences, but I have no recollection of Prokofiev, who died in 1953, ever sitting upon my mother's couch. I remember "Maestro," as Rachmaninoff generally was referred to, although my mother always called him Sergei Vassilievich. To a small boy, Maestro was frightening looking, although in truth he was a handsome, even princely looking man. What scared me was his frail body, and the skeletal nature of his shaven head. My impressions, apparently, were not wholly idiosyncratic, for in describing Rachmaninoff, Ernest Hutcheson likened his face to a "saturnine mask,"[1] while Harold Schonberg described him: "The tall, dour, lank, unsmiling figure of Sergei Rachmaninoff, with its seamed face and head of close-cropped (almost shaved) hair invariably reminded the public of a convict on the loose."[2]

Rachmaninoff must have sat on my mother's couch, though I have no recollection of it. I do recall, however dimly, spilling a glass of milk at dinner on the occasion of his first visit. This kindly man, who had been sitting directly opposite me—I always sat to my father's left and my sister's right—walked around the table and told me there was no problem, as he helped me clean up the mess I had made. It's not much of a stretch to interpret my little "accident" as a plea for attention. Rachmaninoff knew it, and acknowledged it. I suspect, however, my attempt to gain attention was short-lived, for the conversation quickly returned to music.

A childhood nightmare spawned by a stage production of *The Three Bears* in which a nefarious fourth bear frightens the baby bear, has Rachmaninoff as the central figure. I see him stealing records from the antique wooden cabinet in which my parents housed their record collection. The marble-topped piece stood behind the piano in the music room adjacent to the bay window. It now stands in our dining room, its drawers housing photographs of my parents and the people of their generation. Its lower cabinet, once holding my parent's records, now stores bottles of liquor. My parent's recordings, not so incidentally, are stored in the junk room, not that far from my mother's couch.

The nightmare bespeaks theft, perhaps Oedipal in nature, for I always feared that my mother was more involved in the lives of these male musicians than she was with my father or me. There were several women musicians with whom she was also close: Myra Hess, Ania Dorfmann, and Guiomar Novaes, but never, I imagined as close as she was with the men. I always feared that she would run off with one of them, perhaps Rachmaninoff. He seemed to provide a perfect opportunity. Truth be told, he whom I imagined to be a potential suitor, was for my mother an ideal, or an idealized father figure. She worshipped Sergei Vassilievich; she dreaded any negative thought he might entertain about her. One dared not whisper the slightest slur about him in her presence. Even the rumor of his anti-Semitism would be deflected; she loved him far too much to even contemplate such a possibility.

There were endless stories about the Rachmaninoffs, Horowitzes, and Cottles, all of whom summered together in Switzerland. The Rachmaninoffs lived in what my mother remembered as a magnificent house, but the Cottles and Horowitzes rented rooms in a hotel where, on one occasion, Sigmund Freud was staying:

> We had a big suite with Volodja [Horowitz] . . . and we'd have coffee at four o'clock in the afternoon, and I never had anything like it in my life, such rolls. So anyway, we get off the funicular and I said, "Oh, my God, look at the Rachmaninoffs, they came up from downstairs and they're trying to wave to us." [Horowitz] says, "Don't wave!" . . . We are going up the stairs and Horowitz gives me a pinch in the derrière and I go "Whoop!" and, of course Rachmaninoff is walking up with us. He says, "What's the matter with you?" I said, "I think a bug bit me. . . ." I never had a peaceful moment with Volodja, and we were so afraid of Rachmaninoff that when they served the raspberries, we ate those raspberries with the mosquitos right in the plate, and if you think I'm lying I'll get Volodja on the phone right now. [Rachmaninoff] looked at us

and said, "I never saw such good looking raspberries, but how can you eat them?"

If I had one regret in my life I think it would be, now that I look back, at that time I didn't think it was such a loss . . . that I didn't stay with him for three months. Never. You know, when I went to play for him at the Congress Hotel [in Chicago] where he stayed, I did the Beethoven First like he did. I did everything he did. The Beethoven First, and I played the *Paganini Variations* [of Rachmaninoff] both in one evening with [Chicago Symphony conductor Frederick] Stock. We did it three times. So I play [for him] and there comes this one part . . . tutti time, you know, and Maurie started to sing the orchestra part, and with that Rachmaninoff's dentures nearly fell out. He started to laugh. "Doctor knows the orchestra part?" He just adored him. He loved him—he was nuts about him. He'd look at me and say, "You're damned lucky to have him, you know." He thought I was a great pianist, but not in his class. Not as good as his class, oh, no.[3]

I feared as well that my mother had a little something going with the pianist Oscar Levant, who brought his nonstop coffee drinking and chain smoking habits to our home on more than a few evenings. You could tell that Oscar Levant was somewhere in our house the moment you opened the front door, for the odors of coffee and cigarettes pervaded every room. What a wreck he was. Even as as a child, I remember Oscar Levant sitting at our kitchen table, in my father's seat, his blue suit always shiny, his tie never tied tightly, his billions of nervous ticks, and his cigarette smoke permeating our home. I am certain my mother sensed my displeasure with him. She never requested any of the artists who came to our home to perform for me. They, of course, played together, double piano—sonatas, trios, quartets, and sextets. But when Oscar visited our home, she made him play one of Gershwin's songs, or the theme from one of his recent movies. She also urged him, I'm certain for my benefit, to speak about the movie stars that he knew. It always felt to me that the only movie star Oscar Levant cared about was Oscar Levant.

On the Jack Paar program, Oscar was asked by the host what he wanted to be as a boy. His answer—an orphan. Clever and telling as this response may be, I suspect there was something about the orphan quality of the man that made me distrust him. His presence in the house, in the kitchen actually, where visitors rarely went, made it seem as though my mother were acting as a foster parent, which perhaps meant that I was being displaced, for an afternoon anyway. Yet, bizarre as it may have seemed, he, too, must have struck me as a possible suitor, when all along my mother's lover was music.

Oscar wasn't the only musician my mother turned to in an effort to amuse her young son. One year, she arranged to have a handsome young composer named Norman Dello Joio take me to the Cubs opening day game. Mr. Dello Joio, who years later would become chairman of the Boston University School of Music, was evidently a baseball aficionado. As we walked to our seats in the grandstands, I could tell by the stares and gawks that he was well-known throughout the baseball world. Was it possible that all these fans knew of his compositions and I had never heard of him? The mystery of his fame was revealed when someone approached him and requested an autograph. It was then I learned that the spectators believed him to be Joe DiMaggio. In fact, there was a resemblance. My mother, too, had noted it.

Besides popular cultural figures like Oscar Levant, my mother palled around with the composer and song writer Victor Young. Victor, who I always believed to be an uncle through marriage, visited my mother on most every trip he made to Chicago. He was sitting on my mother's couch when he described how he wrote "When I Fall in Love." He wrote the song on a napkin en route to an airport. Victor also wrote "My Foolish Heart," a song my generation danced to on a million nights. For me, however, his crowning achievement was a ballad that in his lifetime had already become a jazz staple. Everyone in the business knew "Stella by Starlight." As an aging man, it saddens me that so many young people have no idea of that beautiful ballad, but thanks to Nat King Cole and his daughter, Natalie, they *do* know "When I Fall in Love." When I hear this song Victor is still alive, and, because he sat on my mother's couch so admiring and loving of my mother, she is too.

Actually, there was another popular songwriter in my mother's life, but their relationship ended with his death before I was born. Upon her own death, I discovered a green file box with silver locks and a silver carrying handle; it contained letters from someone named George. Not at all sexual or erotic in nature, they were profoundly warm and admiring notes. George had loved the way she played at some party and hoped with all his heart that they would see each other soon again. He delighted in the pure chance of their being seated together at a gala; he couldn't wait to hear what she thought of his latest work.

Upon reading the letters and knowing no one named George, I telephoned my sister, informing her that I thought our mother may once have had a lover named George. Judy was interested; she was neither shocked nor incredulous, just interested. Finally, it dawned on her that the admirer was George Gershwin.

There are at least two occasions described by my mother involving Gershwin, both having to do with chance encounters at parties where he played some of his compositions. The first was a party given in honor of Maestro Toscanini by the sister of Jascha Heifetz, who was married to the the music critic Samuel Chotzinoff, known as "Chotzy." In fact, Chotzinoff had written a glorious review of one of my mother's New York concerts:

> So he [Chotzinoff] invited me to their house and they had a wonderful party in honor of Maestro—Jascha was away on tour. . . . Can you imagine that party? And there sat George Gershwin. George and I took a good shine to each other; we were a couple of Americans there. And he said, "What are you doing afterwards?" I said, "Nothing." "Can we go out for coffee?" And we were sitting in the presence of Mr. Toscanini, and Mr. Toscanini asked him to play, and George played. He wanted an autograph so badly from the old man . . . [Toscanini] wouldn't give it to him. Doesn't even answer him half the time. We're listening to him play and then George says, "Where'll I meet you?" I said, When am I going to have the chance to go out with George Gershwin? Why do I have to go back to the suburbs [Toscanini's home in Riverdale] with the two morons [Vladimir and Wanda Horowitz]. And I said, "I have to go back with them." "So, I'll take you back. What's so terrible about that?" Volodja says, "She goes home with us. She stays with us. She cannot go anywhere." And when [Gershwin] died, the old man conducted *American in Paris* . . .
>
> The first time I met George was after my Carnegie Hall Concert. A reception was given for me and he was sitting at the piano playing some of his songs . . . and I was in awe of him. . . . Who in the hell was I in spite of the fact that I already had a Steinway contract. . . . Somebody said to me when I made my debut, you should listen to this young

composer because he's very talented and maybe you can use some of his works for your recital in New York. . . . I played his compositions in New York. Then Rachmaninoff wanted to know the [big deal] about him. "Why do you play that?" "Well, Sergei Vassilievich, he wrote twenty-four preludes and if you don't mind I would like to bring you a copy." "All right." And he opens up the score and he says to me, "Why," in Russian, "does anyone write twenty-four preludes and start in C-major when Chopin did such a gorgeous job?" But Rachmaninoff liked them, gave [Gershwin] a nice autographed picture . . . couldn't get that out of anybody else.[4]

My mother's friendship with George Gershwin seemed almost as auspicious as her relationships with Arturo Toscanini, Sergei Rachmaninoff, Marian Anderson, Jascha Heifetz, Paul Robeson, Rudolf Serkin, Nathan Milstein, Mischa Elman, Gregor Piatigorsky, Isaac Stern, and Vladimir Horowitz. However, I know Gershwin never sat on my mother's couch.

I remember all the laughing that went on when Marian Anderson came to our house, which she did every time she performed in Chicago. Miss Anderson, for I never could get myself to call her Marian, sat on the left end of the couch, my end. When she arrived, I sat in my chair and never entertained the slightest intention of moving. I just stared at her. She sat, royalty that she was, erect, elegant, enjoying everything that went on around her, requiring not an instant of personal attention. From time to time, she would lean forward, pat my hand and say, "Tommy."

Miss Anderson always arrived with two of the most unlikely sidekicks. The first was a jolly, rotund man called "Jofe," pronounced *Yo*-fee, which in fact was his last name. His first name was Isaac. He served as her personal manager. Jofe not only loved Marian Anderson, which he did with all his soul, but he also loved the state of Israel where he always hoped to spend his later years; he spoke openly of wanting to die there. Mercifully, Jofe never sat on the couch, for I feared that his weight might be more than the poor couch could endure. I enjoyed listening to him tell stories, but no one loved his accounts more than Marian Anderson, though I noticed she rolled her eyes toward the heavens when Jofe spoke of being buried in Israel. "Oh, Jofe," she would implore. "Please." At some level, I know that this elegant queen found discussions of death, no matter how tender, to be socially improper. There was demeanor in life, unalloyed civility, decorum. Miss Anderson lived these ideals, respected them, and required them of her unlikely entourage.

She didn't always get decorum from her beloved accompanist, a short, compact German man with a somewhat greasy face and a high-pitched hyena-like laugh named Franz Rupp, a man who appeared to be utterly uninhibited. He wasn't in the house a second before my father gave him a scotch. From a pinched bottle, my father poured Haig and Haig into a large drinking glass with ice and no water. Within a few minutes, Rupp, now on his second scotch, was noisy, profane, telling jokes, and cackling his way through every sentence. It was almost impossible to believe that this rowdy guest was the same man who accompanied Miss Anderson with such loving support and inconspicuous perfection. He always sat in the corner opposite Jofe, thereby looking across the length of the living room to Miss Anderson who, I am sure, must have wondered just how sober he would be at the concert the following afternoon.

A host of musicians were part of this concert eve dinner circuit. The person I remember most fondly is Nathan Milstein, the great Russian violinist whose pristine yet passionate playing, I have always felt, never received the attention and fame it deserved. I remember my mother describing her first sight of the man we called "Nathan," pronounced Na-*taahn*, but whom she called "Natanchik." She described being on a train with my father and the Rachmaninoffs; they arrived at a station in Gstaad, Switzerland. The families often vacationed together during the summer along with the Horowitzes and Piatigorskys as well. A handsome young man with slick, straight, black hair, dark brown soulful eyes, accompanied by a magnificent looking woman, his wife Rita, was standing on the platform. They became fast friends for life, conversing in English, Russian, German, and French, each of them having heard of one another, although at that point my mother had not heard Milstein play, for he had just recently departed Russia. How, precisely, he got out is a story I never heard, although whatever it was, it couldn't have been more fabulous than the story the cellist Gregor Piatigorsky, affectionately known as Grisha, pronounced *Gree*-sha, recounted, sitting at our dining room table, his long legs and arms splayed out in all directions.

Grisha, apparently, escaped his tormentors and murderous government by floating down the Dneiper River on his cello case.

Luckily for him, the current flowed in the right direction. My father always wondered, his characteristic British smirk starting to form on one side of his mouth, what was more amazing, that Grisha was never caught, or that the cello case never took on water and sank? Any child would have loved Grisha, for every child adores magical storytellers and magical stories that go on and on, each twist and turn as exciting and improbable as the journey of life itself.

"Grisha never lies," my mother always explained at the end of the evening as she and my father began their cleanup routines. "Maybe he embellishes, maybe he embroiders; *that's* different."

"So," my father would reply, "maybe it wasn't a cello case? Maybe it was really a viola case?"

I loved the way Nathan, with his thick Russian accent, said my name, *Toe*-me. I loved the open way he expressed his adoration for his daughter, Jill, who, for him, was the personification of perfection, and the way he harangued practically every conductor with whom he ever performed. Nathan had the final word on everything political, social, psychological, and philosophical.

Four months younger than my mother, Nathan became a citizen of the United States soon after his first American tour in 1929. From that point on until his death, he was acclaimed and admired everywhere. He traveled nowhere without wearing cologne 4711, a scent I shall forever associate with him. It was the final touch to his elegance, for he dressed in magnificent English sport coats, gray flannel slacks, always the most beautiful shirts and ties, and a tiny red cloth bud emblematic of *La Légion d' honneur* (The Legion of Honour) in his lapel buttonhole. As dogmatic as he could be, Nathan could always laugh at himself as he did when he described how he shined his own shoes, which were eternally spotless. I recall an evening at the dinner table as we ate his beloved kasha—everyone received normal servings, but my mother arranged to have Nathan's kasha served in a huge soup tureen—when he told of an obsessive compulsive fetish that had to take place before he could walk on stage.

Immediately prior to performing, he would work up a bit of a sweat, like a boxer, while he practiced in the green room. Then, carefully, he would place the violin on a table with the bow, go to the case, close it, clicking the two metal catches simultaneously with his thumbs. Simple enough, except if both locks didn't catch on the first try, he had to repeat the entire ritual: open the violin case, remove the violin from the table, take the bow in hand, practice a little something as he paced around the room, place the violin and bow back on the table, close the violin case, and then make absolutely certain that both locks caught simultaneously on the first try. I remember we all laughed at the sheer foolishness of the backstage ritual. The audience, however, would never know.

When my mother laughed, there was a lightness and a peace in our house. That feeling usually went away when the musicians did. "The thought of the eternal efflorescence of music," Romain Rolland wrote, "is a comforting one, and comes like a messenger of peace in the midst of universal disturbance."[5]

Nathan was a spectacular performer, both on and off the stage. Like many of the musicians who visited us, he possessed a sublime sense of the dramatic, something that served to tantalize a small child. Like the others, his stories often involved boisterous exclamations and exaggerated hand gestures. Often he rose out of his seat to accentuate some point. Sitting across from my sister and me at the dinner table one evening, Nathan, in his inimitable manner, was gesticulating wildly as he rose from his chair. Suddenly, his right hand smashed against a large crystal bowl that stood on a blond fluted pedestal in front of the dining room windows. We were all horrified. The suddenness of the accident and the noise were shocking.

My first concern, truthfully, was for the bowl. Knowing that it was valuable, I feared what my parents would say, only, of course, after Nathan left that evening. Poor Nathan was horrified. Instinctively he reached down toward the shards of glass, as if he could magically rescue the bowl. My mother, a look of terror on her face, reached over and grabbed his hand and pulled it away. "To hell with the goddamn bowl," she blurted out. "Is your hand all right?" Thankfully it was, and within minutes the conversation continued; Nathan's flourishing gestures having diminished not one iota.

I don't remember my father's precise response to the accident concerning the bowl, but it would have been the same as my mother's. He always valued life over material possessions. On one occasion, as my sister reminded me, two years of work constructing an elaborate medical exhibit was completely destroyed in minutes in a Chicago hotel fire. My sister learned of the fire on the radio. Judy was so upset she went immediately to the hotel, which was filled with the smells of smoke and burning materials. She expected to find my father totally devastated, but instead discovered him calmly working at something. She expressed her sorrow, and he replied that as long as no one got hurt there was no problem; the burned exhibit could always be reconstructed. As my father always said, "If money is the answer, the question's not profound."

Felix Borowski, a composer, teacher of musical theory, for a time president of the Chicago College of Music, and the music critic of the *Chicago Sun-Times*, also sat on my mother's couch. On one particular Saturday evening, following a performance by Rudolf Serkin, Borowski was seated at the far end of the couch. In time, the discussion turned to the interpretation of the Brahms first piano concerto. Truthfully, it could have been the second; I have a fifty-fifty chance of being correct. I cannot recall who might have been in attendance that evening, although I am sure other musicians were around. Members of the Fine Arts Quartet might have been there. Leonard Sorkin and George Sopkin were two members of the Quartet I remember well, along with violist Sheppard Lehnhoff. My mother always laughed at my inability to remember who was the cellist, Sopkin or Sorkin? Who was the first violinist? Sorkin or Sopkin? Our amusement was later expanded when a pianist by the name of Seymour Lipkin came on the scene. Imagine the fun a mother and son could have with names like Lipkin, Sopkin, Sorkin, and Pushkin!

Paul Stassevich, pronounced Sta-*say*-a-vich, was in attendance that night as well. Mr. Stassevich, once the head of Chicago's De Paul University's violin department as well as the conductor of the university's orchestra, was a remarkable man with a bald head and luxuriously bushy eyebrows. I always imagined he let his eyebrows grow when he realized that no other hair on his head was developing. A classmate of Nathan Milstein's in 1917 when they studied violin under Leopold Auer in Petrograd, Mr. Stassevich owned a distinction of which few could boast. He had once given a concert in which he performed a Brahms piano concerto in the first half and then, after the intermission, played the Tchaikovsky violin concerto in the second half. On numerous occasions, Stassevich had accompanied violinists like Auer himself. It was all rather amazing to a small boy who always wondered what happens if you pick up the fiddle and start playing the piano concerto?

The discussion on that one Saturday evening winds around to the tempo of the second movement of the Brahms First, or, as Groucho Marx might have muttered, fingering his cigar, the first movement of the Brahms Second. And one person on the couch says, "it should be played like this," and they warble a melody. "Not at all," comes a rejoinder from another part of the couch. It's much faster, *con brio*, and they, too, warble something. Suddenly, Mr. Borowski makes the following announcement which instantaneously silences everyone: "Well," he begins, "I recall that when I heard Brahms play it . . ."

Now wait just one miraculous moment, we all surely thought. Borowski heard Brahms himself play the Brahms piano concerto? For a few minutes, the entire room of adults no less was perfectly silent. Each person was dazzled by this utterly astonishing pronouncement, and each was calculating historically and mathematically to determine whether, in fact, it was possible that a man alive at this time in the twentieth century had heard Johannes Brahms. One could practically hear them thinking: Brahms died in 1897 . . . let's figure he was concertizing late in his life . . . this is 19. . . Felix is now, how old? It was true. The historical facts and the mathematics proved it. Unlike Grisha, Felix Borowski neither embellished nor embroidered. So much for the tempo of *that* movement anyway!

When Arturo Toscanini came to our home for dinner, preparations took on a special intensity. My mother moved about frantically, her concerns strictly with the condition of the beef tenderloin purchased that morning from Mannie Stockenberg, the butcher on Broadway near Aldine. Everything had to be perfect—spiced peaches, dripping in their sugary syrup, small red boiled potatoes, their skins barely beginning to crack open, a salad of the freshest lettuce and cucumbers with a tangy dressing, and finally the various flavors of hand packed ice cream, often five or six different varieties of chocolate alone, from Vala's, a store also located on Broadway. The huge frozen ice-cream balls layered in different shades of brown were served in a Steuben crystal bowl so that everyone might first see this modernistic sculpture.

Kasha, of course, had to be prepared for the Russians, but quite frankly, I don't remember anything about the Toscanini menu. I do know that years before moving to Hawthorne Place, my parents took Maestro to some favorite club of theirs in Chicago where they dined on spaghetti, at least this is what the *Chicago Israelite* reported on their society page. In that same column, the violinist Fritz Kreisler was noted to have "smashed his right hand in an auto door."

In the world of classical music, my mother taught me, the highest award a musician could receive was a trumpet fanfare at the moment of their entrance onto the stage. What she called a *touche* involved the horns blaring a welcome of recognition as the entire orchestra stands in appreciation. Musical in nature, the *touche* is the honor shown the musician by his or her peers in the only appropriate setting.

I actually heard the *touche* played every so often, although nowhere near as frequently as I hoped, for after hearing the first *touche*, any child waits with anticipation to hear it once again. To my knowledge, my mother never received one, but like an actor, hoping one day to receive an Oscar, I sensed that she always wished to have this musical fanfare blown in her direction. No one in her eyes deserved it as much as Maestro Toscanini, who I know heard a *touche* on many occasions. When Maestro dined at Hawthorne Place, he was assigned my mother's seat at the head of the table; it was her way of showing how deeply she honored him. He was the only person ever to usurp her.

My mother's relationship with the Toscanini family began in the years that she and my father became friendly with Vladimir Horowitz and his wife, Toscanini's daughter, Wanda. Trips to Italy almost always involved visits to the Toscanini's, and there was rarely a journey to New York City when my mother failed to visit the Toscanini home in Riverdale, a huge mansion that my mother always described as having rooms the size of barns:

> They had a house in Riverdale that no person in his right mind would have the courage to walk into. The reception room to sit down was twice the size of what we have here, with a great big monumental fireplace there, and that's where we always sat and had our cocktails before we went in for dinner. And I thought, Oh, God, it's gruesome . . . I never saw such a mansion in my life.[6]

In fact, on one excursion to the Riverdale manse, my mother, who had been invited to sleep over, could not find peaceful rest in rooms so enormous. Her first option was to sleep in a bathroom, which she also found terrifying. Wanda discovered her pacing in the living room. When my mother described her restlessness and discomfort in such a residence, Wanda advised her to go upstairs and sleep with her mother, Mama Toscanini. The only problem, Wanda warned, was Mama's loud snoring, but you can combat that, she counseled, by making a little clicking sound with your tongue. And so, my mother followed Wanda's admonition and crept into Mama Toscanini's bed where, sure enough, the woman snored loudly, and sure enough, the tongue clicking temporarily halted the irritating noise.

The next morning, as my mother described it in an interview with Steven Heliotes, Maestro asked her how she had slept. Always forthright, my mother recounted the travails, and travels, of the previous evening: "I slept and I clicked, I clicked and I slept."

Maestro listened intently and then replied: "You should have come into my bed."

None of these stories, however, could mask the occasional fright of Maestro, the fear of his wrath or disapproval. A musician had to be on her best behavior when Maestro was near:

> . . . He attacked some musician when he came to our house.
> I said, "Maestro, after all, he's a good musician; he plays
> chamber music so wonderfully . . . ," [He said] to me, "You
> know, you're an idiot." I say, "Why?" He said, "I don't un-
> derstand what you mean. He plays chamber music so well?
> Are you a musician or aren't you a musician? Do you have to
> be a special musician to play chamber music? What do you
> do?" he said. "Do you pick up a sonata and it says, 'I'm a
> sonata, I'm going to play you one way?' I don't know what
> you're trying to say, but you're an idiot!"[7]

I, too, visited with Maestro Toscanini on several occasions in New York City where, whenever possible, my mother would take me to rehearsals of the NBC Symphony Orchestra in an almost completely empty Carnegie Hall. Wanda would be there, along with Mama Toscanini, renowned for owning a different pair of eyeglasses for every possible occasion. She spent her time, my mother described, going through her shopping receipts. Recognizing that rehearsals could become tiresome, although there is probably no better way to learn a piece of music, my mother allowed me to abandon the rehearsal for Maestro's limousine, what she called the "black mariah," under the watchful eye of his driver, a lovely man named Luigi. Luigi let me pretend to drive Maestro's long Cadillac; I recall thinking, although this is fun, I'm probably missing something important inside.

At one rehearsal of Mendelssohn's *Italian Symphony*, I spied Richard Wagner. He was sitting in practically the same row as we were, only at the far end of the Hall.

"Mother," I whispered, "look, it's Richard Wagner."

For obvious reasons, my announcement caught her attention, even as the orchestra was stopping and Maestro was bellowing out something, partly in English, partly in Italian, for he often seemed impatient with the musicians. She looked where I was pointing. Either the combination of the Mendelssohn, Toscanini, and Carnegie Hall had produced a miraculous time warp, or her only son had become delusional.

"You're right," she whispered, and I felt the pride that she suddenly displayed in me. "You're absolutely right."

The person at the end of the row was, of course, not Richard Wagner. For that matter it was actually a woman whose profile along with the angle of the dark beret she wore had reminded me of a miniature plaster cast of Wagner that sat on a shelf in my bedroom in Chicago, along with the busts of Handel, Bach, and Beethoven. In fact, the woman was the granddaughter of Richard Wagner, but I felt my mother was proud that I was making such visual associations, for they meant I was growing up to respect classical music, the people who composed it, and the people who performed it.

As I said, Wanda was also at the Mendelssohn rehearsal that afternoon. It was she who turned around from the row in front of us and scolded us for talking. My mother pretended to be properly chastised, but when Wanda turned back to face the stage, my mother stuck her tongue out at her.

During the Hawthorne Place dinner with Maestro Toscanini, I remember first that a man my mother had hired to serve the dinner cried when he entered the room and saw Maestro for the first time. I remember, too, that in the middle of dinner, Maestro beckoned me to come to his side. Although frightened, I obeyed his command. Walking to the end of the table toward him, somewhat diffidently I am certain, I recall that others at the table were not paying much attention to us. "Come close," he said, and I did. I cannot properly convey how precisely I recall his features, the thinning white tussled hair, and the smooth face that was also Wanda's face. Maestro bent forward and suddenly, like a magician, pulled off his tie. He was wearing a black jacket and a striped black, silver, and white tie, and there it was in his hand, knot completely intact. I had never seen a snap-on tie before and probably appeared mesmerized. Like the other Maestro, Rachmaninoff, who had dined at this same table years before, Toscanini knew the little boy, who occupied the seat to the left of his father, was growing bored with adult talk about music and musicians. "You want it?" he asked me. All I could do was shake my head and return to my seat.

I remember nothing else of that evening. I am told by my sister, however, that Maestro was not yet finished with me. Seeking to relieve whatever tension or boredom he perceived, he let me play with his expensive watch. I took it completely apart and discovered I could not put it back together, thus destroying his valuable possession. Maestro, apparently, thought it was all perfectly charming.

What Maestro didn't find charming in the least, however, was one particular Saturday afternoon, years later, on the occasion of an NBC Symphony concert, broadcast nationwide, where the program's final symphonic piece concludes with a soaring and thunderous crescendo, followed by a long rest of silence, one final blast from the entire orchestra, and then at last total silence. The problem that one afternoon, was that some uneducated, musically illiterate, utterly insensitive, and moronic bore exploded with applause and screamed a giant "BRAVO!"—also broadcast nationwide—at the precise moment of the penultimate silence, thereby destroying the entire dramatic effect of the finale. At his Riverdale home that evening after the concert, it was all Maestro Toscanini could talk about; he was raving mad.

The end of this story may now be told, for Maestro will never know that the culprit whose neck he would have most certainly wrung sat but a few seats away from him at his own dining room table. The culprit was Gitta Gradova. Wanda, who had sat next to my mother at the concert, and my mother were the only people who knew the truth. Like two schoolgirls, it was all they could do to keep from laughing.

The cavalcade of visiting artists continued during my years as an adolescent. Each visitor producing some unforgettable scenes not only at Hawthorne Place, but in Union Pier as well. Some of Chicago's prominent citizens owned homes in Indiana and Michigan along the lake in towns with names like Michiana Shores, Lakeside, Bridgman, and New Buffalo, which, extraordinarily, the Eisenhower administration once considered designating as an emergency national capital in the event of a nuclear attack.

Farther west was Michigan City, Indiana with its Monkey Island Park and two invaluable movie houses. To the east were Benton Harbor and St. Joseph, where men in long beards played softball games, and the Silver Beach Amusement Park beckoned to families like ours.

Somewhere in Michiana Shores, Frank Leahy, the Notre Dame football coach owned a home, and down the road from us lived an attorney named Clarence Darrow, who, it was said, was a rather significant figure, but nowhere near as exciting as Sid Luckman, the Chicago Bears quarterback of those years, who summered in Lakeside; Luckman was a graduate of Columbia University, no less. Every so often, if you happened to hit the beach when he did, he might throw you a sixty yard bomb which you caught, ideally, flying into the lake. What parent worried when their child was in sight of Sid Luckman of the Bears? I always thought Aunt Sally missed the boat by staying in Salt Lake City and not spending more time in Union Pier.

The one man from that region, Sawyer, actually, who struck me as truly peculiar, however, was a frail-seeming soul with long, silver hair, unusually white skin, and oversized clothes that seemed to hang down too low on his body. On several occasions, I remember him coming to our home and reading his poetry while my mother spontaneously composed background music to words she had never previously heard. The scene offered gentle confirmation of Pierre de Ronsard's notion that "music is the younger sister of poetry."[8] Everyone seemed to enjoy these little performances, though frankly, I couldn't for the life of me understand what all these people found interesting about Carl Sandburg.

All of the visits with artists, however, didn't end on a pleasant note. For years, my father volunteered in a veteran's hospital on Chicago's south side. As the story was told to me years later, an account of a well-known actor and musical comedy star, who had been staying in our home, appeared in one of the Chicago newspapers. Clearly the implication was that if my father was offering sanctuary to a "known Communist," he, too, must have been a Communist. As a consequence, he lost his volunteer position at the veterans hospital, an act that profoundly disheartened him.

Quite a few people, actually, with leftist leanings passed through Hawthorne Place, one of them igniting what was to become the first political protest of my childhood.

Larry Adler, a man with dark, wavy hair and thick glasses, arrived at our house carrying his musical instrument in his pocket, something that greatly appealed to my mother. He was the world's premier harmonica player. I was stunned when I first heard Mr. Adler play a recital at Orchestra Hall. Now *this* was fun! Larry Adler walked on stage ostensibly carrying nothing at all, and everyone knew he wasn't going to sing or dance. Then, when he was actually playing, his hands were cupped around the instrument in a manner that made it possible for him to create a vibrato as well as pump the instrument's single valve with his palm. No one could see either his mouth or the source of the magic. He covered his mouth, his fingers flying up in front of his face, and from his instrument the audience heard glorious music—Bach as well as Gershwin. My mother always marveled not only at Adler's talent, but the fact that a harmonicast can go anywhere with his instrument tucked in his pocket. Quite a contrast from pianists, especially those like Horowitz who had their own personal pianos shipped from concert hall to concert hall.

Larry Adler not only visited our home, but in response to a request by my mother, consented to perform with his friend, the dancer, Paul Draper, at our school. For these "morning exercises," as they were called, those of us in the lower school sat in little chairs at the front of the old auditorium; the rest of the school and faculty occupied the permanent and wholly uncomfortable wooden theater seats. I was quite excited on that morning to see Larry Adler. Having heard his recital the day before, I told my second grade friends how terrific this one morning exercise was going to be. Before Adler played, however, we watched Paul Draper dance. I remember only bits of that performance, but I recall the sleeveless purple jumpsuit he wore over a pink silk shirt; all of this was new to me. Then it was time for Larry Adler to perform, or so I thought.

At the conclusion of Mr. Draper's performance, a teacher stood up and announced that the lower school would now be excused before "morning ex" continued, which meant that we weren't to hear Larry Adler. I protested, loudly, strongly, and angrily. "What do you mean, excused? This was totally unfair. Didn't the school think little kids could understand a harmonica? Did they think it was going to bore us? How could they just decide we were too young?"

Within minutes of the disturbance, my mother received a telephone call from the school's principal. Herbert Winslow Smith, an erudite, Harvard-educated man, who wore only suits and bow ties, and who died on the same day as my father, May 5, 1981, *Cinco de Mayo*, was a good friend of my parents. He and his wife, May, had attended many of the dinner parties with musicians at Hawthorne Place. However, he was very displeased with me; my behavior was inexcusable.

I don't know what my mother actually said to him, but I do know that I was neither punished nor disciplined. It was one of very few decisions made by the school that my mother totally disapproved of. "Children," she preached, "are never too young to experience the art forms of any culture." They may be too young to be sent on the road alone as child prodigies, but they cannot be too young to sit safely in their own school, listening to someone like Larry Adler.

The violinist Leonid Kogan, on the occasion of his first trip to America, upon being released from the Soviet Union for the purpose of playing concerts in the West, was another of those who sat on my mother's couch. What made the visit memorable was that in addition to the people who had assembled in our home to meet him, was a member of the KGB, a large man dressed in a wrinkled brown suit, and assigned to accompany Mr. Kogan everywhere. I think that when Mr. Kogan was in a public setting, Mr. KGB even accompanied him to the men's room.

The conversation with Kogan was about music, of course, the usual stories, moments of forgetting a passage, being anywhere from a beat to thirty minutes ahead or behind the orchestra, and any problem of any concerto inevitably being the fault of the conductor. Then, initiated surely not by anything a guest had said, Leonid Kogan, who had been speaking in Russian with my mother, began speaking both in English and Russian about the oppressive conditions in the Soviet Union. I wondered how he could say these things with the KGB agent ten feet away and clearly wide awake, though probably bored out of his mind? We knew the man spoke some English. How did one respond? Would they take Kogan back on the spot? Would they transport us all to a gulag somewhere? For the moment, I could tell that the guests and my parents were terrified. Americans might have freedom of speech, but would it be accorded Mr. Kogan by Mr. KGB simply because he was a visitor? What would happen to him once he left Hawthorne Place?

Then suddenly, everyone was laughing hysterically, even Mr. KGB. And between all of the gasps for air and the uproarious laughing there was even more talk of the oppression of the Jews, and how Fascist the entire *Sovietzky* regime had become. "The country was utterly unlivable," Mr. Kogan reported. Still, everyone laughed, presumably out of sheer terror.

The Hawthorne Place preparations for the mystery guest linger with me in the same way as those undertaken for Maestro Toscanini. A few moments of that one evening remain, nothing more. Yet this one night was different, for on this occasion, prior to the arrival of the guest, my mother made me sit down, in the living room no less, and listen to her. Her earnest manner encouraged me to take notice, for had she revealed anger or melodramatic fright, I would not have listened to one word. In effect, she told me that the person about to arrive was a wonderful man who I had met several times before. This particular visit, however, had to be kept secret from everyone, even my school friends. I wasn't to tell a living soul. "Like a mystery story," I think I said. "You have to promise," she commanded. Oh, for sure, I promised. The expression from Seinfeld born decades later could not have been more relevant: "Mother, it's in the vault!"

Who was coming? And what was the reason for the secrecy? Normally, I found activities to pass the time waiting for guests to arrive. What could be so great anyway? Marian Anderson's visits always excited me, but as much as I loved Nathan, Grisha, Mischa Elman, and Horowitz, I could wait for them to arrive. I played in my room, listened to the radio, or, in later years, did some homework until I heard the doorbell. Not so this particular evening. With the arrival time approaching, my mother, as always, fretted about everything as though life and death hung in the balance. I told her once in anger, "You don't know any other way to live but by worrying. God, if nothing else came up, you'd worry about sea level!"

The doorbell rang and I rushed to answer it. This time I was the one who let this visitor, this Elijah into the mahogany-walled reception room and then the entrance hall. There he stood, a gigantic man exactly eighty-five feet tall with a voice that boomed so loudly I feared it would shatter the three stained glass leaded windows that adorned the staircase leading to the second floor. He wore a camel-haired colored coat and a chocolate brown man's hat which he removed with grace, even elegance. He gave them to my father who placed them carefully in the closet at the bottom of the stairs behind the French blue-louvered doors. Then this giant looked down at me, bent over so that he was no longer eighty-five feet tall and said, "You must be Tommy." Oh, my God! I thought.

Robert Goulet once described Richard Burton's great voice, which, he said, he literally felt in his feet, the sounds traveling down through Burton into the floor boards, across the stage, and then up inside his own feet and legs. This was the same sensation I experienced when Paul Robeson, our visitor, spoke to me. I not only heard his voice, I *felt* his voice, its power, and its resonance. I remember nothing else of that evening; my memory ends with those four words, "You must be Tommy." Sadly, too, I have no recollections of Mr. Robeson's other visits when, accompanied by my mother, he sang Negro spirituals.

Well, that's not completely true. I remember going to school the next day where I kept my mother's secret for precisely a nanosecond. I told everyone I met about the eighty-five foot colossus with the booming voice. I think I also told people that he was a king; my parents probably had showed me pictures of Mr. Robeson in the role of *Othello*.

I have no idea what my friends thought of my tale, probably not all that much. Perhaps they all had encountered kings in their lives. At around ten o'clock in the morning, as my mother would tell the story, which she did with relish, Principal Herbert Smith once again telephoned our home. This time he informed my mother that her son was running around the school telling everyone who would listen that Paul Robeson had not only dined at our home, but was hiding out there.

My mother couldn't keep from laughing. She had to admit to Mr. Smith that her son was telling the truth. Paul Robeson was indeed living in our home for a few days so that he would be protected from "authorities" seeking to "contact" him, and possibly arrest him. The amusing portion of the story was now officially over. Mr. Robeson had to be moved to another sanctuary, a precarious arrangement given his politics and the furor his public statements and professed political ideology had aroused. If he were a Communist, which, according to his son,[9] he never was, it bothered my parents not one iota. My parents worshipped Paul Robeson, were probably sympathetic to his politics, and stood totally prepared to provide him asylum. Until that is, their son blew their cover.

I never saw Paul Robeson again. For certain, I was never told where he would now be hiding. I do remember feeling relief, however, when, months later, someone recounted his latest activities. It meant he was still alive, which meant that although I was often reminded by my mother that I was the source of many family problems, at least I wasn't the cause of Paul Robeson's death.

Chapter 4

The Physician

The oldest of seven surviving children, my father assumed the role of head of his family by the time he was ten. Grandpa Louie, his father (originally Leib), who had emigrated to England from Sedziszow Mal'opolski, a small town in Poland east of Krakow, was a ne'er-do-well tailor. Proudly, he strutted about the streets of London in mourning clothes and spats while my father and paternal grandmother, who was born Rachel Kraska in Przasnysz, Poland, also in Galicia,[1] were left to earn money and raise the other children. While my father's mother and siblings slept in the cramped flat behind my grandfather's tailor shop, my father actually made his bed on the cuttings of fabrics beneath his father's sewing table. An outstanding student, he was awarded a prize for excellence in July, 1906 at the Raines School in London. Eight at the time, he was presented with a copy of James Fenimore Cooper's *The Pathfinder*.

Our family always believed my father was born in 1898. Upon his death, however, we discovered his birth certificate; it indicated he was actually born two years earlier, which would have made him twelve at the time he became the family's male authority figure. Then, many years after his death, we learned that the original information turned out to be valid; he was born in 1898 after all. Wishing to enter the University of Illinois College of Medicine at an age under the legal level, his parents altered his birth certificate to make it appear as if he were older. Had anyone investigated the forged certificate, they would have discovered that my father's birth in 1896 preceded his parents marriage by fifteen months.

As the story was told by his siblings, though rarely by him, around the age of twelve, my father and his mother determined the Cottles would have a better life in Paris, so they picked up the family and moved to a small flat near the Rue Mouftard and Rue de la Balette. My father attended school, and among other things, his mother gave birth to my Uncle Philly. Even with housework and school responsibilities, my father found time to study the violin in a cramped studio above the gendarmarie near the Pantheon. He also worked in a pharmacy on the Rue St. Germain des Près, several miles from the family's apartment.

How my grandparents made do is anyone's guess, but my father's job at the pharmacy evidently helped to some minimal extent. The problem, however, was that no matter how many hours he worked, he never could bring home sufficient wages, and so he regularly stole a few centimes from the pharmacist's cash register. However, the family was unable to survive in Paris. Thus, Rachel and her eldest son decided to move everyone back to London, to the East End, not that far, actually, from St. Paul's Cathedral. After a few years this move, too, got them nowhere and so, when my father's Uncle Sam invited the family to come to America, the Cottles booked passage and set sail on the Lacania for New York. My grandfather actually preceeded his wife and children by a few months. The year was 1913.

There must have been great excitement for the Cottles at the time, for Uncle Sam, how fortuitously named, had indicated that he had plenty of room in his west side Chicago home. Surely, the family imagined a veritable mansion awaiting them. The excitement of the trip, however, was almost immediately dashed when my father encountered the steerage class accommodations that had been purchased for the family. As he told the story, he could not bear the indignity forced upon his mother, whom he clearly worshipped, living for fourteen days in wretched conditions. What, then, does a young boy do? He went to the captain and made him an offer: If the captain would move his mother into better circumstances, he would play the violin for the guests, free of charge. The deal was struck. My father played morning, noon, and night, mostly the Kreutzer Sonata which he had studied in Paris. His family settled not in first class accommodations exactly, but acceptable ones.

Like millions of immigrants, my father's family passed through Ellis Island but remained in New York only a few days; they were eager to reach Chicago, where, as it turned out, the "mansion" at 2053 Evergreen Avenue was nothing more than a small apartment in which my Great Uncle Sam had two spare bedrooms. The Cottle boys were assigned to one room, the Cottle girls to the second, and my father's parents slept, I'm not sure where. Still, everyone seemed to believe that America was the land of opportunity; there would be no returning to London or Paris.

In time, my father attended Chicago's Hoffman Preparatory School, becoming a member of the mandolin club, Omega-Tau fraternity, and the very first H.P.S. Orchestra. By 1919, at the age of twenty-one, he was on the faculty of the school where he taught zoology, French, and mathematics. He made additional money teaching violin and guitar. My father was admitted to medical school in Chicago, a rather expensive proposition even in those days. While still a student, he was offered an opportunity to teach in the school; this is rare in contemporary medical education. My father, apparently, was an exceptional scholar. As a second-year student, he taught the first-year students, and as a third-year student he taught the second-year students. Even with all these efforts, plus a job at Sears, a store he veritably worshipped, money was still insufficient. Again music bailed him out.

This time my father appealed to a man by the name of Mike Fritzel, who owned a brassy downtown eatery; some people claimed it was a hangout for Chicago mobsters. Since solo violin music was hardly coin of the realm at Fritzels, my father proposed that he earn his keep playing banjo for the guests. Once again a deal was struck: A student by day and a banjo player by night. And may I say, better renditions of "I Ain't Got Nobody," and "The Sheik of Araby" have rarely been heard. In fact, my father became so good at the banjo, he actually formed a small jazz band with the assistance of his younger brother Charley, a first-class drummer, or as my father always said, "top quality." Charley would later tour with the Ted Lewis Orchestra, as well as front his own bands. On several occasions, the Cottle brothers allowed another young Jewish kid from Chicago's west side to sit in with them, but only if he promised to behave. Young Benny Goodman wasn't old enough to perform in restaurants, but his talent on the clarinet was undeniable. My father maintained vivid recollections of Goodman arriving at the sessions, his instrument wrapped in the Yiddish newspaper.

Benny Goodman, it turns out, had vivid recollections of the Cottle brothers as well. Raised as we were on classical music, it is probably not surprising that early on my sister fell in love with popular singers like Frank Sinatra and Ginny Simms and I with jazz, especially pianists like Art Tatum and, later on, Theolonious Monk and Oscar Peterson. I discovered all the Benny Goodman records as well, loving especially the trio, quartet, and sextet playing with musicians like Teddy Wilson, Gene Krupa, and Lionel Hampton.

Imagine my excitement, then, the night my father took me to The Blue Note in downtown Chicago where Benny Goodman was performing. I was thrilled. I could barely remain seated during the performance. Afterward, I almost died when my father arranged to have Mr. Goodman come to our table. I was stunned to see how his top front teeth had been ground down by years of biting the mouthpiece of his clarinet.

Mr. Goodman, to whom I uttered not a single word, drank a glass of water. Well before he had finished, I had planned to steal his glass as a souvenir. I vowed never to wash it. Indeed he did remember my father and Uncle Charley very well; with fondness he told of the days they allowed him to play with them. The story of the clarinet wrapped in the Yiddish newspaper was true; instrument cases were extravagent expenses. Then suddenly, overcome with memories, Benny Goodman, no more than three feet away from me, began to cry. Soon afterward, he left the table. We never spoke with him again.

I brought the glass home and found my mother not at all surprised by my desire for a keepsake. She too, had a thing for celebrities, and who was to say that Maestro Toscanini's baton, which had been a gift from him to her, was of greater value than Benny Goodman's Blue Note glass? "Please," she said with a grin, "sleep with it, bathe with it, go to school with it, double date with it, just don't drink from it. Who knows where Benny's been lately."

My father's medical school tenure was followed by an internship and a residency in eye, ear, nose, and throat, his medical training being momentarily interrupted by World War I. This time, as my father recounted the story, he was called to register for the draft late on a Friday afternoon. Men from the Chicago area were being inducted and assigned to boot camps all over the country. But this could not happen, my father argued, as he was the main financial support of his family. The military didn't buy it, but there was one final musical deal to be transacted.

"Can you play the bugle?" the commanding officer inquired?

"Absolutely!" came the answer from a man who had never once even held a bugle.

How difficult could it be, he reasoned, and how many melodies did one have to learn? You bugled people up in the morning, then you bugled up the flag. At sunset you bugled down the flag, and at night you bugled people back to sleep. It wasn't unaccompanied Bach! So apocryphal or not, my father taught himself to play taps and reveille in a week, and the bugling job allowed him to remain in Chicago. He always joked that he had to stay home in case axis armies invaded Grant Park.

Following his residency, my father set off to Europe with his good friend, the urologist Irving Shapiro. They were headed for Vienna for postdoctoral fellowships, but a stop in Paris was mandatory. For years, the robberies of the pharmacist on the Saint Germain des Près, a good and decent man, had haunted my father. A righteous and moral person, he could not live with the memories of his transgressions. So Irving and he went to Paris ostensibly to catch the train for Vienna, but not before my father visited the pharmacy one last time. The proprietor remembered my father well; he was thrilled that his former employee had become a physician. At last my father admitted to his crimes. The man's response stunned the young visitor: "Of course you stole. Who do you think left money in the till for you to steal? My wife said I overpaid you, but I knew your family had nothing." He refused compensation of any sort.

My father's ingenuity extended to the world of art as well, but here, truthfully, he may have capitalized on a somewhat haughty attitude. Somewhere along the line, he had fallen in love with Asian art which he found in droves, actually, in Marshall Field's Department Store on North Wabash Avenue. Statuary, vases, and bowls from the Ming, Han, and T'ang dynasties, literally thousands of years old, lined the home furnishing shelves selling for ten, twenty, and thirty dollars. My father purchased every piece he could afford. He would have bought a lot more had my mother not felt the house was turning into what she called a "stable for camels, horses, birds, and water buffaloes." Ironically, she may have unconsciously been resisting this second coming of Asian art into her life, as Madame Herz's studio too, had been filled with art from the Far East.

At the same time, he developed an interest in Japanese wood block prints of the eighteenth and nineteenth centuries. Once again, several department stores carried these "items" as people desired them as accessories to their room decor. It dawned on him, however, that such pieces might be found in the junk shops of Chicago's west side, where, quite possibly, proprietors would have little appreciation for their value. Quite a few prints were purchased by this "artful dodger" from those west side "junk" shops, which my father visited allegedly hunting for unusual frames. When he found what he wanted, he extolled the virtue of the frames, saying nothing about the prints, and in this way got the prices marked down.

Partly his ingenuity was predicated on people's ignorance, which he could barely tolerate, and partly on their lack of sensitivity for the beauty of art. My father believed art was not only to be loved, it was to be displayed, enjoyed, but most definitely to be distinguished from mere decor. Aaron Copland expressed in a musical context what my father believed true for all the arts: "Music can only be really alive when there are listeners who are really alive. To listen intently, to listen consciously, to listen with one's whole intelligence is the least we can do in the furtherance of an art that is one of the glories of mankind."[2] A Chinese vase sat on a shelf because it was glorious, not because its ox blood color went perfectly with the living room drapes. My cousin Frankie and his new bride learned this lesson all too quickly.

On the occasion of their wedding, my parents gave the young couple a Chinese maiden of the T'ang dynasty. Making the piece unusual was the fact that it was fabricated not in the traditional terra cotta, but instead carved in wood. Standing almost two feet high upon a round mahogany pedestal with gracefully sculpted legs, the figure revealed more than hints of the original bold green, yellow, and blue paints characteristic of the period.

Alas, as beautiful as she might have been, she didn't quite go with the color scheme of the couple's Salt Lake City home, and so, when my father visited and wondered, as he would, where the figure might be? he was told that it was sitting on a shelf in the guest closet. That's all he needed to hear. I can only imagine the lecture the young couple heard, but my father returned from Utah with the figure, wrapped in towels, under his arm. I encountered it for the first time on the dining room table at Hawthorne Place. Carefully avoiding any discussion of whether one has the right to reclaim a gift, or even ask where it is, I went on about the beauty of the figure.

"You like it?" my father asked.

"I love it," I answered.

"Then it's yours." And it sits this very day conspicuously displayed in our dining room.

In the early 1950s, his love of Asian art now shared by hordes of Americans, which meant that no longer did one just pop into Marshall Field's to buy a few T'ang horses, my father set out on a mission. Where, he wondered, might these pieces exist where people have little appreciation of their value? The west coast was an obvious answer, but where, precisely? He reasoned that one needed a community where the *nouveau riche* buy the right stuff for the wrong reasons and then change their taste, or more precisely in his eyes, their lack of it, only to discard beautiful treasures.

Concluding that the place to visit was Santa Barbara, California, he set off to explore junk shops and antique stores. The trip proved to be a bonanza. He discovered a slew of pieces, a few of which he purchased. As he anticipated, the prices were laughably low; many of the shop owners had no idea what they possessed. One of the pieces, actually, was the five foot high wooden figure that stood behind my mother's couch. Another piece was the figure owned by my cousins, well, for a few months anyway.

When my father loved something he wanted others to take a deep and abiding interest in it as well. When that something was as precious as Asian art, a part of him wondered how it was that someone would not be moved by such beauty. Ask him about this or that piece, as many visitors to our home would do, and two hours later the lecture, "Asian Art 101 at Hawthorne," would come to a begrudging conclusion. Some people departed the lectures more knowledgeable but unmoved, and still others, it is fair to say, had their lives changed by my father's appreciation of the artifacts of various Asian cultures.

I maintain vivid recollections of my father rising from the dinner table, going to the piano upon which his violins sat, opening a case, unwrapping a fiddle from its silk wrap, and then selecting a bow from its position on the inside cover of the case. Tapping middle A on the piano, he would spend minutes tuning, measuring the tone of one string against the tone of another string. Finally, he played, but always while pacing around the house, looking at the shelves in the living room on which many of his beloved Asian artifacts rested. Slowly, he wended his way through the living room, then through the music room, past the antique marble top chest that housed his record collection and on which stood a *blanc de chine* figure of a maiden, and finally into the dining room where he continued his practicing standing before the glass door breakfront that protected still more art pieces. This was for him sublime sensuality: The music and the Asian art in concert. It also meant that he never came up to my room, or asked about school, or sports, or much of anything. Our house was the breeding ground of the infamous exchange: "Where did you go?" "Nowhere." "What did you do?" "Nothing." I never even told my parents I had been elected president of the student government. They found out weeks later from a teacher.

In fact, I remember only two events that brought my father to my bedroom. One was when I was sick; he would come with his little black medical bag and give me an injection. The other was years later when I returned home from college. Then he walked around my room making certain that everything was in order: lamps worked, appliances were plugged in, and there was a sufficient number of hangers in the closet.

More than anything else, medicine stood at the epicenter of my father's existence. For him, it was the most noble work any person could undertake, and God help anyone who violated its sacred tenets. As a surgeon he railed against a nurse for picking up an instrument that had fallen on the floor during surgery and replacing it on the tray. My father, known in his operating room as somewhat of a tyrant, railed against anyone for dropping the instrument in the first place; one simply didn't do those things. If anyone, even his children, did something unacceptable, he would say, "What do you mean? I don't understand. How could you have . . . ?" He was the same apparently in the classroom, for he was described as demanding "complete attention during his lectures, however, he treated everyone with equality. Those who came with inflated egos were soon deflated and some voluntarily left the class. They were the losers. Paradoxically, he could single out an inattentive student, give him a lecture, often abrasive, before the entire class, and yet shortly after show that same student a great kindness and concern for his progress."[3]

To spend more time with my father, I occasionally accompanied him on his Sunday morning hospital rounds. I was barely able to keep up with him in the long hallways and stairwells. I never liked this activity, for he was constantly occupied with significant medical consultations, which meant I spent a great deal of time alone, inhaling medicinal odors and peeking into rooms at gravely ill people, many of them with contraptions of one sort or another coming out of their bodies. I always felt as if I was going to vomit or choke to death. Often, I hoped if a professional ball player was in the hospital, perhaps I could get an autograph, although an athlete clad in a hospital Johnny was more than a trifle incongruous.

Conversely, I enjoyed visiting my father at his North Michigan Avenue office where his head nurse, his sister, Sarah Udell, a highly efficient woman walked as quickly as some men run; her fingers raced through the little tobacco brown books in which thousands of patients records were kept, with the speed of light. The waiting room, where I sat waiting for my father to complete his work, opened into a long corridor; examining rooms were situated on either side and his private office was at the end of the hall. Sitting in the waiting room on one of the tangerine leather couches—Mr. Walsh had been here as well—I studied his patients, hoping, of course, that a celebrity might emerge; on occasion they did.

The best part of the office visit, besides the relief of not having to be a patient and have my sinuses blown out, was going downstairs to DeMets, the coffeehouse in the lobby; I often had tea and cookies with my father in the corner booth near the rear exit. The booth had an internal window which meant I could observe people walking along the main corridor of the building. Wearing his white medical coat, tongue depressors and pens sticking out of the left breast pocket, my father was, in my estimation, the most important man in the entire restaurant.

These were the times I had my father to myself, if only for fifteen minutes, but I relished them, even if there was minimal conversation. To join my father for afternoon tea was more than a treat; it was an honor he reserved for the special people in his life; my cousin Billy, his brother Jack's son, was one of these people. Years later when Cousin Billy, whose law office was close to my father's, told me the significance to him of the afternoon teas with my father, I told him I was jealous. "The teas meant you were really loved," I told him. Cousin Billy could only respond, "Really?" It was difficult for me to think that after I left Chicago, Cousin Billy and my father had tea together almost every week.

From my father's conception of physician emanated a thoroughly moral approach to living. "Always do the right thing," he taught, "and you'll only regret the things you didn't do." One didn't lie, steal, misrepresent, nor mention any patient by name. One did not cheat the government in taxes, and one did not sue, no matter how egregious the offense. "You don't make money suing people," he admonished my sister and me many times. "You make money by working. Then again, if someone passes on a good stock tip, you don't have to look the other way."

Early in the 1940s, a cigarette company hired him to conduct research on the effects of smoking. He took the money and reported to them that he had never found anything more deleterious to the human body.

He also taught me that a physician didn't pursue patients for unpaid bills. If people either couldn't pay or, for whatever the reason, chose not to pay, that was the end of the story. One neither degraded oneself chasing after accounts receivable nor engaged someone to perform this work. Doctors saved lives and sought to prevent illness. Patients either paid, or they didn't. At the time of his death, when he had practiced medicine for almost sixty years, a family friend advised me that if my father had collected one third of the money owed to him over the years, my sister and I would be very wealthy people.

To say the least, my father was an inveterate reader. His night stand and several desks always were piled high with books on medicine, psychiatry, literature, art, biography, history, philosophy, and poetry. I don't think he was the novel reader my mother was, though he did enjoy great detective yarns, especially authors like Erle Stanley Gardner and Raymond Chandler; they consumed his summer vacations. Several of his friends shared his passion for reading and the pure joy of discussing books, but no one I knew had a more genuine intellectual curiosity. A telegram he sent to my mother in 1927—they had been married about a year and a half—announces only that he has attended a "Nietzsche class at Eisendraths." In a letter, he tells her of being at a party where he has discussed "the theory of color perception and its relation to the theory of relativity and gravitation of Einstein."

My sister relates the story of finding our father studying a journal one afternoon and asking him what he was reading? He told her it was an article in a medical journal having to do with the testing of a new drug. "Why are you reading *that*?" she asked. His response came in the form of an expression that he often used, and one that never left her heart.

"Because," he said, "if you can't keep up with the times, you don't deserve to live *in* the times."

Decades later, on the eve of a trip my sister had planned to Chicago, he telephoned her. Knowing that she was coming home for a visit with a man with whom she had been living in New York but to whom she was not yet married, a man my parents had only met once, he wanted to tell her of the sleeping arrangements he had made for them. My sister assumed that my father was going to assign David to a bedroom on one floor, and her to a bedroom on another floor. Instead, he advised her that they would live in his house as they lived in *their* house. Suddenly the meaning of that earlier expression came forth: "If you can't keep up with the times, you don't deserve to live *in* the times." At the time of that telephone call, he was seventy-nine years old.

An ear, nose, and throat surgeon, his specialty eventually turned to the anatomy and physiology of the nose, and in particular the relationship of the nose, heart, and lungs. He loved performing surgery, but this work was guided by the research he conducted. Toward the end of his life, he was immersed in work wherein by measuring the amount of effort required by the heart for normal breathing, one might be able to predict whether a patient is prone to sustaining a heart attack.

In order to do this work meant years of researching nasal anatomy and physiology, which in turn meant constant explorations of cadavers. In time the entire basement, a space equal to the entire first floor of our house, had been turned over to his writing area, research area, and an office in which he and several colleagues founded what in 1954 became the American Rhinologic Society and in 1961 the International Rhinologic Society, both of which saw him serving as the first president. This meant that until the end of their lives together, my mother accompanied my father to cities in America and abroad as a member, albeit of special status, of the contingent of doctors' wives. Some of these women, presumably, knew of her earlier life, others probably did not.

Every Thursday afternoon, a group of physicians and secretaries went down into the basement with my father to work on the research and administer the medical societies. They would come up briefly for a bite of food in the kitchen and then descend once again. All his spare hours were spent in the basement that in time my mother called "Dr. Jekyll's laboratory." He was always in the basement doing something, usually viewing and cataloguing his thousands of photographic slides.

The laboratory area, what was once a room where the family did some woodworking and played ping pong, was now a place to work on human heads which were wrapped in toweling saturated with preservatives, then placed in plastic bags and stored in garbage cans. An appreciation written of my father after his death declared: "He insisted that all laboratory material be treated with the same care and respect shown to a surgical patient and he, himself, strictly followed these admonitions."[4] Despite his ethical treatment of the cadavers, my mother, for obvious reasons, rarely visited the basement. She said she didn't relish the idea of accidentally bumping into Mrs. Goldstein or Mr. Pishkin, names, of course, for the heads. Because of the somewhat ghoulish idea that heads were actually stored in our home, I called them "Mr. and Mrs. Gottsengoul."

"*Nu*," my mother would remark, "maybe we could get your Mr. Gottsengoul together with my Mrs. Goldstein, they might make a lovely couple."

"Yeah, they could kiss but they couldn't neck," I would reply. Then we would laugh.

When I say that wherever my father went, his research went with him, I am being almost perfectly literal. Driving a young woman home late one Saturday evening on Chicago's outer drive, my father's car developed a flat tire. Ironically, I was able to pull the car into a turnout no more than a couple hundred yards from Hawthorne Place. Chivalrous to a fault, I opened the door for the young woman and made certain she was safe on the grassy median strip of the highway, and then proceeded to open the trunk in order to fetch the jack, lug wrench, and spare tire. Since the car was stopped beneath a street lamp, I had all the illumination I required. When I opened the trunk, the light fell directly on Mr. Goldstein who was "sleeping" in a cardboard box, looking not unlike a character Señor Wences created on The Ed Sullivan Show. "Is all right?" "Is all right." I remember that Mr. Goldstein needed a shave. I was so surprised I let out a yelp and slammed the trunk shut. I couldn't get myself to open it again, much less reach my hand inside.

Fearing my parents' reaction to my cowardice, I nonetheless walked with the young woman to our house; I woke my parents with the news that the car had a flat tire and that I couldn't quite get myself to fix it. My father responded with his characteristic: "I don't understand. What do you mean? How could you have . . . ?" Excusing myself from the young woman, I explained the presence of

Mr. Goldstein, who, apparently, had chaperoned us. With that my parents exploded with laughter.

The medical research went to Michigan as well for the summers, where a sleeping porch off my parent's bedroom was turned into a study. Papers, journals, patient reports, manuscripts, books, and the ubiquitous slides and photographs of operations, patients, and cadavers were everywhere, though I don't think the Gottsengouls and Goldsteins ever made it to Michigan. They did, however, make it to Israel, where they were accompanied by a host of their *mishpocha* (relatives).

In the early 1960s, my father accepted an invitation to offer a two week postgraduate course at the newly opened Hadassah Hospital in Jerusalem. For years he had been teaching courses at major medical centers in New York, Chicago, Baltimore, New Haven, Los Angeles, Pittsburgh, Portland, and New Orleans, as well as Mexico City, Leiden, Odense, Bologna, and Budapest. The Israel trip was for him a crowning achievement. Israel opened its doors, providing him almost everything he needed, including an entire floor in a wing of the new hospital which was, at the time, starting construction of a small chapel that eventually would house the stained glass windows designed by Marc Chagall. The only item the Israeli government could not provide was human heads; these would have to be transported from the United States. Happily for me, my father asked me to join him on this trip, but I was going to have to work for the International Rhinologic Society to earn my keep.

My first job commenced at New York's Kennedy Airport where the twenty-five of us, mostly doctors, constituting the American entourage, faced the task of escorting Mr. and Mrs. Goldstein, Mr. and Mrs. Gottsengoul, and their relatives to Israel. Many hours of conversation between my father, the Israeli government and transportation bureau, and El Al Airlines resulted in an expedient solution: Each American would transport one head in an El Al carry-on bag that would be stowed in the luggage racks above our respective seats. It was understood that airport officials in New York and Tel Aviv would not inspect these bags.

"Come on, Mr. Goldstein, Tommy's taking you to Israel," I muttered under my breath as I approached the man inspecting our luggage. Seeing that it appeared as if I were carrying a bowling ball on to the plane, he jokingly asked me, "What have you got in there? A head?"

I am my father's son, and he taught me never to lie. "Yes sir," I answered. "It's a head. It's Mr. Goldstein. The guy behind me's got his wife."

The man appeared completely unfazed.

Having graduated from college and living through a somewhat low moment in my life, my father's suggestion to work for him for two weeks seemed immensely appealing. I had nothing better to do, nothing resembling a career to pursue; besides, Israel represented an ideal jumping off place for trips to Greece and Italy. As it happened, I fell in love with the country and asked my father if I could remain after he departed. He was delighted and at once gave his approval. The first question, however, was where would I live? A telephone call to my mother brought news that the violinist Isaac Stern was staying in a hotel outside Tel Aviv. Perhaps I should contact him.

Normally, I would never impose on my mother's musician friends. For all I knew, they hadn't the foggiest knowledge of who I was; there was always that matter of my being little more than my mother's son. Surely these people didn't expect to see me anywhere outside Hawthorne Place. Nathan Milstein was so shocked to see me backstage at a concert in Lucerne, Switzerland, he instinctively blurted out, "Where's Mommy?" But there was something about Isaac Stern that made me feel he always had room in his heart for one more friend, especially someone who needed him for something. Indeed, one of the many things that endeared me to Isaac, a man who made his New York Town Hall debut at almost the same age as my mother, was his optimistic, joyful approach to concertizing and living.

I had met Isaac at Hawthorne Place during one of his numerous trips to Chicago, but never really got to know him. Like most of the touring musicians, he was my parents' friend. My first trip to Israel, however, afforded me the opportunity to learn first hand what I had always heard about this generous and fun-loving artist.

I didn't even call the Stern's hotel, I simply showed up and introduced myself. I don't remember his wife, Vera's, response, but Isaac was wholly enthusiastic and delighted to see me, as were his two children who saw me as a potential playmate. Within a few minutes we were at the beach in Netanya splashing in the waves together as if we were old buddies. In that instant, I proclaimed him my godfather. Later that evening, sitting on the veranda after dinner, Shira Stern, Isaac's oldest child, ran toward me holding a present behind her back; it was a key to a room at the hotel. After that I never left the Sterns' hotel. I headed to a kibbutz only after they departed for America.

Isaac Stern's effortless generosity and thoughtfulness, coupled with his manner of treating me not as my parents' child, had won me over. The lasting image I have is the way we all played together in the surf, something I never did with my own father.

Swimming with my parents was a rare occurrence, even though we owned a summer home on Lake Michigan. My father didn't seem to relish the beach. As he said, and a phrase I now confess to muttering from time to time, "If it weren't for the sun, the sand, the crowds, and the water, the beach would be terrific." My father would go in for a dip, but it wasn't a long one. He'd get used to the water by splashing small amounts over his shoulders and back. Then finally, after all of us prodded him along, he would stoop down until he was submerged up to his chin and do a few breast strokes. "That's it," he'd shout as if to say, "You wanted it, you got it. I'm done!"

My mother, on the other hand, wearing her two-piece yellow bathing suit and cream-white bathing cap, seemed to enjoy swimming once she got over the preparative ablutions. More flamboyant and theatrical than my father, her entrance into the water was performed directly for us children who, for minutes, had been submerged up to our noses waiting for the big event. It came replete with yelps, screams, shouts, and Russian swear words strung together like an aria, as if the water were freezing, which it never was, and she was never going to survive the ordeal.

This theater only happened a few times each summer, so it was an event when Gitta Gradova entered Lake Michigan. Five minutes and it was over, an étude, never a concerto. Then she was back on shore toweling herself off, and appearing like Gertrude Ederle having just swum the English Channel. Was this really the same "athletic form" that had captivated the *New York World* critic?

"Please stay in," we'd shout. "Please, please!"

"No chance," she answered. As my Uncle Charlie used to say, "The water was too wet."

Then there was Isaac Stern. No warm-up, no getting used to the temperature, no *schmunzes*, my mother's word for all the unnecessary behaviors that distract from one's artistry. Isaac just went swimming, and body surfing, in the formidable waves of the Mediterranean. Not only that, he stayed in as long as his children wanted him to. And then, before we finally got out of the surf that first evening in Netanya, I saw Isaac standing waist high in the water, his hands planted on his hips, blowing out his chest, and pulling himself up as strongly as possible as if daring the waves, nature itself, to knock him over. What a wonderful way to face life. What a gift to be fearless, or at least know that genuine courage, as the ancient Greeks taught, is to know precisely what one should fear.

I loved accompanying Isaac to concerts. He practiced, of course, in the various hotels in which he stayed, or at the Orchestra House outside Tel Aviv where the Sterns often resided in Israel. I always sensed he practiced for the purpose of learning music and honing skills, not to silence lurking demons intent on sabotaging him in the middle of the final movement.

Not so incidentally, Isaac, like my mother, struggled with the matter of leaving his children when his concert schedule—which was constant—required him to go on the road. Life was relatively easy for him during his stays in Israel; concertizing meant only a few hours away from home. Living in the Orchestra House, I often babysat the Stern's two children, Shira and Michael—a third, David, was born several years later. Every night when there was a concert, Isaac and Vera left their children in the care of their full-time nanny and me. Night after night we endured the heart wrenching scene at the front door. Michael looked sad and confused, and his older sister wailed her unhappiness no matter how comforting her parents tried to be. Finally I would say, "Just leave; they'll be fine," words my own mother probably successfully uttered to hundreds of parents, but never to herself. Other parent's children would survive separations, but not her own. Nor would she.

Then one night, Shira's wailing came to an abrupt halt. Everyone just looked at her as she stood perfectly silent before the front door. When asked, how come you aren't crying? this remarkable child responded: "I just realized it doesn't do any good!"

One other experience from that first trip to Israel remains with me. Connecting me psychologically with my own family, it occurred well after my father had returned home and I was alone to travel and work; the Sterns too, had left for America. Shortly before my own return home, I was invited by a young nurse for a weekend to her parent's house in Haifa. Previously, the woman had moved into the home of a friend in order to allow me to live alone in her

Jerusalem apartment. We traveled together by train, a slow but enjoyable journey that made me wonder how it was I hadn't gotten to know her better. The trip put me in mind, as well, of a joke my mother told of the huge Texan bragging to a little Israeli gentleman about the size of his revered home state.

"You can stay on a train all day, and all night, and well into the next day," the Texan bragged, "And you're still in the state of Texas," she announced affecting a Texas accent.

"Well," the little Israeli answered, in a Jewish dialect, naturally, "to tell the truth, in Israel the trains aren't much faster."

Arriving at the Haifa train station, we were met by the young woman's mother. Within minutes we were passing the B'hai Temple and beginning our ascent up the glorious Mt. Carmel, the road lined with luxurious vegetation, when the young woman's mother leaned forward for the purpose of studying me. "And so, young man," she said in a disarmingly severe tone, "and just what do *you* do to justify your place on this earth?"

Her words were not those my own mother would ever have uttered, but there was something in her dark eyes and her tone that flung me back to Hawthorne Place. Fourteen years of progressive elementary and secondary education, coupled with four years of private college proved a complete waste. I had no answer for her. Still, there was something valuable about the moment, for it was a reminder that I was hardly the only one to live in the shadows of parents with powerful temperaments.

The woman's demeanor and flashing eyes took on an even more familiar quality that evening at dinner in her elegant home. Seated around the long dining room table, along with the young woman's father, a well-known attorney committed to having American corporations open plants in Israel, were prominent businessmen from Israel and America. My own dinner partner was the CEO of a major American drug company. I had conversed with him about Indiana for fifteen minutes before his position and prominence dawned on me.

Then, suddenly, sparked by heaven only knows what, I leaned forward to study my hostess at the head of the table. Before all the dinner guests, I announced:

"I have an answer to your question," the one she had asked literally hours before.

"Oh," she said.

"I love."

My words fell as a thud, a perfect confirmation of what this woman must have originally thought of me, which presumably prompted her question in the first place. Better to ask me that hostile question, however, than inquire of her daughter why, of all the interesting visitors to Israel, she would bring home this *schlub*? I know that the question in the car troubled the young woman, a person I knew only slightly, even though I had received such generous gifts from her. Years later I would show a photograph I took of her that weekend in Haifa to my mother-in-law, a gifted portrait artist and photographer and, hence, a keen reader of faces. She looked for a moment and declared: "This is a person with a strong feeling, who might well do something about it."

How extraordinarily accurate was my mother-in-law's perception, for within months of my return to Chicago, I learned that the young woman who had been so kind to me had committed suicide in the bedroom of her Haifa home while her parents were on holiday. Her body was not discovered for several days. Unfairly, of course, I have never stopped blaming her mother for her death, just as a part of me always fights off a tendency to blame all parents for the turmoil and sadness of their children.

Equal to his passion for research was my father's love of music. One night a week like clockwork, unless, of course, Chicago was hit simultaneously by a blizzard and cyclone, what my mother called, in a Yiddish accent, "a wizard and a Cyclops," my father played chamber music. Joined by three businessmen, Emil Horween, second violin, Harold Sher, viola, and Warren King, cellist, the four musicians appeared to live for these once-a-week sessions. In the words of Willard Marmelszadt, one could see that for these men, chamber music playing served to "wash away from the soul the dust of every-day life."[5] One didn't dare cut a session or find anything more important to do. The graduation or marriage of a loved one might have been considered a barely reasonable excuse, but the men's commitment to the quartet made one believe that even their own death wouldn't stand in the eyes of the others as justification for absence. Granted, they were amateurs, but this hardly connotes a disparaging term, for indeed until the nineteenth century, according to Homer Ulrich, chamber music was almost entirely "amateur music, confined to small rooms and private homes."[6] Ernest Hutcheson's[7] definition of the term "amateur," moreover, perfectly describes the four musical colleagues who loved music, sight read with ease, were acquainted with a rather large repertoire, and frequently performed rather competently with other amateurs as well as professionals.

Over the course of the years, my mother and I would sit in the small room beyond the dining room listening to my father and his friends during their weekly chamber music gatherings. We would look at each other and grin when we heard them scratching—we used the word *kratzing*—or struggling through difficult passages. When, like beginning skiers tottering on a mogul, it truly seemed that they weren't going to make it, we giggled, or completely lost our composure.

"Where else," Ulrich expressed in his book, "can there be accomplished so much with so little?"[8] (And by so many, one is tempted to add.) My mother, however, was never derisive during these moments. The men's love of the art form carried the night. So did their talent, as Marmelszadt confirmed in his book, *Musical Sons of Aesculapius,* a study of physicians who were also musicians—Hector Berlioz and Aleksandr Borodin being the most famous. Marmelszadt confirmed that my father was "an excellent violinist and is known for his long standing love of music."[9] Significantly, my mother proudly admitted that she learned the chamber music repertoire from my father. On more than one occasion, when she heard some lovely playing coming from the music room, she would look at me and nod approvingly, "That wasn't bad. That wasn't at all bad." Then suddenly my father would stun us by navigating through some treacherous fingering and she would remark, "You know, they tell me he's also not a bad surgeon."

The evening began with a ritual I abhorred. It was my obligation to help my father *schlep* the quartet table from the room beyond the dining room into the music room; it would sit in the middle of the floor, framed by the two Steinways. I hated the task because the table, actually a handsome, oak drop-leaf, with small holes drilled to hold as many as six music stands, was itself not only heavy, but made more so by piles of chamber music stacked upon it. Equally significant, the leverage I could barely achieve in lifting it required me to bend over in order to keep from whacking my own legs on the table's legs. The table had to be carried the entire distance because its wheels might dig into the bare floor or rumple the gold shag dining room rug. My father invariably took the front of the table, holding it with his hands behind him and leaving me with the rear end. Every three seconds he would admonish me to be careful and every three seconds I would resist the temptation to either drop the table or shove it into his back. Dreading the task of moving the table, I often made certain to be asleep, or pretended that I was, when, at the end of the evening, it came time to return it to its back room resting spot.

I hardly need a psychiatrist to interpret my anger at the table. Along with the violins, the medical research, and the Asian art, it symbolized what I always imagined were my father's dearest loves, and as a boy I must have felt that I wasn't among them. I made no sweet sounds, I yielded up no medical mysteries, I rested elegantly on no shelves, and I faithfully supported no music. If chamber music was on the schedule, then he wouldn't be coming up to my room, or playing with my trains, or just being with me.

On the other hand, I loved listening to the quartet and rarely closed my bedroom door so that the sounds made by these four earnest players, musicians my mother would have called "passionately fond of music but not dangerously talented," would waft up the stairway into my room. Each week, one of the men selected the program for the evening. Usually they began with Haydn, for chamber music itself seems to commence with him; then they graduated either to Brahms or Beethoven, Schubert or Mozart, Mendelssohn or perhaps something modern, Darius Milhaud, a twentieth-century French composer. I knew my father was totally enjoying himself, although there were occasional instances of disagreement over tempo or interpretation. Most importantly, the house was happy; the only sounds to be heard were those composed by geniuses.

Now and again, my mother rewarded the quartet by joining them for quintets. On these occasions, I often descended the stairs and turned pages for her; her head bounced an exaggerated nod when she wanted the page turned. I always thought the process remarkable because the turn came with measures yet to be played at the bottom of the page, which meant that she was not only sight reading but also was, at a glance, remembering whole lines of music she rarely if ever played. My father normally led the quartet as all first violinists do, but not when Gradova was playing. Then *she* was the leader, a kindly one to be sure, periodically warning them of rushing or falling behind. Even during the performance she might notice that someone was playing flat or sharp. "It would kill you to tune, Emil?" she would joke. Or, "Gentlemen, if you don't speed up the tempo I'm going to miss *Gunsmoke* . . . which is on tomorrow night." Then, missing not a note of her own playing, she would suddenly begin singing a cello, viola, or violin part in order to rescue a momentarily drowning string player. She had no problem, moreover, admonishing her husband. Like little boys blessed with the opportunity to play ball with a professional, they obeyed her every command and direction. In music, the first and last voice at Hawthorne Place was hers, with perhaps one notable exception:

> Rachmaninoff came for chamber music one night. I begged him to go home. I said, "It's not for you Sergei Vassilievich." He said, "No, no, I listen . . . and where will doctor play?" And I said, "Why don't you worry about where *I'm* going to practice?" "What will doctor play tonight?" I said, "You know Sergei Vassilievich, he's a great doctor and a fine musician. . . . I have to practice, why don't you ask where do *I* play? I play in this room, that's where we play chamber music."
>
> Then I told him I'm not going to invite him again. I said, "Why do you want to come?" He said, "I like to hear doctor play." And he sat in that chair in the room where they played and then he stood up and he said, "I would like very much to repeat the slow movement of the Brahms." So they did that and he autographed a copy for them and sits down again, and at ten o'clock we all stopped and [I] served . . . a lovely buffet, cheese etc. . . . and I go over to the chair, and I say, "I think you should go. Why don't you go? Now we're going to have chai [tea] and all that, do you want to sit?" "I sit," he says. "I can sit here." He goes into the dining room and gets tea. He gets up and goes to every *schlemiel* who's there and the wives of the people and shook everyone's hand, "Thank you for me to be here. Thank you very much."[10]

Whether or not she played with "the fellas," as she called them, my mother always arranged to have the dining room table covered with deli food so that everyone could *nosh* after the music was completed. Fresh salami, bologna, turkey, roast beef, maybe even lox and bagels, were laid out on trays, along with dill and half-sour pickles, potato salad, chilled coleslaw, and fruit. There might be three kinds of bread, none of them ever white, condiments, soft drinks, and beer. There was usually a coffee cake as well. Transporting hard liquor was my father's job. Never once, moreover, did anyone eat on paper plates or use plastic utensils. After the quartet table was returned to the back room—Warren King did more than his share of *schlep*ping—everyone sat down at the table, ate, and talked.

The discussions usually commenced with a review of the music just completed, the men, like golfers, rehashing the recently completed "game," remarking on a measure here or a passage there; mostly they complimented themselves. Then, typically, the conversation turned to political, financial, social, and cultural issues. I learned in these hours just exactly where my father stood on political matters, the attitudes and ideologies that had begun to shape my own political visions, such as they were.

My father was never surprised by my own radical activities during the 1960s. That I skipped a fair amount of classes during graduate school to participate in civil rights activities never appeared to trouble him. I think he felt it was my duty, somehow, to engage in those actions, even though he believed deeply in the ideals of America, civility, and proper decorum. Still, he never questioned me about the organizations I was joining. Nor did I ever ask him about his own leftist propensities. I suspect that although he was never a Communist, he might well have been a fellow traveler. There was, after all, his friendship with Paul Robeson and others, and his subscription to the *PM Daily*, a slim newspaper that arrived every week from New York, and which he read faithfully. Just as there was no question that Franklin Delano Roosevelt was the greatest president, so would there be no question that in the 1948 elections, my parents would become staunch supporters of Henry Wallace, though they wouldn't in the end vote for him because in effect they believed it meant giving votes to Governor Thomas E. Dewey, the sort of politician for whom they had little respect.

I still hear those post-quartet conversations in my mind, the gaiety, the rich expressions of friendship, the concerns for the country. Those were good and peaceful nights, comforting even. Not a bad educational experience either, learning from intelligent people—my first encounter, actually, with talking heads, unencumbered by celebrity—who argued in good nature with one another over a political policy, a recent Supreme Court decision, or a financial market trend, people, furthermore, who had just performed Haydn, Schubert, Mendelssohn, Beethoven, and Brahms, and then served a late night *nosh* on top of it. John Dewey himself could not have designed a better education, and on many mornings, my own school, designed in fact by John Dewey's disciple, Colonel Francis W. Parker, paled in comparison. In retrospect, *schlepping* the quartet table was a small price for admission.

As memorable as the post-chamber music sessions were, they couldn't hold a candle to the colossal manner in which our family celebrated Christmas.

By the first of December, preparations were already underway, the packages arriving by mail and delivery services, and both my parents undertaking their secret discussions and shopping missions that conspicuously excluded my sister and me. "No, no, no, no, you can't hear any of this. You have to leave the room right now!" It was all delicious. My mother's conception of gift gifting was predicated on a mystical mathematical formula: 487 gifts seemed appropriate for each of her children. Opening Christmas presents took us in to late March when we could safely throw out the used wrappings and yellowed Christmas tree.

A few days before Christmas, my mother would go to the window and, depending on weather conditions, say aloud either, "I hope they'll get their white Christmas," or, if there was snow on the ground, "It looks like they're going to have their white Christmas after all." Then, satisfied that all of Chicago's Christians were content, we commenced our own celebration. Annually, we argued whether there should be a wreath on the door, something I thought, somehow, not quite right, but there was no question that there would be a tree as fat and tall as the front hall could accommodate, its top scraping the ceiling. When, after numerous family consultations, the tree was thoroughly decorated, someone, usually my mother, would inevitably say: "This is unquestionably the most beautiful tree we've ever had." And it was.

Gifts were wrapped on the dining room table the afternoon of the twenty-fourth by both my parents who continued to delight in the secrecy of it all, and opened that very evening, Christmas Eve, after a dinner of roast beef, boiled potatoes, and spiced peaches. I'm not certain why we didn't wait until Christmas morning. Perhaps given the impulsivity level of the family, waiting wasn't the easiest thing to do. On the other hand, maybe one is acting slightly less non-Jewish opening presents Christmas Eve. Actually, the real reason is that the entrance hall floor was so filled with presents, there was no way to reach the stairway to the second-floor bedrooms.

Christmas always meant just the five of us, my Aunt Leah being a definite fixture of the celebration, a bonafide contributor to the chorus of: "I can't believe you got me this."

"Where did you find this?"

"Believe me, it wasn't that easy."

"I don't deserve this. How could you?"

"How did you even know my size?"

"What, I can't peak in a drawer once in a while?"

"It's my favorite color."

"Don't look at *me*, your father picked that one out."

"When did you buy this?"

"Three days after last Christmas."

"That's the last time I'll ever mention liking something in front of you again."

How happy we all were, five Jewish children celebrating a Christian ritual and feeling not one shred of guilt, shame, or uneasiness. Who cared that we were adding to the materialistic nature of what should be a sacred observation? None of us wanted it to end, none of us wanted the tree ever to come down. It stood as a monument to sheer delight and enjoyment. And family.

Chapter 5

On Soirées and Skirmishes

No social gathering at Hawthorne Place could ever have been deemed perfunctory. There was always excitement and tension as people prepared for the evening's company, be it a musician traveling on his or her own, a musician with an entourage, or, most significantly, what can only be described as the musical soirées. "The house of Dr. Maurice Cottle . . . and his wife, the remarkable pianist Gita (*sic*) Gradova," Gregor Piatigorsky wrote in his memoirs, "was the home of all 'wandering' musicians passing through the city or traveling long distances just to spend an evening with them. One could never know for sure whom one would meet there—Toscanini, Elman, Rubinstein, Prokofiev, Heifetz, Horowitz—but one could be certain of having enough colleagues for a feast of chamber music." If that were not enough, Piatigorsky added, with a hint of embroidery, "And if a cold needed to be cured, or an operation had to be performed, Dr. Cottle would see to it splendidly, and gratis."[1]

What I observed first hand was something already well known by Chicago's society columnists: My parents were spectacular party goers and hosts.

> April 16, 1933, the *Chicago Sunday Tribune:* [pianist Egon] Petri, Horowitz, Milstein and Gradova, all at the same party—isn't that something to remember the rest of your life if you were lucky enough to be one of forty or fifty invited to the dinner 'Bobsy' Goodspeed gave recently at her Arts Club for Petri and his wife. . . . Some say it was THE small party of the season.[2]
>
> June Provines, *This Gala World*, April 7, 1933: . . . [Conductor Frederick] Stock saw himself as others see him the other evening when Nathan Milstein did an imitation. It was at the Stock's home on Astor Street after the dinner given in honor . . . and the distinguished roster of guests

included: Vladimir Horowitz, [violinist] Mischa Mischakoff, [cellist] Daniel Saidenberg, Gitta Gradova and her husband, Dr. Maurice Cottell (*sic*) . . . There was much laughter . . . and informal music such as few are fortunate to hear in a lifetime.[3]

Mrs. Henry Field, "Week Full of Music—The Social Whirl," January 22, 1934: Vladimir Horowitz and his charming wife, Wanda Toscanini, were given one of the most lovely parties of the Winter last night by the great friends of Horowitz, Maurice Cottell (*sic*) and his wife, Gitta Gradova, in the house on the roof of the Hotel Sherman. There was a sumptuous buffet supper. . . . fifty guests. . . . And later Horowitz and Gitta Gradova played the sonata of Mozart for two pianos . . . one is hardly aware that it is the first time they have ever played together and that they are reading at sight the works of the great masters . . .[4]

Mrs. Henry Field, "The Social Whirl," April 9, 1933: Another party will probably take place when Dr. and Mrs. Cottell (sic) entertain their intimate friend, Vladimir Horowitz. In their beautiful drawing room they have two pianos, and one of the things Mrs. Cottell (sic) and Mr. Horowitz enjoy most is improvising jazz simultaneously.[5]

Glenn Dillard Dunn, the *Chicago Tribune*, March, 1932: Gitta Gradova, of whom the late Fannie Bloomfield Zeisler said on the occasion of her (Gradova's) debut, "She is my successor," has another of Mme. Zeisler's talents, not pianistic. She is a delightful hostess and she contrives to attract to her home some of her distinguished colleagues. . . . Horowitz goes there to play two piano music with her and to indulge in those quaint verbal ecstasies to which the art so often moves him. And be it said in passing that the thrill, which so often emanates from the playing of either of these great pianists in public, is redoubled in the intimacy of the drawing room.[6]

Normally planned well in advance, although on occasion, within a few days of the event, Hawthorne Place witnessed indescribable evenings of musical and culinary feasts. As many as sixty people crowded into the living room and entrance hall, their conversations absorbing and animated. Always there were the regulars, always there were newcomers, musicians and artists, university faculty, people from the worlds of medicine, science, business, and law, and most significantly for me, teachers from my school, something that was often a trifle perplexing. It was one thing to answer the door and greet my parents' insurance man and his wife, but it was another thing altogether to see my social studies teacher who, two days before had given me a low grade on a paper, standing at our front door with a date and utterly delighted to see me.

In the main, the boundaries of teacher and guest were impeccably maintained; what happened at a Saturday night soirée was never to have a bearing on what transpired Monday through Friday at school. Every so often, however, the boundary proved porous. I recall a French class with Helen Richard, a gifted intellectual with more energy than the entire Chicago Bears football team.

On this particular day, Madame, as she was called, was on the edge of having an apoplectic fit; she was utterly frustrated that not one student was able to translate a certain word. Finally she looked at me and blurted out, "I don't understand that *you* don't know it; you have one in your house!" Could you perhaps narrow that down a bit more, Madame? "How do you say 'angry Mommy' in French?" is what I wanted to reply. Still, this was the exceptional experience. The soirées were thrilling; they allowed a young student, his teachers, and principal to coexist with a barely discernible uneasiness. Besides soothing the savage beast, Brahms, Haydn, Schubert, Mendelssohn, and Beethoven have the power to reduce differences in status as well as rank. And, as an added benefit, as a psychological study reported in 1927 revealed, "It is difficult to conceive of a person becoming very angry from the hearing of music. He may become angry at certain circumstances accompanying the performance. . . . But the music alone would never make one really angry."[7]

The Cottle house was packed. People sat on the stairs practically all the way up to the second floor; they settled themselves as the chamber music began. Any number of musicians might sit in, Milstein, Piatigorsky, or Horowitz if they were in town—their presence in Chicago usually the reason for the soirée in the first place. At some point in the evening, my mother joined the musicians. Then the sonatas, trios, quintets, sextets, octets, soared through the house.

Nathan Milstein wearing his glasses, bends over his music, concentrating on a difficult passage. Horowitz sight reading, shrieks with delight when he narrowly gets through a thorny section. Members of the Fine Arts Quartet, the Chicago Symphony Orchestra, or my father and his chamber music colleagues either join in or turn pages for their illustrious colleagues. Surprisingly, Nathan plays a slow movement of a quartet on the cello.

At the end of each piece the audience exploded with applause; they begged for more, and they got it. Although the concert usually started at seven or seven thirty, the encores proceeded until well after midnight; still the audience clamored for one last piece. The musicians obliged. Horowitz played a Chopin waltz, my mother a Scarlatti sonata, Milstein a section of a Bach Partita. The people crammed together on the stairwell, their knees pushed into the backs and shoulders of those on the steps directly beneath them, revealed not the slightest sign of discomfort. Given their location, there was no way the audience could see what was happening in the music room, but the acoustics of the old house were unusually fine; the walls yielded an exquisite sound.

Well after midnight, the handsome five-foot-wide, oak pocket door, which separated the music room from the dining room, was rolled back into its wall envelope, revealing the blond dining room table covered with platters of food. Filled with the joys of Hawthorne Place, the centerpiece being my mother, the guests took their plates and silverware and lined up all the way back to the entrance hall for the buffet repast that turned out to be as glorious as the music. For days, my mother had arranged for the food. Gapers was her cherished caterer. She had agonized over the menu, the presentation of the food, flowers, drinks, silverware, dishes, glassware, and napkins. The apprehensions and agony now vanished, she moved about the crowded spaces accepting compliments, embraces, and kisses. This is the same woman, after all, who decades before had publicly asserted: "The right sort of people can do as much for one's mind as any quantity of reading. . . . I am a very gregarious animal and I still love going to parties and meet important people. I never seem to grow blasé or tired of forming new acquaintances."[8]

Eventually she approached me: "I got rare roast beef 'specially for you. There's more in the kitchen." She turns to my date: "Pretty boring, huh, all these old people with their long hair music?"

Deep into the morning hours the revelry continued, the guests resisting the notion that the evening must come to an end. Finally, my mother stood at the open front door making certain to touch and kiss each guest as they departed. Her comments were quick, clever, and amusing. Yet, as a teenager, I began to detect a sadness that returned after the party ended, just as the song says, "when the music stops."

"Sam, take some food home with you," she insisted. "I can't stand any of it. Don't be a *noodnik*. Take the chocolate cake for your kids. *They* it won't kill, *us* it will."

"What do you look so sad, Georgina? This won't be the last time we'll do this. As soon as I'm out of the hospital we'll do it again."

"Gitta, darling, no, you're going into the hospital?"

"What, you think all that food I just ate in there isn't going to give me cancer?"

"Gitta, may I tell you that I have never heard you play as well. Ever!"

"Lotte, can I can tell *you* that your ear for music is getting worse. I assure you, it wasn't that good."

"Gitta, if you don't record the Schubert sonata with Milstein then you're absolutely crazy."

"It actually wasn't too bad, was it, for two *alte cockers* (old crappers). And what's more, you're right. I *am* crazy."

"Bless you, Gitta. A million thanks for this generous and positively scrumptious concert and dinner."

"Sy, you still going to feel this way when you get the bill?"

"Darling, Gitta, how do we thank you for such a precious night? I'm calling you first thing in the morning."

"Thanking me is easier than you think: Don't call me in the morning!"

If the soirées were joyous occasions, there was another form of encounter at Hawthorne Place. The skirmishes with my mother erupted to full-blown proportions during my adolescence. Our verbal assaults on one another were incessant. They were brutal, and wounding to both of us. What Edward Moore said about her playing could have described both of us during these destructive encounters: ". . . Miss Gradova has certain feline qualities in her playing, the qualities of lithe alertness and furious attack."[9]

My mother directed soul-searing messages at me during these times that I carry to this day, and I am certain I responded in kind. Between the two of us there were, in Henrietta Straus's words, "no hesitant impulses."[10] Our exchanges went beyond shame and humiliation. They exploded as death wishes. We took each other on precisely as that one critic had portrayed my mother's confrontation with a piano: "Miss Gradova swept erect and free of stride upon the platform, bent her athletic form over the piano and plunged with *masculine strength* and decisiveness into the concerto. Its music leapt *rugged and almost savage* from beneath her hands."[11] After a prolonged verbal battle about Heaven only knows what, she would say in a tone that indicated these were to be her final words on the subject, her ultimate assessment of me as a human being: "As my son I *have* to love you, but I *don't* have to respect you." My comeback was equally cruel: "As your son, I don't happen to love *or* respect you." Then she would say, "That's very clever. Is that what they're teaching you at that school?"

As I say, these stabbings have never completely healed. On an afternoon decades beyond my adolescence, and well after my mother had died, I passed through the living room of our Boston home several times attempting to catch a snippet of a conversation between my wife, a high school teacher, and the educator Sara Lawrence-Lightfoot. A scholar and writer, Sara is a close family friend, someone I call "Sister Sara."

On this particular occasion, however, Sister Sara wasn't simply visiting, she was interviewing Kay for a book she was researching, titled, *Respect*. When she first told us of the project, we, of course, did our best Aretha Franklin impressions, R-E-S-P-E-C-T, but the notion of such a book struck me as brilliant. Truthfully, I always felt somewhat uneasy and envious that Sara would be making Kay into a star, as there would only be six people chosen for extensive portraits in *Respect*. Stardom, after all, is what long ago had taken my mother away from our family, so I have always held it in some ambivalence. Thus, I wanted to hear bits of the interview that one afternoon almost as a way to relieve some anxiety, and jealousy.

In retrospect, my concern had nothing to do with stardom, and hence abandonment by my wife, that might accrue to Kay from being included in *Respect*. Sara's selection of Kay only confirmed my childhood insecurity. I wasn't respected. Therefore, I wasn't respectable. My mother's words had spanned decades: Sara Lawrence-Lightfoot had to love me, but she didn't have to respect me. No one else did either.

There was another expression my mother called up from time to time, one uttered with a sense of relief from all the pain in the world, which, of course, meant that I was the personification of *all* the pain in the world.

"When you see me in my grave," she would say, "I'll be smiling." (What had that critic written? "Miss Gradova rose to take her inflammatory applause with a wan aloofness that might have belonged to Virgil himself . . .")

Despite the majesty of the soirées and the magnetism of my mother in which all of us on those evenings rejoiced, mornings were times of despair and gloominess. Afternoons after school were occasions when I looked to attack, and I waited for her to admonish me. Mornings, however, were the worst. Why my mother even got up to help with breakfast preparations is beyond me. Perhaps she felt it an obligation. It was something a good mother did. That she may have forever destroyed the pleasure of breakfast for me remains the perverse dividend of all those mornings.

On school days, I descended the staircase, turned left into the entrance hall, and entered the pantry from the rear of the hall. Just before one reached the kitchen entry, one encountered a wall separating the passageway from the music room. When my parents purchased the house, this wall had been an open space, allowing access to the music room. My mother requested that the passageway be closed off, for it was distracting to be practicing at a piano and having people coming and going behind you. I understood her need. It actually reinforced my own sense of security when I lay beneath her piano, just as I understood her sadness and dismay when, as a surprise, my father had their bedroom redecorated during the summer when my mother was away. Together with Harold Walsh, a decision was made to eliminate the bedroom's Georgian fireplace; this decision deeply displeased my mother. For whatever the reasons, in these moments, over these matters, I could identify with her suffering. All people, not merely artists, make attachments to natural and man-made environments; they are thrown by radical transformations, not to mention the elimination of elements. I grieve when any plant in our garden dies. Besides the psychological and esthetic aspects of these attachments, there was also the matter of men professing such love for her, yet making decisions on how and where and in what settings my mother would lead her life. Moreover, she felt obliged to take their direction.

Passing through the entrance hall I would enter the pantry, its walls lined with glass-front cabinets. After a few steps, I would take a left, past the kidney-shaped stainless steal pantry sink. Patsy, our dalmation, always napped there. The kitchen was the house's only unattractive room, clearly bespeaking my mother's disinterest in food preparation. Its main feature was the wooden table that sat against the west wall. The table was covered with the same homely linoleum that protected the floor. A slim silver edging framed the ends of the linoleum. Beneath the table, the edging was crimped, but I could always find places where there were sharp points. During moments when I felt particularly sad or furious, I would push my fingers hard against the metal, purposely causing myself pain.

Pressed against the wall, the table allowed for only four people, my parents at the ends, my sister and me on the one available side. My place, to the right of my father, was closest to the kitchen's exit. Unconsciously, I was always preparing for a quick getaway. And I *would* get away, often quitting eating in the middle of a meal, for some mornings were wholly intolerable. On these occasions, my father would rise from the table, throw his napkin down, turn and leave. He, too, was close to the exit. To this day, I rarely eat breakfast sitting down. Kay, my wife, always admonishes me: "Sweetie, just put the toast on a plate and bring it to the table." But I prefer to stand without a plate, just in case I need to make a hurried escape.

It is hardly surprising that the passage I remember best in Philip Roth's novel *Portnoy's Complaint*, is the description of Portnoy visiting a young woman in Kansas to whom he refers as "the Monkey." For the first time in his life, he understands that people actually choose to wish one another good thoughts until lunch time. On hundreds of occasions I have heard Kay say, "Good morning, Sweetie," to one of our children. "Did you sleep well?" Such good cheer, in the *morning*? Such expressions of love, in the *morning*? What kind of a childhood did she have! Hardly surprising, her mother was the same way. Bab Mikkelsen was always happy to see you in the morning. And if it were in her cozy St. Louis suburban residence, the smells of breakfast already filled the air. Every item, the bacon, the sausage, the eggs, all foods I wouldn't touch with a ten foot pole as a child, I gobbled up at Bab's table. It wasn't that I didn't like eggs, bacon, and sausage. I was terrified of them.

On some mornings, I entered the kitchen before my mother. On other mornings, she was already there dressed in a light blue sweater and dark plaid or black wool skirt over her cream-color nightgown, which could be seen poking out here and there. I think she wore slippers. I know she wore frowns, grimaces, and offered up generous servings of frustration and anguish.

I actually grew up imagining that every child in the world entered their family's kitchen for breakfast to find a depressed, furious, unkempt mother, complaining about everything from the overcooked toast to the height of the Alps, and harping at her older sister.

It was the same way with reading. Before anyone properly diagnosed me as being dyslexic, I assumed that everyone struggled with reading as I did. Oh, people claimed they loved to curl up with a good book, as my mother always said about her cherished afternoons in the New York Public Library, but I knew they were lying. Reading was awful. One's eyes raced over the page. One struggled with the temptation to mouth the words. One forgot a sentence as fast as it was read, and the mental strain of it all made the activity an irritating nuisance.

Then came the overnights at various friends' homes and the opportunity to witness firsthand how other mothers not only prepared breakfast, but also prepared themselves for breakfast. I saw Mrs. Abrams, George's mother who was utterly beautiful, and a portrait artist to boot, and Mrs. Friend, Kenny's mom, who was just as beautiful, and Mrs. Oldberg, George's elegant though somewhat severe mother. Each one of these women was beautifully though never ostentatiously dressed, her hair brushed and her makeup applied at seven in the morning. Never was there a sign of a nightgown sticking out from beneath a sweater. Not only that, these women seemed happy to greet their sons and their son's house guest. Tables were handsomely set, food was already in preparation, no task seemed burdensome, and pleasant conversations were acceptable and expected. For the first time, like young Portnoy, I understood how it could be that people found breakfast to be a wholesome experience. But it rarely was that at Hawthorne Place.

Getting together a few pieces of toast and some juice was nothing short of monumental for my mother. It was really the job of eighteen very strong men. My mother accomplished everything with flared nostrils, grunts, long, heavy sighs, and complaints. They're the very sounds I make when gardening. Partly they are the sounds of physical effort. Mainly they are the sounds of "why can't people see I'm dying here and come to my rescue with words of love and admiration!" Nothing was ever right, nothing was ever easy; every piece of food consumed became a reminder of food that once again had to be purchased. "We're already out of jelly? I just bought jelly two days ago. It's not to be believed. What happens to this stuff?"

Breakfast was to be eaten quickly. Three minutes tops, before significant psychic damage could be done. I rarely fought back in the mornings; I didn't have the energy. My father ate as quickly as he could. He never arrived at the table for any meal without being shaved and groomed. Most nights he wore a tie and jacket to dinner, never demanding, however, that I do the same. Nor did my mother, but always she questioned me, "Did you wash your hands?"

"Yes, mother, I washed my hands." Soap and water should have dripped from my fingers like the sarcasm that dripped from my every word.

"Good." But I didn't wash, which she had already observed. "Tommy, you'll wash your hands, please."

"How come Dad doesn't ask me to wash my hands? *He's* the doctor."

I hated washing my hands. I still do. I hated bathing and washing my hair as well. I still hate getting dressed up. If I had my way, I would sleep in my clothes and wear them the rest of the day as well. I think my mother was the same way. (The only reason I don't put my clothes on over my pajamas is that I don't wear pajamas.) Neither one of us would ever be called "clothes horses." Come to think of it, my mother was a saint not to have smacked me from time to time.

The ugly mood that hung over the breakfast table was as palpable and lugubrious as the kitchen itself. I am certain that sleeping pills were partly to blame for much of my mother's morning struggle. She was crashing before our eyes, not that any of us ever defined it in these terms. She was, I am sure, depressed. We begged her to stay in bed, just as we begged her to return to concertizing, but we got nowhere. No matter what her protestations, she hated preparing breakfast. Exactly ninety-one million times I heard her say that breakfast was the most important meal of the day. So why do you ruin it everyday? I would think. "You know, you don't need to be here, mother. We're fine." But she *did* have to be there, sitting at the table's end, the sturdy backdoor behind her, alternating be-tween scowling and holding her head in her hands, constantly communicating exhaustion and despair. She had to be there be-cause a "good mother" prepares meals for her children. It's part of the food-nurturance, take-an-interest-in, and love-them chain. She wouldn't dare allow herself to break it, even though she did break it almost every morning. She even broke it on occasions when all her best intentions were in the right place.

I grew up to become a rather serious baseball player. It wasn't what my parents expected. Jewish boys were born to attend law school, medical school, or graduate school. Of course, it was per-fectly permissible to be a musical prodigy as well. The thought of my becoming a professional athlete didn't go down particularly well with them—the career of Hank Greenberg notwithstanding. If only Sandy Koufax had been born five years earlier, a door might have opened for me.

My baseball activities were tolerated but rarely celebrated. In the resentful spirit of my adolescence, I told my parents nothing of my successes. I never even told them there was a game, insisting they find out on their own if they were that interested. But want-ing to be a good parent, my mother decided finally to attend a game, and for years she told the story of that experience, believing it to be utterly charming and poignant.

Standing on the sidelines, she only viewed a few innings before she broke down and cried. She was immediately comforted by David Wallerstein, the father of one of my classmates.

"What's the matter?" he asked with obvious concern.

"Tommy throws the ball," she answered, "but the other boys don't hit it. He doesn't let them hit it."

Mr. Wallerstein, of course, laughed and explained to her that that was the whole purpose of the game. In fact, he told her, I was performing brilliantly. From that point on, my mother loved the experience, though she attended very few games.

The story, however, always troubled me. Of course it showed her desire to take an interest in what I was not merely doing, but to what I was totally committed. It showed her as charming and inno-cent. I should have been more understanding, even as a teenager, but I wasn't. A *good* mother, I would think bitterly, would find out about baseball. She would know what her son was doing, and when she discovered herself to be ignorant of the one essential feature of the game, she should never have revealed this to anyone! Couldn't she see her interest wasn't innocent and well meaning, but that she was appearing disinterested? If you don't like baseball games, I would think alone in my bedroom, don't go and pretend that you do! No one needs you to go! You're only patronizing me. I don't do that at concerts, do I?

One particular anecdote illustrates the character of the afternoon skirmishes with my mother, especially the anger that seemed always to be lurking. The story begins with a reference to the aforementioned Claudia Cassidy, who, along with my mother, shared a love of William Kapell, the pianistic genius whose career might have rivaled even those of Serkin, Rubinstein, and Horowitz had he not died at such a young age. Kapell, whom my mother called "Willy," was playing in Australia where, one story goes, he was devastated by a hostile review. As a result, he changed his flight reservation in order to return to the United States at once. His plane crashed. In his mid-thirties with so much to offer, he perished along with his fellow passengers.

William Kapell was one of many young musicians my mother had believed in to carry the torch of her profession. Worshipping her colleagues and predecessors, and particularly, of course, her mentors, Rachmaninoff and Horowitz, she nonetheless believed that a host of young performers would turn out to be anywhere as good as those of her generation. She also appreciated the fact that many of them seemed so smart. There was never a feeling with her that they "don't make 'em like they used to," a sentiment shared, apparently by a Boston critic in 1924, who heard her when she was twenty years old: "One by one the young pianists smoke and smolder past. Then at last—say in Gradova—darts the flame."[12] Her bets were placed on Martha Argerich, Daniel Barenboim, Itzhak Perlman, Pinchas Zukerman, Jacqueline DuPré, and a host of young Russians, most notably Vladimir Ashkenazy who, on one occasion, used Hawthorne Place as a practice studio before a Sunday recital, and at the same time introduced the Russian style of drinking vodka to a good friend of mine. Young Eddie Wachs tried to keep up with the slightly built Ashkenazy, but to no avail. Forgiving the pun that my mother employed, classical music was in good hands.

I was riding the bus home from school when I read the news of Kapell's death in the newspaper of the person sitting next to me. It was one of those many days during my adolescence when I had fought with my mother in the morning, our competing angers creating an insidious dance, our words intended to destroy one another. So with relish, I raced home from the bus stop with the news of Kapell's fiery crash. With sadistic glee, I ran up to her bedroom carrying directly to her the news of Willy's tragedy.

Predictably, she was lying on her bed watching her precious soap operas, about which she would discuss every detail with Nathan, who also watched when he could, which turned out to be most of the time. The two spoke of soap opera characters with more passion at times than they spoke even of music.

"Willy died!" I shouted out.

"Willy who?"

"Willy Kapell, of course. What other Willy do you know?"

She was broken by the news. At first I felt triumphant, but then so guilt ridden I had to leave the room, but I would never let myself cry, a rather common symptom, incidentally, of male depression. I could make *her* cry, but *I* never would.

My mother's stories about William Kapell show her as caring, compassionate, understanding, appreciative, and at the same time combative, acerbic, antagonistic, and, whether she chose to admit it or not, competitive. And God help those who threatened her idols, even idols about whom she revealed more than a tinge of ambivalence. All of these emotions, like actors ready to appear on stage, could be called upon at a moment's notice, and be part of any drama with anyone, including her own family. At any point, one of these emotional actors could suddenly make their entrance and either win over the entire production, or make it seem as if utter catastrophe had occured:

> I had a big fight with that kid [Kapell] when he first came here. I said, "Get out of this house!" My mother said, "How can you say anything like that?" I said, "How dare you [Kapell] compare yourself with Horowitz!" He comes and says, "You know, Horowitz is annoyed with me because I'm playing ninety concerts the first year, or something. How many did *he* play? A hundred and twenty five?" I said, "In this house, you don't compare yourself with Horowitz. You can take your hat and coat and leave right now!" I hated him and Willy knew it. . . . He played Bach for me and I said, "So you got the proper ornamentation?" He says, "How'd you know?"

I say, "'Cause I know where you got it. From [the pianist Abram] Chasins." We could get on each other's nerves.

But I was so glad I went to hear the last concert because he did the Third Prokofiev, and he called up my house because [the pianist and wife of Chasins] Constance Keene was staying with me, and he called me up and I said, "Well, Willy, I can thank you for a memorable performance . . . that's the best Third I heard in a long shot." And you know what Jascha [Heifetz] told me after he died, because Jascha did the Franck Sonata with him and that's really unusual— he recorded it with an American kid, so he must have thought well of Willy . . . [Kapell] had that kind of an irritability in his nature and impatient and [Jascha] said, "Why in the hell did he have to go and change his airplane ticket because the critic said he was lousy!" [Kapell] was so offended by the press that he took an earlier flight. For a long time I thought about his wife . . . Whatever happened to her? . . . I think he was the most promising American kid we had. He would have been number one . . . today . . . as American.[13]

My mother mourned Kapell's death for weeks. I don't know what she made of my almost ferocious tone in announcing the news of the accident. I am sure there were many times when we felt hatred for one another. I also know there were times when I felt it was perfectly justifiable for me to loathe her, but that nothing could ever justify a parent hating her own child, especially not a mother! That issue probably will never be resolved.

In retrospect, the two person drama that unfolded at Hawthorne Place during my adolescence, a drama of which no one at my school had even the slightest inkling, was as sad as it was wounding. Clearly the two of us were depressed and employed anger as a way of deriving some sort of psychic energy, or at least fabricating some semblance of human armor. Equally clear was that our depression, anger, armor, and perverse energies served only to torture one another and further our depressions. I blamed her for every ounce of unhappiness I owned. She too often appeared to blame me for the very same thing. Of course, at some level, I knew other things ate away at her, but during those afternoon skirmishes it seemed as though the weight of her despair was being transferred onto my shoulders and into my soul.

"The trouble with you is very simple," I would state in the ugliest tone I could muster. "You should never have had children!"

"Is that so," she would respond with the exact same tone.

"Some women simply weren't meant to have children. And you're one of them. Just because you have a uterus doesn't mean you can be a real mother!"

"So now you're God, making these decisions?"

"You don't have to be God to see what you've done to both of us. And to think you wanted more!"

Nothing, I think, could have hurt her more than this. Her own child pronouncing her a failure. Her responses were equally cruel and wounding. On more than one occasion she used the retort: "I was meant to have children, all right, but not one like you!"

"But Judy, yes, right?"

"Could be."

"Careful, careful," I would come back in a sardonic and condescending tone. "Mothers aren't supposed to talk to their children that way. Or maybe you aren't a mother and so you let yourself say anything."

"Do you call yourself clever? Is this all supposed to be clever? Because I can tell you that it isn't at all clever. Not even by *your* standards!"

"Hey, if I have rotten standards, who's to blame for them?"

"And you wonder why I don't respect you. Just listen to your own words and you'll see why no one could respect you."

"But *you* they respect?"

"In fact, young man, they do. Sorry that that troubles you."

"Nothing troubles me but you. And it's too bad you don't know what they *do* think of you."

"But you're going to tell me."

"Me, blow my cover? Never!"

"You know, I think you're right about one thing. You're not *my* child!"

And so it would go on week after week, year after year. We rarely if ever swore at one another, and never during these skirmishes did I refer to her as "mother" or "mom." Similarly, she never uttered my name. In fact, continuing this theme of my complications about her being a good mother, something I did in fact speak about with her in sanguine terms later in life, I recall a nickname I invented as a child rather than call her mom or mommy.

The word was "Mumineer." Later on when I thought about the odd neologism, two associations came to mind. One of them seems to involve her yelling at me, the other a more generic significance of her presence in my soul. Mumineer: Mom in ear; mom in here.

Making our battles even more pitiful—my mother would have described our drama as "funny like a child's open grave"—was that because of our long-standing involvement with psychotherapy, both of us were fully aware of everything that was happening. We were, in other words, performers as well as critics, and the foundation for this was constructed from our individual insightfulness which the skirmishes, ironically, only perpetuated. The best word to describe this awareness of self and other, and most especially the suffering of self and other, was "sensitive."

In many ways, "sensitive" was the password into Hawthorne Place, just as "insensitive" was the quickest way out. The highest accolade was to be deemed sensitive. To not be moved by a Scarlatti sonata, a Bach partita, a slow movement of Brahms, the mystery of Scriabin, the romanticism of Rachmaninoff, a painting by Picasso, the stage presence of a Heifetz, the textures and weaves in a man's sports jacket, or the lavender color in the alcove and ceiling of the dining room, was to be something less than human. Sensitive, was Nathan sending a New Year's note on the back of the New York Madison Hotel stationary on which he had taken the time to paint a small watercolor scene of a stately tree standing aside a lake. The note ends: "The word that I looked for in connection with the mood of Schubert's Quintette is 'Conjuration.'"

Insensitive was to be uneducable, incorrigible, unworthy. It was to be labeled "common." Sensitivity extended not only to a thank you note, but to the words and form of that missive. My parents would have abhorred the idea of a dinner guest thanking them by e-mail, a mode of communication, mercifully, neither of them lived long enough to encounter. A dinner party meant both a telephone call the next day *and* a note. Don't think for a moment that Marian Anderson, Arturo Toscanini, Nathan Milstein, Frederick Stock, Misha Elman, or Sergei Rachmaninoff had earned a status in the world excusing them from such mandatory gestures. Notes and calls came from all of these people, along with flowers and gifts. Even Horowitz wrote, as did Wanda, although an inspection of my mother's few memorabilia reveals that he never knew her first name contained two "t's." "But what would you expect," my mother would say like a gratified teacher, holding a handwritten letter from Marian Anderson. "What you are on stage is what you are in reality. Such a beauty!"

You aren't, I would think, oppressed by the endless stream of criticisms and judgments made about people, as well as the constant list of men and women, though never other children, falling short, a list on which I seemed always to place first, even though I knew both my parents believed that I was sensitive. I was moved by the Scarlatti sonata, Harold Walsh's lavender in the alcove, and the romanticism of Brahms, just as I was put off by those who would call Rachmaninoff's music saccharine. Somewhere in my mind I think of these critics as superficial, and insensitive, and support Harold Schonberg's succinct dismissal of them,[14] as well as Hugo Leichtentritt's characterization of Rachmaninoff's music as a "last enthusiastic glance backward toward the beautiful regions of nineteenth century romanticism."[15] Truthfully, however, I shall never know whether what I feel is caused by the hearing of the music or the vision of the painting, or the fact that I can't hear music, especially Rachmaninoff, or look at art or even the color of walls with my mother's soul not rising up within me, with all its life-affirming glory and all its soul-destroying anguish. "From persuasive lyricism to brittle hardness,"[16] is how critic Edward Moore had described the breadth of her pianistic temperament.

At bottom, of course, she was a romantic player, a romantic person, much of her life composed in minor keys, as are all of Schumann's concertos, her music, in Willi Apel's words,

> . . . the immediate expression of the soul, with all its emotions of joy and sorrow, of passion and tenderness, of exuberance and despair. More specifically, [romantic music] is the expression of those feelings which cannot be satisfied, or which want to remain unsated even though they could be satisfied . . . the Romanticist includes reality in his dream world, instead of facing it as an objective phenomenon."[17]

Another passage regarding romanticism, this one from Abraham Veinus, also fits my mother: "An expansive temperament counted more with the romantics than cold form. . . . The romantics possessed a fatal talent for good theater."[18]

Finally, Leichtentritt's attempt at a definition of romanticism captures well what my mother expressed in her music, although rarely in spoken language, most notably her transformation from what he called "the sober drudgery of ordinary life into the fantastic world of the imagination:"[19]

> . . . The romantic inclination seems to be immanent in the human soul, a natural propensity. . . . Whatever appeals primarily and very strongly to the imagination and the emotions, and stresses the fantastic and emotional qualities with all the means that are available, may justly be called romantic. . . . The language of the heart means more to the romantic artist than the cold clarity of logic. For romantic music inspiration in its literal meaning—something breathed into the soul, something of heavenly origin, given by the grace of God—is the divine spark which ignites the fire of artistic creation.[20]

It wasn't just manners that the concept of sensitivity subsumed, it was the expansiveness of the mind and the heart, and the lack of histrionics on the concert platform. It was, somehow, the most noble combination of vulnerability and civility, even if it came with pain. Sensitivity even extended to assessments of animals. Patsy, our beloved dalmatian, who literally cowered in terror under the pantry sink when my mother grew angry, regularly displayed sensitivity. She knew precisely when to befriend, and when to back off. Her kindly willingness to take the morsels of food my father, but rarely my mother, offered her from the dinner table into the kitchen rather than munch them in the dining room where she might leave stains on the rug confirmed her sensitivity. (I'm not sure what my mother made of Patsy sleeping under the piano's keyboard, her head resting on the pedals. I assume it meant that Patsy loved piano music, which further confirmed her sensitivity.) I never can see the scene in *Pretty Woman* in which Julia Roberts, having been taken by Richard Gere to an opera for the first time in her life, weeps at the beauty of the spectacle, and not think of this matter of innate sensitivity. This was the sort of sensitivity my parents hunted for in every human being. It was not about social status, formal education, nor exposure to "high culture." Neither was it about money. It was merely the capacity to feel deeply human engagement, accomplishment, and most especially, art. Sensitive people don't store T'ang statuary in a guest closet!

Brady had it. A lovely young man who exuded kindness, André Brady ran the parking garage on Wabash Avenue and Lake Street. It was here my father parked his car five or six days a week when he went to his medical office. Brady, as he was called by everyone, had an uncanny knack of knowing when my father was coming, and he would run, not walk, to fetch my father's Oldsmobile, the only brand of automobile he drove in the last decades of his life. "Comin' right up, Doc," Brady would call out, but not loudly, for that would be crude. "And how are you, young man?" Brady always inquired, his lovely face looking down at me. Brady loved my father, and my father loved him. It was all about sensitivity. The difference in their social rank, the difference in their occupations, the difference in their skin color meant nothing.

Once, during a fight, I asked my mother, "You think I'm sensitive, that big word of yours? You think I'm sensitive?"

"Indeed I do," she said, suddenly crystal clear, even calm in the midst of the skirmish, the closest we ever got to pure intimacy, for she was always truthful. One frequently felt what that one *New York Times* critic had called her "rare force of temperament and personality," not to mention the penetrating white hot irons of her truthfulness.

"Well, I'll tell you how I got it."

"I'm sure you will." Having disappeared for a millionth of a second, her sarcasm had returned.

"You can get anybody to be sensitive. All you have to do is beat 'em up during their childhood and they'll be sensitive."

"Oh, is that the truth, Dr. Freud?" she would respond. "Is that what they're teaching these days? That's what you read? And can you think of one time in your life, one time, that I ever raised my hand to you? Can you give me chapter and verse right now, one time I raised a hand to you? I never spanked you. I never slapped you. I never touched you!"

"You did worse, pal. And that you don't even know it is the saddest thing of all."

"I did worse? This is your great analysis? This is what I've been waiting for? This is what I have to hear when you get home from such a tragic day at that terrible school of yours where everybody beats you and tells you how terrible you are? I did worse? You have it so bad? Oh, my God, you have it so bad here. Oh, poor, poor child. Please. Then *leave!* To save your life, go away from here. If we did so bad, and you have it so bad, then leave! What, what could you possibly miss if it's so bad here?"

"Who said anything about *we* doing so bad?"

"You're so clever. So it's just me, Dr. Freud?"

"Great deduction, Mrs. Schopenhauer."

"You know what, this is over. That's it. That's got to be it. This is over. I don't want any more of this. This is sick. You're sick. You need help. You have to learn to understand *yourself*. You better look in the mirror. Let me tell you something, as your mother, I have to love you . . ."

Then the two of us in unison: "BUT I DON'T HAVE TO RESPECT YOU!"

There was something else she would say when the battles escalated to this level, a piece of her inimitable philosophy that she held for children, but not, interestingly enough, grandchildren: "There is no such thing as a bad child, or a naughty child. There is only a tired child, or a disturbed child." Early in life I deduced an obvious conclusion: I was rarely tired. Thus, I was always being sent to a psychiatrist. I can't remember any time when I wasn't consulting a psychiatrist, not that anyone ever told me what symptoms in particular had them worried. Amazingly, I actually imagined that neither of my parents had detected my sadness. As a consequence, the only career I could ever imagine for myself, not wish for, only imagine, was being a psychiatrist. If only to protect myself, I needed to study psychiatry.

Immersed in the writings of Freud and the entire psychoanalytic movement which reached its apex during the 1940s and 1950s in Chicago with the rise of the Psychoanalytic Institute which was eventually housed on North Michigan Avenue, my parents filled Hawthorne Place with psychoanalysts and sent their son to them as well. A Dr. Bradley was my childhood analyst, Dr. George Mohr my later childhood analyst. Dr. Robert Koff, my adolescent analyst, was someone who helped me through some of those difficult adolescent times, even though I always remained somewhat troubled by his habit of languorously rolling a cigarette in his mouth over and over again. Then there was a doctor somebody at college, and a doctor somebody else in graduate school, and finally the "real work" with Dr. Abraham Fineman after the birth of our first child.

Analysts were always in our house, many of them, like Robert Gronner, Franz Alexander, George Mohr, Helen Ross, and Roy

Grinker, close friends of my parents. My parents bought into psycho-analytic theory hook, line, and sinker, including, presumably, the notion that, like it or not, mothers stay home with their children or undertake analysis if they find themselves resisting this "natural" process. In the same way, they followed every suggestion of every pediatrician, including the technique of wrapping my infant hands in transparent plastic cuffs for months at a time, presumably because I always had my hands in my mouth. I learned of this as a teenager by discovering a photograph and promptly confronted my mother about it. She explained that the cuffs were meant to keep my teeth, that were still nowhere close to erupting, from becoming disfigured, which they would have had I continued sucking my thumb. That I would spend the rest of my life putting my fingers in my mouth, something that always bothered by mother—"I'm telling you, listen to me, you're going to break a tooth someday"—was a small price to pay for straight teeth. Still, I always found it peculiar that of all the people in the world, my mother would go along with a directive that denied a child his sense of touch. Who would know better than she the sensations that can only be incorporated through the fingers? To be sure, these sentiments were expressed during the skirmishes. Similarly, given his extensive psychoanalytic knowledge of the infamous "oral stage" of human development, who would know better than my father the child's need to explore and incorporate the world through the mouth?

It was almost as though the adherence to popular medical and psychoanalytic dictates and fads bespoke a lack of confidence in parenting. It was as though my mother felt others always knew better than she how to lead life, invest money, decorate homes, and raise children. In music, she trusted her gut—she used the Yiddish word, *kishkes*. But in everything else, others had their way with her. Fearing that she wouldn't be loved or approved of, perhaps, she didn't have the confidence to urge her children to play the piano, study Judaism, or even stand by the names she herself had selected for them.

In truth, my sister, Judy to everyone, was born Rachel, my father's mother's name, and with no middle name. Similarly, I was given the name Joseph, my mother's father's name. Again, there was no middle name. Even Patsy, the dog, was Cleopatra. During both her pregnancies, apparently, Uncle Charley would inquire about Judy and Tommy. It happened so often she must have felt disloyal calling us Rachel and Joseph. The cellist Raya Garbousova, who plays a significant role in my mother's life, the South American pianist Guiomar Novaes, and on occasion, Wanda Horowitz, were the only people ever to call me Joseph. More importantly, I used this perceived act of cowardice on my mother's part in my adolescent battles with her, admonishing her for letting other people dictate our very names. I reminded her that it revealed an unforgivable lack of respect for our grandparents, which, of course, was untrue. I wondered why she needed us to have such American names, instead of traditional Jewish names like Rachel and Joseph? Unbeknownst to my parents, I arranged to at least get the initial "J" back into my name at high school graduation where my diploma reads "J. Thomas Cottle." Talk about affectation. And revenge. Yet at the same time, it may have been a contorted way of honoring my parents and maternal grandfather.

The name business took on a truly serious dimension at college when, after my first hourly examinations, I was called into the dean's office and advised that because I was employing a fictitious name, I was, in effect, attending the school illegally. As my birth certificate read "Joseph," and my exams were signed "Thomas," I was obliged to return to Chicago to have my name officially changed, or I could not continue at the university. Even though my parents had to come up with the transportation costs, they found the matter amusing. I was enraged, although at the time I probably would have said that Joseph was a perfectly atrocious name. If I hadn't felt it to be an affectation, I would have changed my name back to Joseph years ago. I think my mother would have liked that. Then again, in her own life, the figure of Joseph, her father, loomed as a complicated one. No doubt he drove her hard and at times must have been overly severe in his efforts to bring forth her greatness. No doubt she hated many of the practice sessions under his more than watchful eye. No doubt, too, she adored him. She recalled, for example, the first time she discovered that he played the piano. The composition was "Asa's Death (*Asa's Todt*). "I stood there and wept. I said, 'What, do I live in a crazy house?' . . . He never touched the piano." In the end, perhaps, it was easier for everyone for me to remain Tommy. Certain people just require compartments in their lives.

One of the sadder repercussions of the seeming omnipresence of psychoanalysis in our home was the subscription to the tenet that the parent is not meant to respond naturally to the child's utterances and accomplishments. Not only that, telling someone that you love them somehow might destroy the delicate relationship between parent and child. One remains comfortably nondirective by asking that ubiquitous question. "And how does that make you feel?"

This particular matter came to a head during my junior year of college. At the end of the second semester of my sophomore year, I flunked a course and was placed on academic probation. The action prompted a meeting with my father that summer at his hospital. We met at the end of a corridor on a window bench looking west over the city. Essentially, he was profoundly disappointed in me, but predictably, he reasoned the failing had a psychological foundation, which meant that I would have to consult a psychiatrist, which I did when I returned to college for my junior year.

Then, astonishingly, not only did my grades improve—studying proved a better medicine than psychotherapy—I won a major award in comparative literature. My paper was an interpretation of Kafka's *Metamorphosis* in which I argued that the metamorphosis of Gregor Samsa into a cockroach was actually a form of suicide in which the child could once and for all not only learn what his parents thought of him, but hear as well their expressions of love for him.

On the heels of my ignominious probationary status, I could barely wait to notify my parents, both of whom happened to be home at lunchtime when I telephoned. Consistent with their alleged Freudian nondirective posture, they responded to my news with an almost impeccable flatness. "This must make you very happy." Sitting erect in our dorm room's soiled yellow chair, I angrily hung up the phone, then sat perfectly still. I knew that as fast as one could dial the number, my parents would be calling back absolutely aggrieved at my atrocious manners and lack of sensitivity. They did.

"Doesn't *anything* I do ever make *you* happy?" I shot back. "Must something always just make *me* happy? Don't you *ever* get tired of all that Freudian crap?" I tend to think the remarks were eye opening. My parent's style changed from that point as if they had been liberated from a prison of stultifying (not to mention misinterpreted) psychological theory, and discovered the legitimacy and pleasure of expressing the joy one feels from a child's activities. In Yiddish, we say that parents *kleb nachus*, "take pride," but someone neglected to tell an entire generation that after you *kleb* you should pass it on so that children know they bring *nachus* to their parents, and hence, they are worthy and lovable people, even when they go on academic probation.

Then again, perhaps, some people, many of whom have been traumatized, cannot openly express their love for their children, or anyone for that matter. They remain emotionally aloof. Perhaps they cannot gain access to these recesses of the mind, and heart, in the same way that one sometimes cannot locate documents on their computer. Others may feel love but they conceal it, which often makes everyone in the family that much more frustrated and unhappy.

In response to hearing the words, "I love you," some people reply, "Me, too," or simply, "thank you." Or perhaps they offer up a nondescript nod. The sad truth is that while some children are convinced their parents love them, others are not quite certain. Or more sadly, they gain their certainty only years later, as in my case when my parents' notes in birthday cards suddenly, that is, after the Comparative Literature Prize, contained effusive expressions of love and admiration. I am reminded, in this context, of a story of someone else who longed to hear something about love from a parent.

I knew the psychoanalysts hadn't come to our home on the request of my parents to spy on me, although evidently the thought did cross my mind. They came for the soirées and the discussions in which Nathan, filled with what James Francis Cooke called "universal information,"[21] lectured them on the workings of the human mind. They merely listened, something for which they all had elaborate practice. I loved it when Nathan told them off. For the moment, he was a mouthpiece sent by God to speak for the voiceless, which of course wasn't an accurate depiction, because my voice was heard all too much in that house. It was my soul that was never heard from.

Doctors George Mohr, George Wilson, Franz Alexander, Helen Ross, Roy Grinker, Robert Gronner, all sat on my mother's couch listening and seemingly loving the guests and every minute of the talks and the music. George Mohr, who had been my therapist, Roy Grinker, who my father consulted from time to time—there was a general agreement in the family that my father didn't require a "complete analysis"—and George Wilson, a man who treated my mother and several of her women friends, all attended the Hawthorne Place soirées. My father, the perpetual chronicler, using his old Leica camera, once photographed Dr. Wilson sitting in one of the living room chairs with my mother and another woman—they were both patients of his—sitting on his lap, and two other women, one a patient, the other his wife Doris, draped over his shoulders. I can't even begin to contemplate what Oedipal terror I must have known imagining my mother lying on a couch in the same office with the man on whose lap she was sitting for a photograph. The terror is etched in my mind, and, I have recently learned, my sister's mind as well.

"You remember that photograph, Judy?" I inquired of her over the phone shortly after writing these paragraphs.

"Oh, yeah," she replied, and I could practically hear her head nodding, not unlike I remember my mother nodding when "big" truths came out.

"Did mother ever apologize to you?" I asked, apropos of nothing at all.

"Once," Judy answered. "Just once."

"How old were you? Fifty?"

"Maybe. Something like that."

Then Judy quickly alluded to the final horror show with my mother, a terrifying scene of rage and anguish, which was motivated by fear and insecurity, I'm certain, that took place on the occasion of Judy and my wife driving my mother to Logan Airport in Boston. It was a scene neither woman has ever fully described. They don't need to. I was present at all too many other scenes. Still, there is tremendous sadness, along with fright and disgust, that inevitably come forth with these recollections, or even oblique allusions to them. Here she was, yet again, traveling away from a home base, alone, the terrors of the past very much alive despite all those hours of psychoanalysis.

Whatever went on in that office with my mother and Dr. Wilson, whose office was in the same medical building as my father's? Why did my father permit any of it? Why, when after completing a series of psychological tests with a professional psychologist, a family friend, naturally, Rusty Miller—you didn't have a bonafide personality or a single legitimate aptitude until Rusty officially determined them—it was recommended that I consult a psychiatrist, did my parents arrange to have this one consultation be with Dr. George Wilson?

Chicago in the 1940s and 1950s was one of the world seats of the psychoanalytic movement. By pure chance, every other person was an analyst, an analyst in-training, or an analysand. You weren't anything unless you had been psychoanalyzed, but your final status was determined by the reputation of your analyst. The whole degrees of separation issue hinged on how far you were from Sigmund Freud or Anna Freud. And amazingly, just as every great movie actor was Jewish, at least according to Auntie Bessie, everybody's analyst had been analyzed by Freud. That is, everybody who came to Hawthorne Place. Which meant that contrary to popular knowledge, Freud treated twenty-seven thousand analysands four times a week, and nineteen thousand of them ended up in Chicago, and of these, fifteen thousand ended up on my mother's couch happily abiding the dogmatic harangues of Nathan Milstein.

There was one more thing. What good, pray tell, was any of this psychoanalysis doing any of us? I was always sad in our home—my Cousin Dickie remembers me crying all the time—and my mother's temper and sadness didn't recede one iota during the three hundred and ninety-seven years of her analysis. And don't think I wouldn't tell her this. As a child, I hadn't yet learned about the concept of countertransference, of course, in which the analyst unconsciously transfers his or her own feelings onto the patient, but I surely had a primitive sense of the unethical nature of analysts holding patients on their laps. During our fights I brought it all out to her, punctuating my oration with, "Tell me, can *you* see any difference in you? Talk about looking in a mirror! All these years and you're as miserable as you ever were." I actually meant by this two meanings: Miserable to me, and miserable in the sense of her being tortured by her own demons who simply refused to quit Hawthorne Place.

Truth be told, I never felt that I was any happier for having seen Doctors Bradley and Mohr. With Dr. Bradley, a kindly woman whose office was also located in the same building as my father's, I played cards and checkers. Together we learned that I badly needed to win. With Dr. Mohr, a kindly man who wore slender, silver *pince-nez* glasses, I played ring toss and looked out of his Ohio Street office building every week to watch the progress made by the workers at the construction site of a parking garage.

I loved watching these men work, just as today I love watching carpenters at work. I spent glorious afternoons observing craftsmen remodel the home of Ruth and Ed Weiss situated on almost an acre of land across the street from ours on Hawthorne Place, thus providing it the name, "Weiss Acre." I can still see them adhering an avocado green fabric—Harold Walsh had been there as well—in the bays of Ed's upstairs study closet doors. Then again, how genuinely therapeutic was this weekly observation of the parking garage? A calming meditation to be sure, but did it genuinely qualify as therapy? Moreover, from my vantage point across Ohio Street, who could tell whether any of those Chicago laborers were sensitive?

Interesting, or as they said in those days, significant, that I don't remember my mother's response to these jabs about her (and my own) lack of " progress" in psychotherapy. She, of course, knew how troubled she was, how troubled I was, and how completely unhappy she became when the music stopped and the musicians disappeared. She must have felt that sending her child into therapy meant that at some level she was admitting to failure as a mother. She knew as well that the analysis was helping only so much, although one cannot underestimate the fact that despite her depression, she did get up and go to her sessions. Only later did I allow myself to recognize the degree of her agitated depression and the fact that the sleeping pills she took almost every night only exacerbated her dark moods, especially in the morning when evidently she was chemically crashing. Come to think of it, my parent's medicine cabinets were always stocked with medicine vials. The comic London Lee's line, "there was so much medicine in their bathroom, their neighbors once petitioned them to remain open on Sundays," could well have applied to my parents.

When I was especially sad, I went across the street to the Weisses, entering the house through the backdoor off the driveway where their maid, Naomi Ziegler, a tall, stately woman, as handsome as she was thoughtful, let me sit at the kitchen table while she prepared dinner. Naomi never asked why I had come. Always she found food for me, sometimes bits from the Weiss's dinner several hours hence, but never was there any surprise on her part that I had appeared. She knew that if I were looking for one of the Weisses, I would ring the front door. A backdoor entrance meant that it was her I needed. She knew something else. My appearance meant that I was sad. I only pretended that it might be fun to kill a few minutes with her rather than do my homework. Sometimes I imagined that Naomi was my mother.

I prayed that Ruth Weiss wouldn't come downstairs and find me, for I would have no reasonable excuse for being there. Why would I be in the house and not look for their son, Jimmy, a boy four years younger than I? Ruth did make unexpected entrances into the kitchen every so often, but always Naomi covered for me. "I needed Tommy to take some rolls over to Mrs. Cottle for me. Lucky I saw him walking down the street." Strange, that just sitting quietly with someone, as I often did with Leah, even someone who may well be unable to pay full attention to or even speak with you, should bring such calm. Perhaps that's why a small child prefers to play in the vicinity of its mother; it's just safer that way.

I have never attempted suicide in my life, but as an adolescent I thought about it more than I think is normal. I never once mentioned these thoughts to anyone, not to the psychiatrists I saw, not to any chum, not to any girlfriend. I just lived with images of driving a car into an abutment, or taking pills from my parent's medicine cabinets, or letting a car engine run in the garage while slowly I lost consciousness. I grew fascinated with an article I had read describing the ecstasy of losing consciousness in an airplane as it climbs higher and higher, thereby gradually reducing the intake of oxygen until the brain goes dead.

Reflecting on it now, it may be that when I was overwhelmed by thoughts of destruction, I would wander over to be near Naomi. It was then I would think of "making it easier for everyone by not being there anymore." I usually spoke this phrase to myself when contemplating suicide. Truthfully, I thought my death would bring peace to everyone; for so often I imagined I had brought nothing but anger, disruptions, and unhappiness to three other people. I never counted Leah, because I choose to believe I neither disappointed nor depressed her.

The fantasy of "making it easier for everyone by not being there anymore" always concluded with specific scenes I imagined would ensue, the very themes I would explore years later in my essay on "The Metamorphosis." I envisioned my parents broken with sadness, remorse, and shame to a degree no other parents had ever known. At my school, everyone would utter the same words: "Of all the people we know, Tommy is the last person we could ever have believed would do this. He seemed to have everything a young person could ever want, and he was so happy all the time." And then, in a grandiose and melodramatic ending, I envisioned reporters going to my aunts and uncles, all of whom would demur and agree to speak only off the record, for they would never have done anything to besmirch the reputation of my parents. But in the end, all of them would say how they had always worried about me, and how regularly they not only witnessed my sadness, but also recognized that I may have had just enough strength to enable me to undertake something drastic. I am certain my mother-in-law would have detected something, even from a photograph. Yet of all the people who might have seen it coming, I always imagined it was my mother who would have said, "I knew something like this was going to happen. I just knew it."

I appeared once on a television program produced in Chicago and hosted by the late Irv Kupcinet, one of the city's popular journalists. Appearing on the show were the actor Nick Nolte and the late Eppie Lederer, known to her millions of readers as Ann Landers. Interestingly, I can't remember whether Dr. Timothy Leary was on that program, but I do remember saying at one point that if I were a kid living in dire conditions of poverty, and feeling there was no way I could ever "make it" in society, I, too, might very well be doing drugs.

That's all Eppie needed to hear. She came at me like a tiger. She couldn't believe that I would say something so irresponsible. Drugs were *never* the solution, and it was unforgivable for me, a professional psychologist, allegedly concerned about young people, not to mention the child of outstanding parents, to utter such a remark.

She may have been right. Only years later did I ask myself from where that comment sprung? Did I honestly believe it? Part of me did, actually. Then again, I don't like being judged, particularly when I never gave my main judges anything with which to find fault. I always tried to be a star, for me and for them. I was always working on their behalf, and mine.

But I was not myself the afternoon of that taping. Earlier in the day, I had visited for the first and last time with Leah in her new setting, a nursing home on the near north side, not far from the Esquire movie theater on Oak Street where I spent so many Saturday nights during high school. I visited a more frail and sickly woman than I had ever known her to be. Before the visit, I couldn't believe my parents had put her in a home; it felt as though they had sentenced her to some foreign outpost. How could they have been so cruel? Yet when I saw her condition I realized it was the only humane thing to do. In these last moments of her life, Leah required precisely what she gave us all those years, round the clock attention, what Aunt Fanny called A.M./P.M. care.

Who knows what we discussed during that brief meeting. I remember asking her several times, "Do you need anything? I can bring you anything, you know." I remember forcing myself not to cry. I told her that I loved her, something I never remember once having told my parents, and she nodded. She said nothing, but she smiled weakly. "I'm *your* son, too," I said, to which she did reply, "I know." She patted my hand, something she would do in the kitchen when, alone together, she watched me devour my "concoction." All the while I knew I would never see her again. I had to return to the east coast the next day, and anyone could see she was not going to last much longer. I said that I would come back soon to visit her, but I knew this to be a lie.

From the nursing home I walked south on Michigan Avenue to the television studio, knowing I would never fully recover in time for the taping. I imagine that the remark about young people and drugs, appropriate or not, came from my sadness and a desire to pop some magical pill of my own. I wanted to make a host of memories and feelings disappear on the spot, a sentiment with which I had lived through much of my adolescence. Now, as I write this, I wonder whether my mother experienced some of these same thoughts, and reached some of these same conclusions about magical pills.

Chapter 6

Identical Sensibilities

How do I convey the relationship my mother maintained for sixty years with Vladimir Horowitz? Anyone who knew our family knew this connection, or involvement, to be complicated, rich, at times neurotic, magnificent, nightmarish, gratifying, liberating, stultifying, colleagial, competitive, exasperating, and as thrilling as any relationship between two human beings in the history of the world! Who else would conclude a telegram to a friend as Horowitz did when he wrote to my mother on April 7, 1931: "My best wishes—Love and constipation—Vladimir Hor."

In my mother's words: "He wanted it to be like whore, you know, HOR period. Couldn't live with that man. . . . Couldn't say w-h-o-r-e 'cause that wouldn't be funny, but he's . . . arriving with constipation. Love, Hor."

As time went on, Horowitz and my mother even began to resemble one another—aquiline noses, with nostrils that flared, and when they laughed, glottal hiccups punctuating their sounds. Their hands, too, were similar, for they had "strong, spatulate fingers," a phrase I borrow from the January, 1932 issue of the *Chicagoan*. Even the texture of the skin on the back of their hands was identical. And truly identical were their sensibilities, the sensibilities, Marc Pincherle reminds us, of the virtuoso: charm and speed.[1] They even had identical photographs of Toscanini and Rachmaninoff sitting on their pianos.[2] (The one from Toscanini, dated 12–31–1939 is inscribed: "Happy New Year, My Dear Gitta, and many good wishes.") Horowitz also had a photo of the pianist Ignacy Paderewski on his piano, whereas my mother had a photo of Horowitz, dated 1931. It is inscribed to both of my parents with the words, "With my love, Volodja."

My mother and Horowitz often acted like mischievous students, making faces at the children at the dinner table when they knew others weren't looking, and then turning to the adults with exaggerated expressions of innocence. They also shared a similar childhood experience that neither may have ever overcome: the early separation from family and friends in order to pursue music. Horowitz departed Kiev, my mother, born almost exactly ten months later, pulled away from Chicago.

Horowitz's facial contortions were sublime, as were my mother's who, on one occasion, was actually chastised by Rachmaninoff for mimicking another pianist. I would crack up at Volodja. He would point at me and say, "What you are laughing at? Is time now for to be quiet." So I would attempt to compose myself never taking my eyes off him until he threw another face at me, this one even more grotesque. "Gitta, why the boy laughs all the time?" Then, lightheartedly, she would admonish the two of us: "If you can't behave you'll both have to leave the table." One last glance from Horowitz told me, stay alert, there will be more mischief coming in a few moments.

There was nothing more energizing than seeing these two people together, nothing more thrilling, even for a small boy, to hear them play double piano. Not so incidentally, I remember my mother usually playing the first piano parts with the man she adoringly called "Volodja" playing the second piano parts. Together with Rachmaninoff, Horowitz remained her most important influence. Early in her career, during a stretch when Horowitz fell ill and had to cancel several concerts, he nonetheless stayed in Chicago and coached her through the Schumann Concerto. She more than paid him back, nursing him through a series of illnesses, my father overseeing the medical consultations, that forced cancellations of numerous concerts in 1940. Some of the consultations even made the gossip columns:

> If you see a tall, slim dark Russian walking thru Lincoln Park early every morning, it's Vladimir Horowitz . . . the great pianist, who has been in Chicago for some weeks undergoing treatment for the injured finger . . . injured last May that made it necessary for him to cancel his concert tour this autumn. Few persons know that Horowitz is in town. He spends much of his time with Dr. Maurice Cottle and his wife, Gitta Gradova, who are intimate friends. . . . It was Dr. Cottle who suggested to Horowitz that he come to Chicago for treatment.[3]

As my mother would have said, it was Rachmaninoff and Horowitz who taught her that the piano, albeit a percussive instrument, could be made to sing. This, despite Ned Rorem's declaration: "The piano is the least expressive of all musical instruments."[4] Ernest Hutcheson avered that "the piano cannot sing like the violin or the human voice, for the simple reason that it cannot sustain an undiminishing tone, let alone swell on a note."[5] Claudia Cassidy was correct when she theorized in February 1936 that Gitta Gradova had been listening to Horowitz, as was Robert Pollak, another critic, who observed in 1941: "[Gitta Gradova's] command of the small crescendo and diminuendo resembles that of her good friend, Horowitz."[6]

Saturday night soirées with the great musicians usually augured Sunday afternoon recitals; my mother always referred to them as "rectals." None of the recitals put our family on edge as much as the Horowitz concerts, for it was at this time that I could see that Volodja and my mother were truly attached, and not merely at the hip.

When Horowitz performed, my mother sat so erect in her Orchestra Hall seat that I thought her back would break before intermission. I always sat on the aisle in case I had to go to the bathroom. During most concerts, she would look at me from time to time to see how I was getting along. She knew a particularly lengthy passage of unaccompanied Bach, even performed by Nathan Milstein, could be a trifle tedious for a child. Mainly, I imagine, she looked to see whether I was absorbing the sensitivity of the playing, whether I was able, in other words, to *feel* the emotion a performer draws from himself or herself as well as from the composer. It was as if she had memorized Aaron Copland's two fundamental concerns for listeners to music: First, were they hearing everything that was going on? Second, were they being sensitive to what was going on?[7] I was sensitive to these emotions, but for some reason I hated to reveal this to her. It would have meant that there was more of her in me than I ever wished to admit. Sadly, I inherited only the seeds of her temperament, too little of her musical gift.

So my mother sat in her seat, seemingly enjoying certain passages of whomever was playing, and worrying a bit over passages about which she and Rudi (Serkin), or Nathan, or Franz, or Jascha had spoken of the night before, passages she knew caused the performer apprehension. But not with Volodja. With him, every measure, every note, seemingly, was torture. Yes, he navigated that part of the Schubert, but oh, dear God, what was about to come up now in the Liszt? That left hand run, those thirds in the right hand, and then those damnable octaves.

Of course I wasn't sophisticated enough in those years to know about psychological concepts like enmeshment, a term which in fact hadn't even been coined yet, but these two people were enmeshed. From her seat in the hall my mother played every note with Volodja, her hands gripping the cushioned arm rests as if she were a passenger in a plane that was going down. During Horowitz recitals, I could have been standing on my head urinating in the middle of Orchestra Hall and she wouldn't have noticed. Her eyes were either glued to him or closed as if in prayer. "Please, God, let him get through this passage," or "*Oi,* he still has the Bach-Busoni, the *Traumere,* the Bizet medley; we're all going to die." She wished for the end of the concert to come soon because it meant the worrying was over, for now. "The horses are reaching the barn," she would whisper as Volodja reached the last page of the composition.

Although I was never there to witness them, it should be mentioned that Horowitz had his own anxieties evoked when my mother played. Quite likely, he, too, sat stiffly in concert halls praying that she would get through the passages that he, better than anyone, knew frightened her. My mother told the story of how when Volodja learned that one of her European tours was going to include the *Wanderer Fantasie* of Franz Schubert, he told her he was certain she could play it error-free, but that it might be a good idea, nonetheless, to have an ambulance waiting for her after each concert.

With Volodja, I sincerely believe, my mother heard more than any other person in the hall save one, Horowitz's wife, Wanda, a woman who thought heaven knows what about the relationship between her husband and his friend, colleague, and perhaps too, at some level, competitor.

Ostensibly, my mother stopped playing because she hated the grind of the concerts, an abiding fear that she would humiliate herself by forgetting the music in the middle of a concert, and the travel which in those days was only by train and boat. A quick trip from Chicago to Detroit, for example, what today might be a ten or twelve hour jaunt, became a several day trek, which my mother would make by train accompanied by one of her dearest women friends, Therese Lackritz or Bernice Caplitz, known to us as "Briny." Although the tours invariably yielded humorous stories and musical successes, she led us to believe traveling was overwhelming. Unlike pianists Gary Graffman and Shura Cherkassky, who loved memorizing air and train schedules, my mother seemed to detest every aspect of travel. She surely shared with her European colleagues the dread of American touring, although she would have been infuriated by Cooke's purposely exaggerated description of "the great ocean yawning between the two continents, and red-skinned savages just beyond New York or certainly not far from Chicago."[8]

Still, with all the depression, sadness, anger, confusion, and pure torture my mother must have known, I have always thought that Horowitz was part of her struggle, or at least one of the main people around whom she wrapped her struggle. I might have been another one of those people. I know she loved Volodja, admired him as much as one can admire another person, especially one in the same field where many strive to become the indisputable leader. She loved introducing piano students to him, as she did with Leon Bates and Coleman Blumfield, the latter having been her own protégé,[9] for she knew that teacher and student alike would benefit from the association. Yet at some level, one that she would never admit to, I think she believed herself to be competing with him. I have always believed that she wanted to be the number one player in the world, a position, she imagined, Horowitz occupied. Whatever their relationship was all about, and Glenn Plaskin[10] observes that my mother was one of only four close friends (and the only musician) Horowitz had, her involvement with his playing was too complicated to suggest that admiration and collegiality alone were at work.

Before they had children, my parents survived a devastating car accident on a highway near Hammond, Indiana. Waiting in their convertible for a traffic light to change, they were hit broadside by a second car going around fifty miles an hour. Without seat belts, they were literally launched out of their automobile into the air. Amazingly, my father landed on a pile of sand probably used on winter days to reduce road slickness. He received minor scratches but required no medical attention. My mother, on the other hand, was not as fortunate. As it was described to me by my father, though never once by her, she flew through the air and was splattered on the Indiana road, breaking bones all over her body, her spine, pelvis, and one knee taking the brunt of the crash. She spoke little of "the accident" over the years, only a brief recollection of her begging the two ambulance drivers to go a bit slower because her pain was so great. They responded, "We haven't placed you on the stretcher yet." She remained hospitalized in Gary, Indiana, for almost a full year. My Aunt Bessie, a daily visitor, traveled back and forth from her Northwest side Chicago home to comfort my mother. (The bottom drawer of her husband Herbie's bureau contained every press clipping of my mother Aunt Bessie could locate.) Music critics wrote of a "brief retirement" during this period; Claudia Cassidy referred to her having been "struck the snag of ill health."

Toward the end of her life, my mother spoke briefly of the accident in an interview with Charles Olin, even showing him her knee which, almost fifty years later, still showed the effects of the trauma:

> It was 1928, six years after I started my career. I broke every bone I ever had. We stopped at the red light, but a guy felt that he could pass the nine cars ahead of him. But before he got there the light changed, but by that time he had gathered so much momentum he couldn't stop, and we were the first one ready to go, and he hit us head on. Gee, you know, I ought to think about that more, because walking out and playing a concerto sounds like paradise next to that.[11]

The accident left my mother not only traumatized, forever dreading automobile travel, but she also never again could walk fully erect, straight, and proud. The closest she got to this erect position was sitting at her own piano and listening to Horowitz play a recital. Gripping the arms of her seat one Sunday afternoon, and sitting perfectly upright, I heard her whisper, "Oh, dear God, he's lost. He has no idea where he is." Horowitz might have been playing Scarlatti, or Bach, or Liszt, but, for what seemed like minutes, I watched my mother grimace, cry, go through the sort of torture I imagine a parent experiences watching her child carted into a hospital emergency room following a serious accident. At long last, the piece was over and the concert concluded and, as always, we were on our way backstage.

To reach the backstage entrance of Chicago's Orchestra Hall, we had to leave the building and walk several doors south. We descended the stairs and marched down the long basement corridor lined with the orchestra's instrument cases; the steam pipes hovered overhead. We then ascended the stairs at the far end of the underground passage to reach the green room where people always gathered after a concert to meet the artist. Horowitz, of course, had hordes of Chicago friends and admirers. But my mother's presence opened all doors and thrust us to the head of the line. Wanda, along with other people, managers perhaps, and of course Volodja waited in the green room. My mother sped down the length of the basement corridor as if she were heading to the physician's office to learn whether her child had survived the crash.

Mind you, in the lobby following the Scarlatti or the Bach in which for two full minutes Vladimir Horowitz had been either playing a section of the piece meant to come earlier or later, or an entirely different piece of music altogether, possibly even one by another composer, we heard people offering comments like, "Absolutely amazing. I have never heard the Bach played that way." "And for good reason," my mother muttered under her breath, hurriedly walking past them, terrified, apparently, that by this point Volodja, unable to handle the shame and embarrassment of such a horrendous *faux pas*, had shot himself. "And you'll never hear it played that way again."

Granted, my mother surely knew the famous line attributed to Anton Rubinstein who was not known to be the most accurate of pianists. After receiving the congratulations of a woman following one of his performances, Rubinstein allegedly remarked, "Madame, I could give another concert with the notes I left out."[12] On this one Sunday afternoon, however, there was nothing humorous about the notes that Horowitz either had omitted or accidentally included. It must be recalled that for Horowitz and my mother, and I am sure other virtuosos as well, if the playing were not error free, it was automatically deemed atrocious. Neither would have subscribed to the sanguine, temperate definition of the great artist offered by Arthur Elson:

> We may, therefore, judge the pianist by his own individual work. If he plays with control and variety of speed and power, brings out his themes expressively without tearing them to tatters, and balances section against section, or voice against voice, in proper fashion, expressing the very best effects of which a piece is capable, then we may feel sure that he is a great artist."[13]

Both Horowitz and my mother, however, would have subscribed to Carl Engel's reflections on beauty and perfection:

Beauty is relative, is a matter of changing taste. Perfection is absolute, is a matter of permanent criteria. The enjoyment of perfection differs from the enjoyment of beauty. Beauty appeals to our senses. . . . Perfection addressees itself to what Walter Pater called the "imaginative reason." This reason must be unalterably fixed, maintained on a level of stable rationality. *The greatest work of art is wholly beautiful, perfect and sane"* (emphasis added)[14]

Granted, people often commented: "But the slow movement was impeccable," and "The scherzo like chiffon." Nonsense! Nothing could compensate for even one false note, what my mother called *"falcha nota."* So the walk through Orchestra Hall's underground corridor was a walk to the graveside, to the site of the suicide, to the pool of blood which had been collecting. Or was it the true home of the *deus ex machina*?

Horowitz was sitting at a table stationed in the entrance to the green room signing his autograph on programs, receiving praise, and being totally gracious, his starched shirt and morning coat soaked with perspiration. My mother, as always walking ahead of us, entered first. Suddenly, their eyes met and not one word had to be spoken, nor, to my knowledge, ever was spoken about that one concert. They merely looked at each other and became hysterical. For minutes they just looked at one another and howled with laughter. Wanda, too, enjoyed the hilarity. She knew what had gone on, or hadn't gone on, in the middle of the Scarlatti or the Bach. She too had suffered in the box with my mother on all too many occasions of a Horowitz rectal, the three of them locked in the most complicated and unsexual *ménage à trois* anyone could have imagined.

My father was part of the menage, but not fully included in it, if this makes sense. He observed it, chronicled it, but never had the stomach or the psychology to make it a *ménage à quatre.* Perhaps it was because he sought attention on a wholly different front, the international world of medicine. I know he felt proud to be the doctor to artists like Horowitz, and on one occasion, the violinist Fritz Kreisler who, at the time, was beginning to grow deaf. As my mother told the story,

He started to lose it, couldn't hear a perfect A. So [the conductor Frederick] Stock told him to see Maurie. So he came to the office and Dr. Cottle said, "I'm amazed at the intelligent questions, medical . . . so intelligent." He said, "You know, Dr. Cottle, I went to medical school." We knew that. I heard that and Maurie knew that, but forgot it. He said, "I think if I had stayed with medicine I *really* would have made a name for myself."[15]

I know, too, that my father was proud to be the cohost of Chicago's celebrated dinner parties and soirées, but not until now did I appreciate the ironic symbolism of a connection he had with Wanda.

My father often wore a gold-linked key chain, which at one end connected to a belt loop in his pants and at the other end held his keys in his front right pocket. However, the problem was that with usage the chain inevitably became entangled, which tended to detract from the suave image it provided my father. Hardly a man to take time to repair these entanglements, my father was only too happy to have Wanda undertake the repair, which apparently she loved doing. I remember her sitting on my mother's couch patiently working like a surgeon untangling each individual link. The chain project was like their own little conceit, their own little *pas de deux*, nothing significant, yet a way to further their connection, entangled or not. For in truth, the spotlight was always on the two other dancers, the prima ballerina and her esteemed partner.

Funny, with all their closeness, I cannot remember my mother and Volodja ever embracing. Often when they parted, Russian, German, and French words would be exchanged, but I cannot remember them hugging and kissing. I do remember an enormous amount of laughing, and Volodja, when excited, speaking in a high-pitched almost squeaky voice.

Laughing, as they say, relieves tension. Laughter means that things aren't all that bad, and not every event holds life or death in the balance, as I fear was the case so often for my mother, a trait that I, too, have incorporated. Laughter means that imperfection is allowed, the improbable occurs, the incongruous exists. It also meant that Horowitz wasn't perfect, which meant that even the greatest artists aren't perfect. My mother didn't always need to be perfect, which meant that she could play again, with the Fine Arts Quartet, with Jascha, Misha, Pisha, Grisha, Sasha, and Kasha. If only she could have worked it out, unraveled it in her mind, for her fingers, and her heart, had been waiting years for the opportunity, any opportunity. Because of Volodja's stupendous blunder during that one concert, my mother, for the time being, I believe, was on an equal playfield with him. She could live with his gargantuan success, even if she couldn't handle the arduous demands of her own ego. *He* had erred, and *she* had survived it. As for the rest of us, I'm not sure anyone was paying all that much attention. Or perhaps people couldn't always summon up the energy to deal with the consternation and histrionics that surrounded the two of them, although it should be said that neither one of them tolerated histrionics or theatrics of any sort during a performance. Overly dramatic behavior—what they called *schmuntzes*—was viewed as unnecessary affectation. Histrionics were perfectly controllable. The music always came first. Some pianists, my mother frequently said, were enjoyable only if one closed one's eyes. (Others, presumably, only if one closed one's ears.)

I have a friend, born in France, who has lived for years in America. Brigitte's English by now is rich and polished, but occasionally she will forget a word or use an idiom inappropriately. She allows me to tease her mercilessly. "Froggie," I say, "your mind's going limp." She always laughs. Brigitte's kindness prevents her from ever responding, "I'd like to hear you speak French half as well as I speak English!" My mother said almost these same words to Volodja. On every occasion he mispronounced something, she would tease him about how his mind clearly was disintegrating, and how extraordinary it was that with each year in America his English, seemingly, had grown worse. He laughed openly when she mimicked him. Walking along Chicago's shoreline and admiring Lake Michigan, she remembered him commenting, "Revue the lac." At the time, Horowitz's English was in its infancy stage; he was actually translating in his mind from Russian to German to French to English. "Revue the lac" was a linguistic derivative, clearly, from the French. But that's all my mother needed; she was all over him. "Review the lac? Do you know where we are?" As always, Volodja laughed. And she laughed. Why is it, I wonder, that I have so many childhood recollections of my mother laughing with people other than me? And why is it that so many of my recollections still evoke sensations of jealousy, literally defined as my being replaced by someone?

There is another memory I have of Horowitz, this one, too, through a story my mother recounted.

As I say, for years, the families Horowitz, Rachmaninoff, Milstein, Piatigorsky, and Cottle summered together in Switzerland.

Somewhere in our basement sits a carton of ancient eight millimeter films my father, ever the chronicler, shot of these larger than life figures. In one film, Horowitz is seen walking in the mountains. It is summer but there is snow on the ground. Standing behind the projector in the basement of Hawthorne Place, my father explained that the couples were hiking on a glacier. I remember not understanding how, precisely, one walks on a glacier, but having my mind turn to the utter incongruity of my mother taking any sort of a hike—she would never have offered to take one with me—but, of course, these movies were shot years before the car accident. Watching her go off in the direction of Broadway to do her shopping, I saw a woman, slightly stooped, shoulders bent forward, hardly elegantly dressed, trudging laboriously. A childhood friend recalls her back as "being sort of hunched, not bent down, but crouched, as if muscularly resisting." I think his observation is exact; without music there was little vitality to her life, and her whole body resisted the ordeal of everyday drudgery. "It is our vitality," Tobias Matthay wrote, "which leaves our muscles unfettered by their fellows."[16] But Nietzsche may have had the last word in describing my mother's frequent lack of vitality: "Without music life would be a mistake."[17]

On occasion I would see my mother join the elegant Louise Eisendrath who lived two houses down on Hawthorne Place. Mrs. Eisendrath was heading for the precise same shops, but she appeared fashionable for a stroll down Chicago's Broadway. The immigrant and the queen, I would think, going off to Mannie Stockenberg's butcher shop together.

Seeing that one scene in the home movie brought back a recollection for my mother in which, on a magnificent day in the Alps, Horowitz suddenly turned his face toward the heavens and screamed out, "OH, GOD, WHY DID YOU MAKE ME THIS WAY?" I have no idea to what he was referring, though I do know that Gustav Mahler was hardly alone in believing that "what one makes music out of . . . is the feeling, thinking, breathing, suffering human being."[18] I cannot believe Horowitz would be angry at having been endowed with the musical genius he possessed, although only geniuses know the sort of intimacy they establish with their own extraordinary talents. I suspect the utterance referred to something else, but suffice it to say it meant that, like my mother, he, too, was tortured by something from which he was never completely emancipated. They both knew this about themselves, and one another. No one else would have dared cut in this dance macabre. When the music was playing, everyone knew to leave them alone on the floor.

Perhaps there is something transcendent about this questioning appeal to heaven. Perhaps, too, it represents the subjective expression of what Paul Bekker called the "romantic attitude,"[19] the expression of all that is unique in an individual, all that constitutes his or her personality. Yet the attitude contains as well the simultaneous desire to impart this personality to others, which the act of performance permits, demands even, and the recognition that this purpose is utterly unrealistic and at times the cause of profound anguish, if not the appearance of classical neurasthenia. Again from Bekker:

> It is the impossibility of realizing such an illusory aim that leads to the tragical mood, the pessimistic temper of this age in which passionate, surging conflicts, dissatisfaction with life, resignation, flight from the world, and retreat into the solitude of self, are characteristic symptoms. A critical and intellectual and psychological attitude is responsible for these conditions and manifests itself in art by making possible a new intensity of dynamic impulses.[20]

Whatever it was, this conflation of attitudes, circumstances, and psychological states, or merely the romantic attitude, which Goethe himself had decried as being "weak, sickly and infirm,"[21] and whatever may have tortured me as a child, could never be expressed to anyone except my mother, and only through the medium of anger. I know that just as easily it might have been her turning her face toward the sky and bellowing, "OH, GOD, WHY DID YOU MAKE ME THIS WAY!" The adult in me weeps for her; the child in me, which lives to this day, wants to say to her, "If only once you had spoken of this. If only once you had told me that story you often said would someday be known so that I might not have taken all the blame upon myself, or, for that matter, thrown it on you, both of us might have been liberated from some of our demons." If only someone could have formulated an explanation for it all. It is not by accident that a man who daily experiences memory lapses, the infamous "senior moments," should remember so well the utterly simplistic yet plaintive line Robin Williams repeatedly speaks to Matt Damon in *Good Will Hunting*, "It's not your fault." As an adolescent, I know I wanted to turn my face toward her and bellow, "OH, MOTHER, WHY DID YOU MAKE ME THIS WAY?" Now I wish to tell her that it was also not all her fault. Nor mine.

If the gossip columnist referred to Horowitz and my mother as intimate friends, she had no idea how intricate this intimacy had become. In my mother's deceptively simple words:

> There wasn't a secret in his soul that he didn't tell me. I wish he hadn't told me. . . . You know, he was a combination of two wonderful things: a child and a monster. Like a little boy, he was. He could make trouble for you.
>
> Volodja told me I was pregnant. [I didn't think I] could have children after the accident. So we went to New York with him which we always did, and I wasn't playing because of the accident, and Horowitz said, "Go along on this thing [trip]." So the lawyer's wife, Oscar Stern's wife, and I went with Volodja. Anyway, we had a beautiful suite at the Waldorf Astoria. We had one bedroom and living room, and every morning our breakfast came up with a beautiful pastel tablecloth, Delft blue one morning, pale pink, corn yellow, and every morning I wanted to vomit my guts out. So I said to Volodja, "What's the matter with you? Why do you insist? You're always so persistent about things. You're such a *nudnik*. Why do you ask me to eat shrimp? What in the hell is so big about shrimp? It's full of cholesterol and dreck . . ." So he said, "So what's wrong with the shrimp?" I said, "I'll be sick to my stomach with this shrimp. I wouldn't have this nausea like this." He said, "How long have you had this with the stomach?" "I've been sick four days." "You know what I think? I think this shrimp will walk."
>
> He's right. And we came home [to Chicago] together because he stayed with us—he was such a horrible guy—and I was waiting to tell Maurie what he said. And I told him, "I'll tell him when you get the hell out of here. Go to your room and go to sleep!" "No, no. I have to wait and see what [Maurie] says." And it was three thirty in the morning. "I won't say a thing to [Maurie] as long as you're in the room." And I told Maurie, and [Maurie] said, "What?" It was all true. "Like I told you. Like I told you."[22]

Such innocent words from a gossip columnist: "[Horowitz] spends much of his time with Dr. Maurice Cottle and his wife, Gitta Gradova . . ." For my mother, that phrase, "much of his time" could mean not enough of his time, or so much of his time she was ready to kill him:

[We had] eight rooms and five bathrooms. Every bathroom had a linen closet. It was made for the people of Lake Forest . . . marvelous . . . and we moved there, weren't there one week, all of a sudden [Horowitz] arrives. I knew he was coming to Chicago. "What are you doing here?" My mother says, "Don't be mean to him." "How would *you* talk to him, [mother]?" I was so aggravated. We had a sixty foot hallway and he comes in there and sees tons of cartons and he's putting his luggage . . . I said, "Do me a favor, for once. Get the hell out of here!" He says, "I will, I will." I said, "I'll tell you what, take my mother with you too. You love her, she loves you, take her with you; she'll have a nice weekend with you."

And everything was quiet. I said, "Mama, you're going to the Belmont [Hotel] with the *meshugana* here," and I went about my business, and all of a sudden I hear water running like crazy. I walk into a bathroom and [Horowitz] is sitting in the bathtub taking a bath! I said, "I'll be damned . . ." Horowitz comes in when we got cartons all the way around the house and he decides to come and move in with us.[23]

Adoration and exasperation, toleration and repudiation, were often at hand when my mother spoke of Volodja. At any moment, he could be either the gentle or chastising teacher or the impudent or penitent student. She frequently referred to his behavior, the boyish charm and naiveté containing its mischief, and the monster, rude and self-absorbed, that lurked beneath it, as a Jekyll and Hyde phenomenon.

[Chicago Symphony first violinist] Jack Gordon's wife, who was a good mouthpiece—she was a lawyer—she invited him Sunday for waffles for brunch. Now, what does [Horowitz] know about waffles and brunch? And everytime he would [shake his head up and down] he would say "please." And he didn't know how to say "thank you," but he would say, "please." And then he wouldn't show up. Well, she wasn't going to take it, and she said, "Who in the hell is he?" She made such a scandal. "Who does he think he is that he can say he's coming and doesn't come!" And he was at *our* house. He didn't know anybody else.

I said, "You know, this was a big mistake you made. You should never do what you did." We spoke in German;

my Russian wasn't good enough for him. So he says, "Vat I say? Vat? Vat? Vat is vaffles?" I said, "You told Madame Gordon, please, and that means in our language yes. When you shake your head like this you're not an animal. That means yes!" So he got so annoyed with me. I said, "You were invited to a brunch with waffles." "Vas mere waffles? Vere are vaffles? I don't care these people. I don't care these people." Then I knew we had a Jekyll and Hyde on our hands.[24]

The expression, joined at the hip, is not altogether mere metaphor. Horowitz's tastes and impulses were the same as my mother's. What he thought he asked my mother to think, which meant that when he changed his mind or his plans, he asked her to do the same. Sadly at times, I think she required an even more powerful figure than he to approve of her going her own way, quite literally in one instance.

David Sarnoff, who my mother described as "a doll of a guy," was throwing a party in Washington to honor Maestro Toscanini following a gala concert. Mr. Sarnoff had invited her and the Horowitz's, all of whom were in New York. All had agreed to go, or so my mother believed.

So Wanda says, "I'm not going." This is the night before. "I'm not going to Washington." So Volodja says, "Neither are you!" And I said, "Why am I not?" And he says. "What for the hell you have to go to Washington?" Everything is "What for the hell." He didn't know how to say, "What the hell." It was, "What for the hell you have to go to Washington? What will you do there? You heard the concert already. Stay home!"[25]

It was becoming the Gershwin story all over again, with Horowitz preventing her from acting on her own desires. More accurately, it was she allowing him a power, on this one occasion anyway, she would eventually reclaim.

So I called up about eleven o'clock at night and I talked to Mama Toscanini and I said, "I don't know what to do. Not only Volodja's not going, but Wanda doesn't want to go now, so I don't think I can leave." So she says, "Achh. Crazy! We pick you up eight o'clock." The big black Mariah, the Toscanini limousine, comes eight o'clock. I get in the car and sit in the back with the old man and Mama and he says to me, "You know, Gitta, these two people [the Horowitzes] living in that house, they are the biggest, boring people that you ever . . . and what you let them talk you not to go along? Why? Those two boring people . . ."

And I never had such an experience in my life. We were traveling in a private train. [The pianist] Ania Dorfmann and I had a suite together; she was close to the Toscanini family. Beautiful brown bedspreads in all the compartments and private dining room—it was fun. And what company, (sic) and young Sarnoff, Bobby, was my escort. He was fourteen years old, and we had dinner in our underwear. Really. I had my hair up in curlers. David [Sarnoff] had his *gotchas* on, and started to tell me stories in Yiddish, I was on the floor, and I wasn't a bad storyteller either, and we had a marvelous time talking Yiddish.[26]

There wasn't a single reminiscence of Horowitz, a single passing thought that failed to arouse my mother's deepest passions. A simple recollection brought all of the emotions tumbling forward. A backstage encounter with him and the arrival of some of his younger fans evoked this story:

. . . girls came in [to the dressing room] one afternoon, because he really had a career like Franz Liszt. There was nobody who'd do that. They'd pull off his shoelaces, they'd pull off his tie, just like they did with Franz Liszt. And two American girls came in—I was in the dressing room with him; where else would I have been? And they said, "Oh, Mr. Horowitz, couldn't you give us something, one of your laces from your shoes?" "A couple of drecks who don't know what they're talking about," [Horowitz says to me]. "How am I going to go home without my shoelaces? Fall down and kill myself." He said, "No, no, I can no do dat." So she said, "We'd love to ask you" . . . I can just hear him, "What do you think about before you play? When you come out and concentrate?" "I think only of my music." I thought, Oh, that will be the day! "I think only of my music." The minute she walked out he says, "If I told her what I think I don't think they're going to bring me that check." He was a cute guy when he was young . . .

He had a wonderful fictitious name that he made up which was marvelous. I love it, it was so nutty. "Chaim Lechner Oilenversnik." Who would think such a thing like that! Chaim, which was a Jewish name, Lechner which was a Polish name, Oilenversnik, which is something that he made up that I never heard; I never heard of such a name. And we got telegrams like that: Chaim Lechner Oilenversnik, in which he had every word wrong. . . . I saved some of these wires; they're right on my desk now. [I] read some the other day [and] I bust out laughing because the man was so insane, he could take such a nutty. . .[27]

Those of my generation enamored with classical music know of the period when Vladimir Horowitz quit the concert stage. For years there were no performances, no recordings, no public sightings, no rectals. The word that reached many people was that he had been under the care of the psychiatrist Lawrence Kubie, for he had become psychotic, actually believing his hands to be made of glass. Thus, any playing would cause them to break forever. To my knowledge, none of this, except for his consulting Dr. Kubie, was true. Yet, had there been anything negative to report about Volodja, it would never have emanated from his Chicago dance partner. She would have protected him from any attack, any morsel of gossip, the slightest disparaging whisper.

Then one night my mother telephoned with news that stupefied us: Volodja was returning to the stage after an absence of twelve years. A Carnegie Hall recital had been scheduled; we would all meet in New York for the weekend. "Mother, if you believe Volodja is going to play a recital and we're going to be there, then you need a great deal of help."

"Don't count your chickens, young fellow," she responded protectively. "This may very well come to pass."

According to Glenn Plaskin,[28] my parents were two of a tiny handful of people who accompanied Horowitz and his wife to Carnegie Hall May 9, 1965, and part of a slightly larger contingency that went home with the Horowitzes after the concert. The night before the concert, however, with New York a twitter over the event, with seats having been sold as quickly as they presently are for rock concerts, and with people practically jumping out of their skin waiting for the four o'clock performance to commence, my parents, sister, my wife, and I were in the Ninety-fourth Street house of Wanda and Vladimir Horowitz. I remember their telephone number from childhood, my mother so often enunciating the numbers to a long distance operator: Sacramento 2–5392. How many journalists, I wondered, would have traded places with me that evening as I sat in the Horowitz's second-floor living room on the long couch beneath the dazzling painting by Picasso of *The Acrobat in Repose*? I know we were all wondering whether Volodja would actually go through with this, or would there be something, some ludicrous non-event that would cause him to cancel at the last moment?

For ten minutes or so that evening, Volodja, my father, and I were alone in a third-floor study, where I attempted to memorize all the objects of art, books, and music that lined the shelves and filled the table tops. At one point, Horowitz excused himself to go to the bathroom, my father taking the opportunity to remind me of his greatness, and sensitivity. His words were superfluous, but something compelled him to once again make certain that I knew I was in the presence of a genius. Perhaps he genuinely admired the courage Horowitz was about to reveal, the courage, perhaps, he wished for my mother. But words were unnecessary; the suspense was chilling. It was beginning to feel a bit like the movie, *Clue*. Was a murder about to be committed? Mr. Horowitz, in the music room, with the piano.

Soon after joining the others in the living room where the talk immediately turned to Sunday's program, my mother, of course, reminding Volodja of every treacherous passage, Horowitz suddenly walked to the piano at the end of the room. With no warning, the room was filled with powerful piano playing. Beginning with a highly difficult passage in the middle of some piece, it was at once evident that the fabled Horowitz technique was back. "Is okay?" he asked her.

"Fantastic," she replied."

"No, really, Gitta, is good, no?"

"It's fair," she said with a straight face. "It's not great, it's not bad. It's fair."

"Fair is good, no?" Volodja asked without a trace of emotion. "Who tomorrow can remember what I used to play like? Some will think, fantastic, some will think, maybe he died and this isn't even him."

And as always, they laughed. Volodja's hiccuping laughter loudest of all, his forehead lined with wrinkles. We all laughed.

Then there was talk about whether such an occasion would mean his playing the famous *Carmen* medley of Georges Bizet, or even John Phillip Sousa's "Stars and Stripes Forever" as encores?

Relieved and thankful, we were once again in awe of a remarkable albeit complex man about to demonstrate an act of courage we had for decades wished for my mother. In the background, I observed Wanda's expression of apprehension mixed with pride. Wanda's own life, after all, had not been easy. She, too, had been jostled about in the wakes of two enormous egos. Who, precisely, did *she* speak to when all her life she had to pump-up the spirits of men who possessed superhuman talents and egos as complex as the human genetic code? We laughed and applauded, when the music stopped as quickly as it had commenced. Volodja had injured himself.

Holding a finger of his left hand, he suddenly looked ashen and afraid.

"No, but now I can't play," he said. "Is not possible."

My father offered to examine him.

"Is here, look, Doctor. Is no good. I can't play with dat. And what will be tomorrow?"

Wanda and my mother were holding their breath. Come to think of it, these three people often acted as if combined they took only one breath among them. I suspect that by this point, my sister and I had glanced at one another as if to say, how could there be an evening starring these two people without the eventual arrival of sheer tragedy? It may start off with cartoons, but it ends with *King Lear*.

Volodja had nicked ever so slightly a portion of a cuticle. Although initially it may have caused him some pain, I choose to believe that for one fleeting instant he indulged in the fantasy of canceling something which both energized and frightened him. It was the sort of act I could imagine my mother undertaking. It is the sort of act I perform all the time, often employing a bad back as an excuse for canceling my own grand returns to the concert stage.

Within minutes, of course, the tragedy had subsided—Volodja made a remarkable recovery—although I left the Horowitz home that evening thinking this concert is hardly a sure bet. As we stood in the living room doorway preparing to descend the stairs to the main floor, Horowitz remaining on the second floor, my mother comforted and encouraged him while Wanda looked on with apprehension and making, as always, that special mannerism with her mouth; she looked as if she were munching on the inside of her cheeks. It was clear to everyone that Wanda suffered the nerves of high-strung performers as if she actually were one. Observing Wanda and Volodja before concerts, it was often difficult to discern just who was comforting who.

My parents assured Volodja they were there for him should he need them at any hour. Then I spoke, and the words were meant to break up the neurotic tension that was so familiar. I hoped to demonstrate the absurdity of it all.

"Volodja, maybe late tomorrow afternoon, say around four, just you and I, we can go out and have something to eat, see a movie. What do you think?"

Suddenly, all of us were looking at him, waiting for his response to this bizarre proposal.

"That I like," he said at last. "We go together and they will go to the concert. I'm not crazy about the program anyway. We've all heard it before. But your wife, she comes with us too, no?"

These last comments are particularly telling. There is, of course, utter incongruity in the notion that while Horowitz is scheduled to perform in Carnegie Hall, he, my wife, and I will be tooting around New York City cafes and movie houses. In fact, my remark was typical of those one employs to momentarily silence a person's demons. How distant was all this from the sentiment expressed by the Lord to Mephistopheles in Goethe's *Faust*? "Man's efforts sink below his proper level, and as he seeks for ease too soon, I send him a daemon for companion to spur him on."[29] Besides, music generally, as Dr. Johnson intoned, enables one either "to enjoy or endure life."[30]

In the onslaught of personal anguish, which I witnessed in my mother all too often, one is faced with the choice of either indulging the demons or ignoring them altogether as though one hasn't even noticed them. Stage fright, cuticle injuries, the dread of the octaves in the left hand, or the running thirds in the right hand, all disappear when one is confronted with the option of getting a bite to eat and taking in a movie.

Cleverly, my mother could do this as well, for she had just minutes before assured Horowitz all was well. Still seated at the keyboard, Volodja asked, "Is okay?" My mother replied, "Fantastic," thereby indulging his demons, and his overriding anxiety. But the demons persist, as did her own on so many occasions. "No really, Gitta," Volodja persists, "is good, no?" Now, consciously or not, she chooses to indulge his anxiety no longer. "It's fair," she responds. "It's not great, it's not bad. It's fair" And these few words for the moment soothe him, as if they cause him to listen to himself and perceive the momentary absurdity of his ways. "Fair is good, no?"

As I reflect on them, neither Volodja nor my mother ever reached the moment of recognition evidenced by little Shira Stern. They never completely ceased their wailing. Their lives were fundamentally constituted of private and public behavior intended to quell, trick, evade, project, and repress demons. It was a task that went on twenty-four hours a day. Their egos must have been exhausted from the work. How could fair ever be good enough when extremely good wasn't good enough? Only playing, practicing, or concertizing, I imagine, restored them, and let no one think they rose from the piano without sweat dripping from them. No wonder my poor mother couldn't sleep well. No wonder she tried to project those demons on to me, and others as well. Sadly, she couldn't stop herself, even when the projections boomeranged. Sadly, too, she selected as targets for her uncontrollable attacks the people she loved the most, her special lifeguards, people who internalized some of her demons and hold them to this day, right alongside their memories of her.

Horowitz's May 9, 1965 New York recital, its *falcha notas* notwithstanding, was the smash hit of the season, of the decade, of the century, for all I know. My mother kept every review she could lay her hands on—and there were many. She even pasted them in a handsome leather scrapbook which she titled "Horowitz 1965." In all of her memorabilia, I have discovered no scrapbook titled, "Gradova."

———— ❧ ————

Gone in the Moment

n interview conducted with my mother for the *Salt Lake Telegram* in 1937—she had performed in the city where she resided in her brother Jack's home—offered not the slightest clue of what in a few years would become the nature of her life. After reporting how my mother loved not only Salt Lake City but all of "western hospitality," the unidentified writer goes on to claim that "Mrs. Cottle is one of those women who can mix a career with marriage."

> I have two children who stay home in Chicago with their father in the winter while I tour. I have made a success of both my marriage and my career and I think other women could do it if they had a little courage and a more adventurous spirit.[1]

I have no reason to doubt that my mother expressed these thoughts with her characteristic ingenuousness. I only wish she could have lived by them and rediscovered that elusive courage and adventurous spirit. She claimed to have stopped playing because of the birth of her children. It was a noble and, well, courageous decision on her part, but it was not a successful one, and we all knew it. She was only genuinely happy when music surrounded her. She denied this on exactly eighty-seven million occasions, but it was true. Still, how does one admit to oneself that one's art may be more important than anyone in one's life! In his book *Musical Chronicle 1917–1923*, which I found in her library, Paul Rosenfeld described perfectly my mother's feelings about her art:

> Music is like love: an expression of the state in which we surrender ourselves in thanks completely to something

higher and purer than anything we have hitherto known. The past, the future, they are both present. All materials, trees, waters, skies, are present; enclosed by the moment as by an integument. The pains suffered, the pangs to come, death and separation, they all become good under its sovereign alchemy.[2]

My mother loved her children as best she could, but one cannot have this prodigious talent, this sovereign alchemy, alive in them and not express it. Simply put, a Ferrari can remain locked in a garage, a Stradivarius housed in its case only so long, eventually they require usage, fresh air. The soul, like the heart, requires regular exercise. I regularly argued with her that if the possibility of forgetting the music in the middle of a concert prevented her from performing, and, I recall that she once endured such an experience, then why not use the sheet music? In truth, concert performers traditionally played with music; Paganini was one of the first to appear on stage with the entire program memorized. She had attended the concerts of Isaac Stern in which he used music. If anyone was bothered by the image of a musician sightreading, let them close their eyes.

Music stands, however, were not for her. True artists walked on stage with the music literally welded to their brain. If one forgot once, one never could risk playing again. "So play chamber music where everyone reads music," we implored her, as if anyone of us were going to make the slightest inroad into an armor forged from that Russian temperament and whatever constituted the stuff of her early experiences. In fact, the aforementioned Fine Arts quartet had made numerous overtures to her to tour with them. What an ideal way for her to get back into the travails of touring and performing. Her children were grown, chamber musicians employ music, the pressure would be off her. But it was not to be.

In this context, I recall an evening when Jascha Heifetz came to Hawthorne Place. Heifetz struck me as a quiet man with a fire raging inside. I can never think of him without hearing my father pointing out that Heifetz could trill with any finger. But that gift was hardly as awesome as seeing him pull a gold toothpick out of his jacket pocket after dinner and watch him pick his teeth, his left hand covering his mouth. Soon he was standing near the piano in the music room reaching for my father's violin. Heifetz was three feet from me, when he said, "Oh, Tommy, you don't want to hear this. This is nothing."

My mother's father, Joseph Weinstock

My mother, photographed on January 25, 1913, at age nine

My mother with her father

My father, the boy violinist

My father (left) at age seventeen with his friend, Charles Fleisher, 1915

My mother at age 20

My parents as a young married couple

Nathan Milstein, left, as Adolph Hitler, with mother as Maestro Arturo Toscanini

Mother with Vladimir Horowitz

A musical gathering: Rachmaninoff is second from the left; mother is second from the right

My mother, middle seat, front row, is flanked by other musicians (this photograph was taken in 1934). Directly behind her is composer Igor Stravinsky. Standing second from the left is Nathan Milstein. Third from right is Josef Hofmann.

Left to right: my father, my mother, the author (age sixteen), Ruth Weiss, Edward Weiss, and my sister Judy (age nineteen)

Mother (standing second from the left) is behind Gregor Piatigorsky. My
father (standing far right) is behind Nathan Milstein

My mother with Jascha Heifetz

Front row: Vladimir Horowitz and Mother; back row: Wanda Horowitz with Mr. Zelzer on her right

My father, music lover and violinist

Mother with author, 1984.

After Heifetz tried the fiddle, my mother sat down at the piano and they played sonatas, just as she always did with Nathan Milstein. I don't recall her playing with Leonid Kogan that one afternoon; she probably feared if she played too well they would both be deported. Later that night, at the dining room table—we were eating snacks, the ritual that invariably followed the completion of the playing—Heifetz offered my mother a deal one would think she couldn't refuse. "Gitta," he said, "come to California." By this point, he was living in Malibu, and with the violist William Primrose and Piatigorsky—my father joked that Gresha had floated to California on his cello case through the Panama Canal—along with several other renowned musicians, teaching master classes at the University of Southern California and playing chamber music. The quartet was completed by second violinist Eudice Shapiro. The offer was heaven sent, and what a messenger! Teaching, playing, colleagues like Bill Primrose, Grisha, Eudice, Jascha, and as we always joked, Mischa, Pisha, Sasha, and Kasha. What else could she want! Could she really enjoy being depressed so often? Apparently, she could want something none of us ever understood.

Which brings me to the problem for many families of just who gets the recognition, and just who gives it. In traditional families, it was the mother who invariably offered recognition, first to her husband for his accomplishments outside the family, then to her children for being good students, good little helpers, or just plain good children. At Hawthorne Place, there may have been some tension over who was meant to receive the bulk of the recognition. For years, of course, my mother had received genuine international acclaim. I doubt that anyone likes to give up this currency, no matter how neurotic its foundation, nor compensatory its rewards. Whatever the source of one's appetite, recognition warms the soul, even if the satisfaction lasts for disappointingly brief spells. The broken spirit seems so hungry.

As the years went on, I suspect my father craved recognition; surely he did from his medical colleagues who regularly bestowed honors on him, honors that he publicly minimized but deeply cherished. Yet I imagine he sought recognition from my mother as well. If Volodja and my mother looked to each other as beacons of mutual approval, although on occasion disapproval as well, then my father looked to his wife for this same assurance and affirmation. Always we need someone to remind us that we are worthy, worthy that is, of being alive. "And so, young man, and just what do *you* do to justify your place on this earth?"

Surely my father was comfortable in his role as partner to the brightest light in the house, his early letters to her while she was on the road performing attest to this:

> To express my delight at your success is to sing Heavenly praises. . . . I just weep with joy . . . I am praying and wishing for your success tonight (and your prompt return home) . . . And it must follow as the night the day that your life with all its details will be majestically happy and as you revolve among us there will be thrown off from your wheel of life large portions of your happiness and content. Those nearest to you will be the proud recipients and thus glorified by you.[3]

And finally:

> You must have felt the great love you left behind when the train departed. The enormous hole that remains with me is unbearable and makes me miserable. It's hard to go away from the station asking yourself what if and feeling despondent knowing how you hate to go away into difficult contacts and foreign environments, unfriendly faces and facts, it makes your going even more poignant. But you do not go for trivial reasons—you go to attempt another step in the accomplishment of a big triumph both personal and professional—the expression of your big beautiful self.[4]

But my father required more, apparently, and her recognition of him must have meant the world to him. As a psychologist, I surely would enjoy the blessing from any colleague, student, or mentor, but imagine if a genuinely famous person in the world of the arts offered his or her blessing! My own fantasy of receiving the Nobel Prize has it being presented jointly by Nelson Mandela and Yo-Yo Ma. If she had heard this fantasy, my Aunt Ann would have said, "*Nu*, go figure!" But the reason is simple: Both men have made remarkable contributions to the world, all the while manifesting loving natures.

All my life I have believed that my mother either gave up her career for her children, or used us as justification for slipping out of a business that, for one reason or another, proved psychologically treacherous. In his biography of Horowitz, Harold Schonberg describes my mother: "One of the most talented American pianists at that time was Gitta Gradova . . . but she was happily married and never tried to make a big career."[5] But this was obviously an assumption, for too much rested on each performance. Too much of what she was as a person in some profound sense was determined by practically every note, every intonation, every arc of interpretation of every piece of music, if only because, as Nietzsche observed, art is a form of self-mastery. If music is not therapeutic, then surely it holds the potential for redemption, and the justification of living. Goodness or shame hung in the balance of the performance, not in the reviews, for she knew better than anyone how she had played; no matter what their public persona, artists usually know better than critics, which is another way of saying that by definition no critic gains access to the sources of the artist's interpretive powers. Of course my mother loved good reviews, just as she derided those people who couldn't make a judgment about a concert until they scoured the notices. "I can't wait to read the reviews," she would say mockingly, "to see if I liked this concert."

Her entire being was at stake in a public arena no less, which hardly makes concertizing easy, but she never found a way to separate her ultimate sense of self from her playing, a tightrope act at best, as if this is even possible, although perhaps it is during moments of rapturous transcendence. Perhaps no artist can truly do this. Perhaps many people define themselves primarily in terms of what they do, or more precariously, in terms of how well they do what they do, and how often they have an opportunity to do it, and make no mistake, musicians long to perform before the public. No one could have convinced my mother that she was the same good person no matter how she happened to have played on a particular Thursday evening or Sunday afternoon. No one could have convinced her that she was the same good person worthy of love even if she never again sat down at a piano. No one seemed able to convince her that she was good and worthy of love, period!

This became her dilemma. If she performed—not merely played, for no matter what her protestations, she loved to play—then she fell into the trap that personal goodness derives strictly from public performance. If, on the other hand, she walked away from the performance, then personal goodness was again forfeited by dint of not doing what God, or her genetic wiring, had intended for her to do, not to mention her father's insistence that she perform. One cannot possess this magnitude of talent and not deal with it as if it were someone else living within one's own soul. One does not blithely dismiss one's neurological hardware. At one moment this immense talent is a friend, one's best friend, perhaps. In the next moment, it looms as antagonist, competitor, enemy even. I have often thought that my mother looked at her own talent as a boarder she would have paid to renew the lease. At other times, I suspect she sought to evict this same boarder instead of merely perceiving it as if it were another member of the family and, for all I know, the most astonishing one at that! Then again, perhaps Horowitz himself was the personification of her own talent, and their relationship the personification of the relationship she maintained with her own prodigious gift. OH, GOD, WHY DID YOU MAKE THEM THIS WAY?

For some reason, I feel that one root of this particular entanglement for her, as it is for many of us, lies in some complex connection with her parents, and especially her father. Although in offering these comments, I share Edmund White's reservation about the impulse to trace all of one's problems to a single event, or even, surprisingly, one's childhood. According to White: "I don't like 'creative' biographies in which the biographer appears as a chatty character in a story that he never witnessed."[6] Formative years to be certain, childhood hardly defines the entire growth of the human mind. Surely there is more to come in the plethora of experiences constituting daily living, experiences that will shape the way one engages the world as well as one's own self, and one's art. Surely, too, there is more to come in the development of the brain which reaches its full physiological and anatomical development in one's early twenties. Still, a brief discussion at this juncture of the role of self-love and self-hate in a child may prove enlightening. At very least, it softens my own memories of those adolescent skirmishes at Hawthorne Place.

Risking reduction of a complex story to painfully simple terms, a child's early years, if writers like Anna Freud, Heinz Kohut, Michael Basch, and Jean Piaget are to be believed, find him imagining that he is the center of the entire universe. Philosophically solipsistic, psychologically omnipotent, all of life's roads, seemingly, wind through him. If his parents divorce, he must be the cause of the dissolution; if his mother is unhappy, then he must be the reason for it. It all seems perfectly normal, for cognitively, the child cannot make other determinations. Whatever he does, whatever he perceives, whatever he communicates, is either rewarded or punished, thus only logically leading him to conceive, however inchoately, of an intimate connection between his reasoning and emotional world, on the one hand, and the actual behavior of himself and others, on the other.

The psychoanalyst Michael Basch held this notion of punishment and reward to be of critical importance in a child's development.[7] If the little boy is rewarded, his narcissistic tendencies are perpetuated and he comes to believe he is pretty darn good, "top quality," as my father would have said. If, however, his behavior, his very expressions are repudiated, he comes to feel shameful, and pretty darn bad. And let us be reminded that the act, the expression, and the self become one: If what I did, or thought, or said, was bad, then *I* am bad, which means, the psychoanalyst W. R. D. Fairbairn instructed, that I must assume all blame for all things. We are, after all, as the philosopher Michael Oakeshott remarked, what we have learned.[8]

The story grows more complicated when we observe that as normal as it is for a child to imagine, to reason, even, that life's roads wind through him, he discovers, first intuitively and later on more analytically, that several of life's significant highways don't wind through him at all. If once, in the development of what psychoanalysts call healthy narcissism, the child learned that others are put on the earth to care for and nurture him, make him feel secure, and hence comfortable with his interior world, no matter how complex and confusing his genetic wiring, he now begins to understand that certain powerful figures require him to nurture *them*, and make *them* feel secure and comfortable with their complex genetic wiring.

In the development of healthy narcissism, I daily learn that I am special simply for being me, the very message that Mr. Rogers imparted at the end of his broadcasts (meant, most likely, for children *and* adults). Pathological or damaged narcissism, conversely, can take the form of my believing that I must do something remarkable in order merely to get others to recognize me, much less reward me for that remarkable achievement. The healthy child, therefore, learns that just being around the house, just appearing for breakfast, makes his parents happy.

The child whose narcissism has been injured, however, believes almost nothing can make his parents happy, or if that remarkable thing he does momentarily lifts the spirit of the family, he knows it is only a matter of time before that spirit will plummet once again and yet another fabulous accomplishment will soon be required. As Felton Earls and Mary Carlson[9] have noted, the child is meant to nurture his parents just as they are meant to nurture him; all families require these acts of beneficence. What happens, however, to the child's emerging healthy narcissism when his erstwhile attempts to love his parents are thwarted and he discovers that little he can do genuinely makes them happy, even though he is slowly learning that one of his major responsibilities of life is to keep making these futile attempts?

To begin, he discovers that in time his futile efforts find their way into defining what he considers to be his remarkable achievements, or his fundamental talents. He cannot perform even at the highest levels without feeling that sense of futility (regarding that other psychological task), a sense that will eventually diminish any achievement he might know. (As much as I hated my mother's story about misunderstanding the role of the baseball pitcher, even worse was the unconscious recognition that no matter how many kids I struck out, I'd never get what I wanted from her, or for her.) Eventually, therefore, the child will confront that very dilemma I earlier outlined regarding my own mother: I must *do* the remarkable, or *be* the remarkable, or *look* like the remarkable, otherwise people won't love me, even though everyday I discover that as remarkable as people seek to tell me that I am, that is, as remarkable as my achievements appear to be, I fail to earn the reward I crave. At the same time, however, I fear that should I forfeit the talent altogether, if I park the Ferrari in the garage, I shall be left alone to die, which I think is precisely what my mother must have experienced.

"And so, young lady, what do *you* do to justify your place on this earth?"

"I play the piano, Ma'am. Like an angel."

"And you, young man? What do *you* do to justify your place on this earth?"

"Well, Ma'am, even with all my private schooling, I can come up with no answer for you."

I thought my justification lay in making my mother happy by being the greatest student, athlete, and person ever to attend my school, but this turned out not to be true. Then I thought I could try to be the person making her the most unhappy so that she might see how foolish and utterly destructive her life had become, and mine, too, along with it. I pledged, therefore, never to tell her one good thing about me, so that if she found out from someone else, the fact that *I* hadn't told her would hurt even though the news was uplifting. At one point, God helped me by taking William Kapell's life, which meant that I could make her deeply unhappy for several weeks. So tonight at the dinner party I shall announce that I justify my life by saying that "I love," when in fact, I struggle with loving, and wish that I had felt certain others' love for me, no matter how well or poorly I performed. I guess I wish too, that I could have conveyed this same message to my mother.

My mother and I were hardly the world's leading experts on sensitivity and sarcasm, but surely we were proficient at what these two forces bespoke: shame. The shamed and repudiated child, as Alice Miller and Heinz Kohut[10] have taught, who comes to see himself as defective, imperfect, bad, is often the child hungering for fame, recognition, a mere look. Or perhaps, as Sue Erikson Bloland[11] writes about her father, the psychoanalyst Erik Erikson, a mere Nobel Prize. He is the child who craves attention, admiration, adulation, awards, prizes, anything if it will temporarily silence the pain caused by a constant felt sense of emptiness. He is the person perpetually seeking perfection, the idealized form, the supreme solution, and heartwarming response. The injured child not only craves the affection and attention, given what he has endured, or more precisely what has forever been denied him, but he also feels entitled to it. In some sense, his sentiment may be justified.

In the end, as Martin Heidegger and Rollo May[12] have instructed, we *are* relationships. We don't simply *have* relationships. The people who form us don't merely live "out there," they live "in here," with us, as us. As long as we have active memory we go nowhere without them. If, moreover, we are in part them, and there is still insufficient love and respect from them for us as the simple human beings that we are, then we go through life with that one special vessel, as Proust may have called it, "unfilled," leaving us unfulfilled, no matter what our accomplishments. The day after receiving the Nobel Prize we will be searching for something even more momentous.

In the terminology of ego psychologists, we don't do well sensing or realizing that we are little more than our mother's or father's "selfobject," a term in part denoting that we stand on this earth essentially for the satisfaction of their needs. It is wonderful, I suppose, that a child develops the sort of sensitivity that was so prized at Hawthorne Place. But this sensitivity, along with the caricatured posture of a teenager acting as a psychotherapist only indicate that the child is desperately trying to empathize with the parent, or become sufficiently attuned to her so that he might find the magical key that will unlock her constant unhappiness as well as the sense of emotional isolation both persons feel.

"So tell me the damn story already!" I would bark at my mother when for the five millionth time she alluded to that piece of history of which I knew nothing. "Give me the damn key," I was never able to shout, "that will make you happy so that I in turn can be happy."

"I know there was something else I wanted to ask you . . ." she would muse at the conclusion of almost every telephone conversation.

"Mom, do you want to know whether I love you, and would love you whether you played the piano or burned the piano? Well, figure it out. Do you really think even a progressive school does well telling a student on every report card that he's not living up to his potential? Do you think it would have killed any of us to sit before the television set and listen not to the great performers of the day, but to Mr. Rogers saying, 'I like you just the way you are?'"

Bloland writes that Erikson, an immigrant, actually "never felt that he had arrived safely anywhere." How can one feel this nurturance, security, and comfort with intimacy, as Earls and Carlson have written, if they are not part of the childhood diet? No one struggling with a sense of shame, an injury to their narcissism, can ever permit themselves to feel they have arrived, finally, to a place of pristine sanctuary. My mother always imagined the "safe home" to be a lakeside cabin overlooking the mountains somewhere in New England. I am certain she read Franz Liszt's description of this romantic yearning, but she never visited New England in search of real estate she knew could not possibly be located on any plot map. I, too, in asking a friend about my relentless ambition immediately resonated to his words that I feared I would be "sent back." It is just another way of saying that when one is not properly loved and respected, there is no safe harbor. Danger lurks in the very vessel intended for love.

No performance will ever cut it because, the theory goes, it cannot compensate for the original wounds. Indeed, the performance, ironically, opens the wounds. At every instant the inner demons threaten to pull away the talent, daring it to fail, almost as if the performer would love to see what would happen if they stood before the world absent of what they imagine to be their greatest human gift, and hence, their ultimate justification for drawing breath. (Intriguingly, this may just be the best cure for a sense of shame: facing it, as the British say, bang on.) Or is it, as Bloland reminds us, that the performer fears that absent the talent, she is not only left shamefully bereft, but exposed as the fraud she genuinely believes herself to be? Where, possibly, would she find a hiding place, much less a safe place within herself, without fame?

"Gitta, darling, please play for us, a little nothing, a *schmuntz*, some Schumann, the start of the cadenza of the Grieg, ten measures of your beloved Scriabin. You know you want to. Don't think for a minute if we could do it we wouldn't play for you. You don't think we'd give our eye teeth to get through a Mazurka? How badly can you play even without practicing? You rotten is better than all of them put together. It's fabulous. Believe me, you'll feel better. You want to feel less sad, I'm telling you, Gitta, a little Scriabin, a little Chopin, a little Bach. They're better than any medicine."

With all the damaged narcissism, all the shame, all the hunting in all the wrong places for all the wrong things, my mother truly was fascinating, and the fascination was not merely in the eyes of the beholders. Everyone genuinely wanted her to play, and they genuinely wanted her to be that thrilling hostess and performer. Understanding the theories of narcissism, it is evident why we all crave cultural heroes and impute to them so much of our own souls. But some of these heroes really have it, they really own the *mana*. Neurotic or not, hungry for all things human or not, injured by childhood experiences or not, they come through a door and we are drawn to them; their presence tugs at us. As Neil Simon wrote, they "charise" us, and in the end, we are left utterly mesmerized and transformed. They do have something compelling, these special folks, which is why we want to see them, and hear them, and read them, and love them, and hate them. They are powerhouses who, when merely idling, are more thrilling than the rest of the population at top speed. It is why we are moved to stand for them, not only in the concert hall, but when they enter a room. They are Edna St. Vincent Millay in this description of Nancy Milford: "Her performing self made people feel they had seen the muse alive and just within reach . . . she not only brought them to their feet, she brought them to her."[13]

There is no reason to believe that anything malignant was ever said or "done" to my mother. There is no reason to speculate about possible abuse or even overly severe forms of discipline, although, as noted, her father could be harsh when overseeing her practicing. Yet I think my grandfather's belief and investment not precisely in her, but in that boarder, her talent, must have caused her to imagine that it was the talent that made her useful (to him), worthwhile, lovable. It was her talent, after all, that brought her recognition. With the music she was beautiful, gorgeous even—the image, critics intoned, of Peter Pan, Lord Byron, and Chopin. Yet without the music, she was, in her eyes, (and his?), homely, insignificant, and invisible. Her humor, which certainly added to her performance luster and mag-netism, might have been as close as she could get to having people see her, be captivated by her. A simple conversation would never do. For her to believe in her own worthiness, every transaction had to be larger than life, certainly larger than her own life, a performance with unanimously positive reviews. And as certain as I am of this as-sertion is as certain as I am that, if she were alive, she would debunk every word of these last pages, except, perhaps, the reference to her father. "That could well be," she would say, nodding her head. "You might have something there."

So she took a dangerous—or is it courageous?—step when she left the concert platform, for it meant that people would now no longer judge her, or love her for her talent, her performing skill, and her artistry. From the moment she quit, all eyes would be on the homely, insignificant girl she believed herself to be. I know my mother never could conceive an image of herself as attractive, potent, enthralling, much less a woman of "masculine strength and deci-siveness" as Richard Stokes had described her. A million times I saw her sitting in a chair, for the moment unaware of what transpired about her, gently pushing up the end of her nose as if this slight anatomical adjustment, for the first time in her life, would render her beautiful. I recall her numerous references to those she called "the world's beauties," the Hedy Lamarrs, the Sophia Lorens, her sisters, especially Rosie and Annie, and her friends, Ruth Weiss, Lotte Wexler, the step-grandmother of the actress Darryl Hannah, and Rhoda Pritzker, all of whom she found magnificently beautiful. She always said that if she looked like any one of them she would strut around the globe making certain that people everywhere saw her.

At a restaurant once, lunching with the Weisses, we spied the actress Pier Angeli at another table. I had never seen anyone as beautiful as she, and was thrilled when young Jimmy Weiss approached Miss Angeli, who had been captivated by the tiny camera he was using to surreptitiously photograph her. Looking at my mother, I detected a hint of sadness on her face. I don't imagine that in that instant she longed for the fame of a Pier Angeli. More likely, she wished simply to be beautiful, as beautiful as the young Stella Adler, who she had brought to Prokofiev as a gift that caused the composer to forgive, as only beauty can do.

An offer from the devil might have had my mother trading her pianistic gift for even a few years of physical beauty. Indeed, I heard her speak with Ruth and Lotte about their beauty, and how she would readily trade her talent to look like them. Both women, of course, told her they would have signed the deal in a heartbeat. If I had her talent, I would think to myself, I wouldn't give it away for all the money in the world. In fact, that's precisely what I would wish to display as I strutted around the globe. I told her as much on many occasions, although probably in contemptuous tones rather than supportive ones. Later in life, I often spoke to her of my admiration of her talent and my belief that most people would give anything to possess one such extraordinary capability. Interestingly, I fear I fell into the trap set by a grandfather I never knew. I am not certain that I ever told her that I admired *her*, the woman, the mother, not only her talent. I know I never told her that I thought she was beautiful, though she told me often I was handsome. Infantile idealization or not, every son, I am certain, believes his mother to be beautiful, and many tell their mothers precisely that. Boys and men attack at the hint of disrespect shown their mother. At three, my grandson was telling his mother how beautiful she was, and she was profoundly moved, as well she should be. He continues to proffer his love in this manner. I never once did.

My mother never fully believed that she was anything of genuinely great value without music. For most of us, presumably, issues of this sort can be worked on in psychotherapy, but I shall never know what child prodigies or virtuosos experience in this realm, inasmuch as their talents become such overwhelming components of their egos, their very selves. "The difficulties which the virtuoso overcomes," Abraham Veinus declared, "are worth overcoming; the impossibilities which he attempts are worth making possible. He is a pioneer even if out of self-interest."[14] Henry Finck said much the same thing, although broadening his observation to a larger group: "Artists are, to be sure, an irritable tribe. More keenly than others they feel the gibes and wounds of life. But by way of compensation, they are thrilled by joys beyond the ken of ordinary mortals."[15] Romain Rolland, too, offered thoughts on the nature of the virtuoso: ". . . a physical pleasure, a pleasure in skill, in agility, in satisfying muscular activity, a pleasure in conquering, in dazzling, in subjugating by his person the thousand-headed public . . . a pleasure mortal to art and to the soul."[16]

Consider in this light, the words of Franz Liszt:

> The virtuoso is not a mason who, chisel in hand, faithfully and conscientiously whittles stone after the design of an architect. He is not a passive tool reproducing feeling and thought and adding nothing of himself. He is not the more or less experienced reader of works which have no margins for his notes, which allow for no paragraphing between the lines. Spiritedly written, musical works are in reality, for the virtuoso, only the tragic and moving *mise-en-scène* for feelings. He is called upon to make emotion speak, and weep, and sing, and sigh—to bring it to life in his consciousness. . . . He breathes life into the lethargic body, infuses it with fire.[17]

On second thought, a musical gift is hardly a boarder. It is a fundamental component of the human spirit, albeit one that often appears to possess a life of its own. The pianist knows she must be in San Francisco on June 23 to play a Chopin Waltz at 3:30 P.M. The question is, will her talent arrive in time? For that matter, as the pianist Eugene Istomin remarked to my wife and me after a concert: "How can anyone know they will even *want* to play Chopin or Mozart three years from the time a concert program is booked? Who knows if one will even want to play the *piano* three years from next Wednesday?" Ignacy Jan Paderewski had described much the same sentiment, adding to it other miseries of concertizing: wretched hotels, playing when you don't feel like it, knowing that savage critics hunt for one mistake, always having to be at your best—"these things are not calculated to make a pianist happy."[18]

If cellists must book a seat on an airplane for their instrument, then every artist must book an imaginary space, equally costly, for their talent, and then pray it boards the plane prior to takeoff. What else could possibly explain all the superstitions and magical thinking like violin cases that must be perfectly locked? One grabs for any sense of control over one's unpredictable gifts which at times appear to tantalize and tease. All of us hope everyday that what athletes call our "A game" will show up, but there is never a guarantee that it will. Indeed, it's the great ones who more than "make do" when both the A and B games suddenly decide to go on holiday.

There is at least one thing more adding to this magical thinking and anxious awaiting one's talent to board the plane. It is, simply, the very nature of the classical concert performance. In the minds of some artists, the act of performing is unforgiving. Inherent in the task is the demand that one reveal one's deepest feelings and emotions, imaginings and deliberations—essentially that which is labeled interpretation—about a composition solely through the use of one's fingers, all the while steadfastly honoring the constraints not only of the composition itself, but also, in the case of concertos, the unpredictable shifts and turns of a conductor and orchestra. According to Josef Hofmann: "The player should always feel convinced that he plays only what is written."[19] "I am no genius," Toscanini himself once remarked. "I have created nothing. I play the music of other men. I am just a musician."[20] "This is it," my mother would tell Charles Olin in a 1985 interview. "I always say, don't pay attention to yourself. I'm playing somebody else's music, don't pay attention to me."[21]

The interpretive component, however, becomes more complicated. Surely a qualification for the interpretive musician is that he or she possess, in John Redfield's words, "the ability to contribute to the composition that portion of it which the composer failed to record in the score."[22] As Adolph Kullak wrote:

> While an objective rendering strives only to follow the composer's intentions, as far as they may be directly specified, or are to be gathered from the spirit of the work, it is the aim of a subjective conception to give expression to that emotion, which the work awakens in the artist according to his temperament or mood at the instant."[23]

For Toscanini, the score, in Neville Cardus' words, "was holy writ; it was as though he were telling us that by taking heed of the letter the spirit would take care of itself."[24] But this isn't, of course, true.

The spirit is in the performer; nothing just takes care of itself, in the same way that no child can adequately just take care of herself.

Whereas on the one hand, the performer must adhere strictly to printed pages of music, she nonetheless must remain free and creative. What appears to be almost a contradiction is clarified somewhat by the words Anton Rubinstein reputedly spoke to Josef Hofmann: "Just play first exactly what is written, if you have done full justice to it and then still feel like adding or changing anything, why, do so."[25] Hofmann was then quick to add: "Mind well: after you have done full justice to what is written! How few are those who fulfill this duty!"[26]

Equally complex, my mother loved jazz. The *Salt Lake Telegram* reported that she also "approved of swing," for it allows the performer to extemporize, fly about in musical space for the moment, free of printed notes. Like the cabaret singer, the concert performer is expected to emote while straying not one inch from the sacred lines and dots constituting the score. As Anthony Storr has observed: "We take it for granted that instrumental music without the voice can express every variety of human emotion, even if it cannot exactly define a particular emotion . . ."[27] True enough, but the performer, we remember, is always "the voice."

As I reflect on the drama that ran so long at Hawthorne Place, I wonder whether my mother felt that she had to give up something, not for her children alone, but for her husband. No one was more sensitive to the needs of an ego than she. She could in a heartbeat step outside herself and recognize what another person hungered for. I am certain she sensed my own mood shifts before I did. Then again, I could argue facetiously, she was often the one to cause these very same mood shifts. It wasn't purely a comedic sense, but a sensitivity to human emotion that caused her to ask Emil, as he recounted the dream of his Carnegie Hall debut, "Did you get our flowers?"

Over the years, as I have reported, usually in moments of defensiveness during one of our skirmishes, my mother would remark, "You just don't know the whole story."

"So tell me," I would shout back, "what *is* the whole story?"

She would only repeat the phrase: "You just don't know the whole story. Maybe someday you will."

"There *is* no story," I would protest, challenging her to come forth with this secret nugget. "You just say that, but it's nothing but an excuse. It's pathetic!"

She never did tell any story. Part of me says there really wasn't an event or series of episodes; there was no story. Her remark stood as a nebulous shorthand for her recognition of her own complexity and the entanglements of historical events in which she had participated, not to mention the perplexity of the artist's mind. The untold story was everything that remained inexplicable, psychologically inaccessible or indecipherable, everything that could never emerge as a coherent narrative but nonetheless constituted an essential ingredient of her interpretive skills and romantic playing.

Another part of me, however, believes there was in fact something for which she had to give up her career that she imagined was more important than her own life-force, a fire within her that could never be extinguished. Her children's well-being? Perhaps it was that, although she always had help; there were always people around to take care of us. Perhaps, too, she saw my own sadness, or something in my sister for which she felt culpable. I know she dreaded leaving us to play concerts. Being on the road on the occasion of one of my sister's early birthdays ate at her to the end of her days. The guilt syndrome here is almost laughably grotesque. First, she perceives her children to be sad because she has left them to play concerts. Then she discovers that to relieve their sadness she might do well to leave them to once again play concerts.

Still, my mother could feel guilty about a host of matters having absolutely nothing to do with her. When I felt I was choking on her own guilt, not necessarily guilt that she was evoking in me, something she also could do rather competently, I would mutter something profane like, "You don't feel guilty about the war? How 'bout that march on Poland you ordered?"

Perhaps it was not only about the children. Perhaps it was the larger than life needs of her husband. Perhaps it was her marriage to a man introduced to her by the mother of the actor Herschel Bernardi, and the wife of the esteemed Yiddish actor, Berryl Bernardi. The Bernardi's lived in the old neighborhood where she had grown up.

"You know the voice of Charlie the Tuna?" my mother once asked. With pride she announced, "I walked that man in his buggy when he was a baby. Herschel Bernardi."

Perhaps, too, she genuinely was a member of her generation, imbued with Jean-Jacques Rousseau's notion "that women exist only with reference to man, and for his comfort and vanity, and that her place is in the home . . ."[28] I have no sense that either of my parents ever contemplated having an affair. Apart from all of my Oedipal terror, I have no reason to believe that my mother longed to be with any of her colleagues, the touring musicians, or anyone else for that matter. I wouldn't have recognized any of this, of course, as a child, but I think I would have as an adolescent. She did however, I will argue to the end of my days, long to be with music.

My mother loved any moments she could spend with Abram Chasins, a man of impeccable musical taste, literary insight, and custodian of a vast knowledge of musicology. Pianist, music critic, author, and composer—she performed his "Rush Hour in Hong Kong"—Chasins was teacher of piano at the Curtis Institute once headed by Josef Hofmann, and for years host of a classical music program on WQXR in New York. Abe knew everything musical. It seemed to my mother that he had memorized every volume of Groves Musical Dictionary. For her, he represented the pinnacle of musical intelligence:

> First of all he has a tremendous wit, and his knowledge is absolutely stunning. I tell you, he took (the conductor) George Szell on . . . [We] came to George Szell's house and George could be as hard as nails. Hard as nails. But brilliant . . . George Szell knew he was up against it.[29]

All it took was a glance and Abe and my mother became hysterical. Often this behavior occurred during formal events, recitals, and piano competitions, and like schoolchildren they had to physically separate themselves from one another. Then came the stories, the gossip, the accounts of this pianist messing up the Schubert, and that pianist getting so lost in the Brahms he ended up in the Beethoven after making an emergency landing in the Dvorak.

"And what did you think of that tempo in the Bach?" she would ask Abe. "People could have gotten terminally ill, died, and been reborn during the slow movement."

"Oh," he would respond, "I'm glad it was just the tempo. I thought I was having a stroke."

"What were we thinking?" she would answer. "We should have gone out for deli. We wouldn't have missed a thing."

"You know, sometimes I think Beethoven had it easier being deaf."

"*Nu*, Abe, did you hear that Firkusny played Chopin in Cleveland a few weeks ago."

"Yeah? Who won?"

And they laughed again, probably relieved, at some level, that they were not the musicians having to perform. Nor were they alone in this sort of professional criticism. Anton Rubinstein, it is said, once remarked: "Liszt plays like a god, Thalberg like a grocer."[30]

None of these comments, dripping perhaps with humor, however, were ever lobbed in the direction of amateur players. They were reserved strictly for professionals, and among the professionals, those whom neither my mother nor Abe considered a close friend.

My mother loved any scene of children involved with music. It didn't matter to her what instrument they played or how well they played, only that they loved the music and the sounds they were learning to create. Pianos and violins, trumpets, even drums were means of human expression; she wanted everyone to have the opportunity to know this pleasure. A concert of school age children for this woman with perfect pitch wasn't at all torturous. She loved their performances because the children were playing music and discovering the art she so treasured. A Suzuki violin class of ten thousand four year olds was for her a perfect event—the louder and scratchier the better. She loved, too, Leonard Bernstein's concerts for children, and especially the faces of the young audience as they encountered for the first time Prokofiev's *Peter and the Wolf*, the *Pictures at an Exhibition* painted by Modest Petrovich Mussorgsky, and the *Carnival of the Animals* of Charles-Camille Saint-Saëns.

My mother treasured Abe's knowledge, and particularly a passage in his book, *Speaking of Pianists*:

> Rachmaninoff particularly admired Horowitz's interpretation of [the Third Piano Concerto], [Benno] Moiseiwitsch's reading of his *Rhapsody*, and a performance of the same work in the early thirties by Gitta Gradova with the New York Philharmonic under [Sir John] Barbirolli. Rachmaninoff was always wreathed in smiles at the recollection of these performances. He wrapped himself in stony silence at the mention of all others.[31]

Abe's inscription in the book to my mother, whom he called his "treasured friend," reads: "Gitta, who has been for me and for many others the conscience of our beloved art."

Abe and my mother traveled to Dallas—need one even mention that they returned with Texan Yiddish accents—where they served on the judging panel for the Rachmaninoff Fund piano competition. At the time of its inception in 1943, the Rachmaninoff Fund, according to Cecil Smith, was the "splashiest performers' contest ever broached . . . floating the claim that this competition, like no other ever attempted, would bring to light the most fabulous talent we could dream of."[32]

In point of fact, my mother traipsed all over the United States listening to literally hundreds of Rachmaninoff Fund competitors. In January 1947, she told columnist Jack Goodman, "I've probably heard more pianists than any living American."[33] Later in that same interview, she allowed us to know the "western talent was a bit weak." In a word, the Rachmaninoff Fund was born in part to perpetuate the name of her beloved mentor, and because the composer himself hoped to help others avoid the sort of rocky start that he himself had experienced. My mother liked this notion of smoothing the path for young musicians. "What could be a better gift," she would say, "than offering someone a career!" As for herself, the same gift, offered by Jascha Heifetz, no less, was rejected.

At the Fund's launching, Mrs. Rachmaninoff served as honorary president, and Horowitz as president. Smaller panels including my mother, Abe, and conductors Erich Leinsdorf, Vladimir Golschmann, and Antal Dorati, winnowed down the candidates who auditioned for them in Dallas, Philadelphia, Boston, and Chicago. The final competition would then be held at Carnegie Hall.[34] Ideally, the winner of the Rachmaninoff competition was about to have his or her career initiated in a most auspicious manner. Unfortunately, although the competition did launch the careers of pianists like Seymour Lipkin who won in 1948, the Rachmaninoff Fund was abandoned in May 1949.[35]

More celebrated was the Leventritt International Competition for pianists one year, violinists the next. Founded in 1940 in the memory of Edgar Leventritt, a lawyer and amateur musician, the Leventritt Award was as prestigious for the winners as it was harrowing for the competitors. Among the more notable winners were pianists Eugene Istomin, Gary Graffman, Van Cliburn, and John Browning.

The Leventritt competition commenced with the selection of applicants, normally just under one hundred performers, through submitted written materials. These people were then asked to play for a panel of judges for precisely twenty minutes. Most of the judges claimed they could assess the performer's talent within the first few minutes. Eventually the judges selected six or even more semifinalists to appear in Carnegie Hall before their families, friends, and a large New York audience.

In 1962, The Leventritt Prize was awarded to Michel Block, who received $1000, along with guaranteed appearances with the orchestras of New York, Cleveland, Detroit, Buffalo, Denver, Pittsburgh, and New Haven. The judges that year, including Leonard Bernstein, pianists Rudolf Firkusny and Rudolf Serkin, conductor George Szell, and my mother, were a bit under the gun inasmuch as their predecessors, in 1960, had decided there was no one good enough to properly earn the highest award, a decision so unpopular with the audience that the Leventritt Committee opted to hold the 1962 finals in private.[36]

In 1976, my mother was once again part of a distinguished list of Leventritt judges: pianists Sidney Foster, Leon Fleisher, Gary Graffman, Richard Goode, Claude Frank, Nadia Reisenberg, and the conductor Max Rudolf.[37] The preliminaries that year were held in the WQXR auditorium; the finals as always, in Carnegie Hall where pianists Rudolf Serkin, Mieczyslaw Horszowski, Rudolf Firkusny, William Masselos, and conductor William Steinberg joined the judging panel. My mother's description of the experience, however, was nowhere near as filled with the sort of hilarity that characterized her depiction of life with Abe Chasins during the Rachmaninoff Fund competition. As it happened, there was anything but hilarity in early June 1976, when the Leventritt judges announced, much to the audience's extreme disfavor, that, after all the hours of competition again there was no winner. As Serkin noted: "Each of the finalists is absolutely equipped to perform in public and the booing of the audience was—in the sense—justified. But this year was the first time we were giving a prize of $10,000 and we felt none were quite ready for it. Each one had something, but no one had everything."[38]

It might be said, therefore, that, unlike her first performance, my mother's last "performance" at Carnegie Hall was not too well received. Still, as Gary Graffman recalled, my mother, despite her pungent wit, had a "logical, no nonsense approach to life,"[39] an approach she obviously brought to the final verdict of the 1976 Leventritt competition.

Affirmed, surely, by Abe Chasins' words about her performance of Rachmaninoff's *Paganini Variations*, my mother, nonetheless, felt intellectually inadequate next to him. Granted, she, along with Abe, could detect good from great playing. Their tastes were practically identical, though neither of them fell into the trap outlined by Joan Last: "Far too many pianists do not listen critically to their own playing, yet have the ability to criticize others."[40] My mother's self-assessments were often merciless, but Artur Rubinstein and Vladimir Horowitz could not have had two bigger fans than Chasins and Gradova. I cannot remember Abe and my mother arguing over a single interpretation of any Horowitz performance. If an E-flat accidentally occurred instead of an E-natural, they both heard it; they both looked to the other, and they both began to laugh. Still, Abe's knowledge reminded her of her own lack of formal education, musical and otherwise, something that forever haunted her.

As it happened, Abe Chasins was married to the young pianist Constance Keene, yet another woman on my mother's lists of the world's beauties. "Connie," as we called her, was as sweet as she was beautiful. As a teenager, I had a terrific crush on her and grew quite excited when my mother informed me that she was going to be staying with us for several days prior to her playing a Rachmaninoff concerto with the Chicago Symphony. I told my mother I wanted to attend both the Thursday night and Friday afternoon concerts. A young man just can't get enough of these romantic composers, even if he feels that his mother "owns" that particular concerto.

Then the thought struck me: A pianist living in our house, in the second-floor guest room, no less, during the days leading up to a concert? What would this be like? Would there be tension, neurotic fretting, boundless apprehension, and exaggerated emotion at every turn? Connie was going to coach with my mother for the Rachmaninoff, which meant that Hawthorne Place was going to witness a solid week of preparations that would make the soirées and Toscanini and Rachmaninoff dinners look like last minute summer barbecues. The psychiatric locked wards were open again for business.

Connie arrived, appearing more beautiful and youthful than ever and bringing with her a fabulous surprise for all of us: her lovely, even temperament. Nothing was complicated nor problematic for her. She was as quiet as a mouse, practiced diligently, worked with my mother, who appeared far more anxious than she, permitted my mother to speak all the time about Abe, and told stories about people she had been teaching, including one Peter Nero whom she thought was especially talented.

On the day of the concert I remember staring at Connie sitting quietly on the curved arm bench in the front hall. She wore a beautiful dress, her hair and makeup were exquisite, and her eyes looked even darker and shinier than usual. An incongruous accouterment were the oversized mittens she wore to keep her hands warm. Looking like a movie star and revealing only calmness, she appeared to be focusing on the task, how appropriately called, "at hand." My crush grew bigger than ever, but imagine too, having a mother this stunning and talented. And this serene!

Then again, I must have wondered, can one really be that serene and still be a great interpretive artist? Can art and life be uncomplicated to the point that others actually are encouraged to befriend the performer minutes before the concert? Can an artist endear herself to her audience even as she emotionally and intellectually prepares for the moment of truth? Would one exchange pleasantries with the matador prior to the bullfight as I often did with Isaac Stern even as he was marching toward the stage entrance? In Israel one time, as together we reached the stage door, Isaac looked at me, his trio partners cellist Leonard Rose and pianist Eugene Istomin a few feet away, held out his fiddle, and asked, "You want to play with these guys tonight?" Would my mother have ever accepted the admonition of coaches to athletes at the hour of their biggest test: "You're gifted, you're prepared, so go out and enjoy it! Have fun." If only she could have.

Lionel Trilling wrote that unlike the literary scholar, a novelist requires "only a quick eye for behavior and motive and a feeling heart."[41] He meant, I think, that thoughtful consideration and deliberation are not always necessary for the execution of this one art form. His description captured my mother, or, more precisely, her sense of herself: A fabulous ear, an eye like an eagle, a heart throbbing with sensibilities, but a brain insufficiently filled with hard earned knowledge. Where she deliberated, if this is even the proper term, was at the keyboard where a passage might be played or interpreted in one way or another, and the fingering altered, then altered anew. Wrongly, I believe, she would not have agreed with Finck's conception that "in its widest denotation, temperament includes everything that relates to expression, and expression in music has much in common with eloquence."[42]

Serious intellectual work she imagined, however, was not necessarily her strong suit, a fact that constantly troubled her. Although the rest of us believed her to be brilliant, a word she regularly employed to describe others, she insisted on delimiting brilliance to intellectual power, the very power a Trilling possessed:

> I feel I'm not so stupid that I can't be effective verbally; I can talk to people. I know enough great people to make conversation interesting. Like Rachmaninoff told me, "Tchaikovsky told me . . ." He looked at me and he said, "You don't believe me? I was seventeen years old when Tchaikovsky died. You don't know your history." I thought, Oh, my god, I didn't realize that.[43]

The art of musical interpretation, apparently, which as E. F. Bartholomew wrote in 1902, is a "study of mind" as well as "another name for the art of thinking,"[44] and in which she excelled, was insufficient for her. Consistent with her own perceptions, she would never have accepted Charles Eliot's vision that "Great music is great thought; no other thought has such perfect transmission."[45] My mother refused to accept the notion that logical thinking and reasoning do not yield up the mysteries of the arts. Her own interpretive gifts should have told her this much. "In music especially," Neville Cardus instructed, "knowledge and fine thinking will go no deeper than the surface, unless directed by feeling and imagination."[46]

Evidently my mother bought into the ancient Greek notion that knowledge was virtue. Everything was a problem of the mind, and a good mind liberated one from any dilemma. Presumably, those who felt imprisoned by life blamed their inadequate minds for their status. One of her cultural heroes in this regard was Mortimer Adler, although she never forgot a passage from Jacques Barzun regarding the need of every human being to be a good custodian of his or her talent.

When, as an adult, I learned that Marilyn Monroe once vowed to read every book in the Random House Modern Library Series, something prompted, perhaps, by the intellectual inadequacy she may have felt being married to Arthur Miller, and a story that well could be apocryphal, I thought, this is precisely something my mother would have pledged to do. Strangely, it is something I always imagined doing as well. No one who reads all the books in the Modern Library series could be called anything other than intellectual, and hence, virtuous and free. All the pianistic talent and romantic gifts in the world were not enough to compensate for the critical looks of children in her school who thought she wasn't pretty enough, or smart enough. So what if she were touring America interpreting Bach, Scriabin, Schumann, Chopin, Brahms, Liszt, and Scarlatti, all the romantics who, according to Rolland, awoke "with the dawn in strange disquietude"[47] while they were preparing for high school. She still wasn't pretty, and she still wasn't smart. She actually lamented being pathetic in mathematics classes where she reported being publicly humiliated by teachers. She never lost the feelings of those wounding stares and remarks. I know our family could never relieve her pain or perpetual sense of discomfort or inadequacy.

There is another aspect to this particular struggle of my mother's, one having to do with the role of the girl as prodigy. Here we were attempting to convince her that she was an outright "genius," the very word used by the press to describe her by the time she was twenty, a person literally of prodigious talent. Yet, she was saying "I'm not pretty," and "I'm not intelligent." For all we knew, she may have even thought of herself as somewhat of a freak, especially when she was young. Historically, as Arnold Schonberg observes: "Early concerts were exhibitions. Emphasis was on the performer, and so great was the novelty that audiences looked on him almost as a freak."[48] Who cares about any of this, we countered, when you can play the piano the way you do? You can do more for the well-being of people than all the beautiful women, and men, of the world combined! Besides, who's to say that a college degree is *the* single indication that one possesses knowledge or intelligence?

In retrospect, our arguments were destined to fail, for we never fully recognized that within the prodigy who resided with us, there lived, still, an unhappy little girl that God, in her eyes, had failed to bless with a pretty face and a brain for mathematics.

The ironies and complexities become as entangled as my father's key chain, and I wish now that I might have spoken with my mother about them. First, there is her father who demanded that she practice and hone her obviously precocious talent. He may well have been tyrannical, in which case he probably would have damaged her friendship with her own talent, not to mention complicate her relationship with him. I am certain, however, she longed to be accepted as a person and not just a virtuoso, although she wasn't at all quick to dismiss that virtuoso tag. Next, there is a powerful culture in which this child grew up, one teaching that above all a girl should be pretty and attractive to men. Nothing, neither brains nor musical talent, not even physical talent, could ever compensate for homeliness. Cultures, after all, define life for us; they teach us the meanings of self and society, just as they instruct us on the nature of values: those actions we are meant to desire as well as find desirable. Said simply, cultures necessarily influence the most private conversations we have with ourselves, conversations we may never share with anyone.

Then there is the matter of esteem, a low one, presumably, that perpetuated in her a lingering image of herself as unattractive and undesirable. The culture taught that a woman unable to lure a man was a failure, a leper perhaps, an old maid for certain. Would any man ever want her? And if he did, would it be for her talent or for her? Could he see beyond her face? Would he love her or merely feel sorry for her? And most significantly, perhaps, would he love her if she toured the world without him?

My father's letters to my mother in the 1920s and 1930s provide responses to these queries. Would he love her if she quit playing? His words clearly indicated that he would. Tyrannical or not, her own father may have actually assumed the feminist position by insisting that at all costs she nurture her talent, even if it meant not graduating from high school. Still, most women of her generation grew up believing that the ultimate acts of womanhood were marriage and bearing children. The fact was that women pianists, like women physicians and lawyers, were often not taken as seriously as their male counterparts. I wonder, in this regard, how my mother would have reacted to these rather hopeful words about women and music written in 1918:

> How many of us ever stop to think that it has come within our span of years to live through the most thrilling moments of all the centuries? . . . The position of women was that of a domestic necessity, a pampered pet, or the tool in a life of cunning, trickery and ignominy. The compassion, the sympathy, the keen feminine intelligence, coupled with women's sixth sense of intuition, the mother heart, the belief in the best, which are natural attributes of the sex and which have made women so important in the musical field were, for the most part, repressed as a matter of course. . . . It seems a leap of only a few minutes to our own day, when

women are playing an all essential part in the music life of the world. . . . America is proud of its musical women.[49]

Quite probably, the combination of her career and huge talent did make her somewhat of a freak in the eyes of certain people. There are those still, after all, who imagine women's "natural need for men."[50] Her experience may be comparable to the contemporary and fatuous notions that a great woman athlete must be a lesbian, and a great male ballet dancer gay. Apparently the nature of women, whatever that may be, is influenced by the culture in which that so-called nature develops. So many of my mother's early reviews likened her playing to that of men. On the one hand, I imagine she took this to be the greatest, albeit sexist, compliment she could receive. On the other hand, it remains just that: a sexist assessment. Lurking in these judgments is the notion that whatever your talent, you should be home with your husband and children. At least, as Claudia Cassidy observed, she looked like an artist and understood "the platform value of the right clothes." Not so incidentally, Cassidy, and others, too, for that matter, even described her as handsome, but I'm certain she always found a way to dismiss such appraisals.

Men like my Uncle Harry and Uncle Jack have always gone on the road to sell insurance, clothes, gadgets, or to play in the world's great sporting and musical venues. There's a whole culture dealing with these occupations, and a veritable literature of traveling salesmen jokes. But there was no counterpart for women in her time, no culture, no jokes, no easy way to be away from home for months at a time, even when there were no children, no easy way to blend career and family, her self-assured *Salt Lake Telegram* statement notwithstanding. Given all of these matters, the early separation from her family, being pulled out of her school environment, her constant need to make it on her own, historically a characteristically male pursuit, and the loneliness and fright she clearly experienced, must have taken a toll almost as monumental as her own talent. Given, too, her temperament and needs, she may well have found the career for which she was destined, or at least the preparations for it, to be at times heartbreaking.

Too young to get married and have children, the child prodigy is safe for a while. Soon, however, she reaches the age when the culture has determined that women should start bearing children, and in her time most women had concluded their childbearing years by twenty-five, if not earlier. She had put off childbearing until almost thirty. So what did that make her? In her eyes, I fear, a failure, for she often mentioned that she wished she had stopped playing even earlier so that she might have been able to have more children. She wanted four, she always said, and herein yet another reason to see yourself as deficient and, with some justification, blame those people who set you on your musical path, a path that ineluctably steered you away from the path determined "appropriate" by the dominant culture. No wonder she loved curling up with a book in the New York Public Library. She was safe in that library with Tolstoy, Dostoevsky, Dickens, Hardy, Stendahl, Chekov, Brontë, Balzac, and Turgenev, her steadfast friends. Then again, she may have also blamed those who were more than subtly encouraging her, if not commanding her to, well, come home, which may have meant to her to give up her career.

This part of the story involves more than pure conjecture. If one examines the often poignant and painful letters my father wrote to his young fiancée and bride in the 1920s, several themes begin to emerge. Clearly he missed her dreadfully when she went away to perform. Many letters involve a despair one never would have associated with my father, a man known for his equanimity:

> You can hardly realize how blue and depressed I was yesterday . . . again you are gone. . . . Life is a dreary nightmare without you. . . . Don't plan too many return trips to New York. . . . I have been utterly miserably lonesome . . . this house is absolutely empty without you. . . . Would appreciate you telephoning tonight. . . . How formless and inexpressive my existence is without you. . . . Please don't say that you are going to stay away long. Make it short and snappy and rush back. I'm very lonely. . . . Just received your note and in the nick of time. I was in such dumps. . . . To tear away from you was the most miserable experience of my life. Depression and despair filled me so that I was just so much human hopelessness. . . . For us who are all to each other, it is a veritable hell on earth. . . . I have to have her. I'm dead without her; I might just as well be extinct; life has stopped; there is no world.[51]

On the one hand treasuring her talent and news of her almost daily successes, he is, on the other hand, laying pressure on her both to regularly communicate with him *and* her family, and return home, the sooner the better! He seems, moreover, to be scolding her for not behaving as she should, using in the process more than a smattering of guilt:

> Your letter just overwhelmed me—you scored a knockout. I was very depressed—and so was Mama—that no word had come from you. We waited for a telephone call last night and were disappointed. But your letter fixed everything. . . . When are you coming home? Please let me know immediately. . . . I miss you terribly. Mama, too, I feel misses you already nearly so much as I. . . . Everyone has been commenting on your correspondence and Mama especially has been almost as delighted as I have been. . . . You really should have dropped me a note. . . . Mama is continuously worried about you and your whereabouts. And I have to call her to let her know what I think you are doing at the moment. . . . Papa goes downtown with me every morning and in general is my protector and shield. . . . Mama is quite cheerful especially now that you are expected soon.[52]

At times longing for her, he appears, in several letters, to be proposing that this painful ordeal called "concertizing" will soon be over, and they will at last be together. Indeed, in some of the letters, he seems almost to be conceiving her career as a grievous period of time; both of them must agree it must all come to an end if they are to be happy. One cannot read these letters—and their impact, obviously, is magnified by reading one after the other—without, once again, sensing this never-articulated agreement that her career can only be a temporary affair. In her absence, he rents apartments for them and her family, signs leases for summer cottages in Michigan for them and her family, arranges for all the decorating, and oversees their financial affairs. But always the message is clear. Ultimately, Gitta Gradova's place is in the home:

> The news of your concerts was certainly good news. That you were content is better news. That you are feeling O.K. is still better. That you are coming home and feeling O.K. is the best news. So hurry it along and bring yourself once again into the family fold. . . . It will certainly be a relief when your season is over and home again is your slogan. . . .

But the sun shines and shines, an "omen" of bright prospects for us—and maybe we shall soon be able to take our little vacation of 20, 30 or 50 years together and stroll along hand in hand and enjoying each other to the utmost and without unnatural or unfriendly obstacles or limitations. . . . It all seems so unnecessary; on such a bright sunny day everything should be so gloomy. Well I hope it won't be long now before this sort of thing terminates. . . . We played bridge and planned the arrangements for Friday evening. If perchance you don't get home by then, then the whole thing's off as far as I am concerned.[53]

Her response to these missives remains unknown to me, but one must assume she felt pressure. First, she is sent alone to New York to develop her talent, and within a few short years, after surpassing everyone's expectations and dreams, she is being told to return home. In the end, only her father, perhaps, remains unequivocal on this matter, although he, too, could chastise her for not writing home often enough.

I have but a few of my mother's letters to my father, whom she often addresses as "Daddy." Predictably, they contain expressions of her loneliness and unhappiness. And, of course, she misses her husband deeply. Yet one letter, from Harrisburg, Pennsylvania, provides a glimpse of a young woman torn between her love for a man and music, which carries the additional joy of being successful in one's work.

I am so lonesome for you that it takes all the control I have to keep from turning back. Although I can't really kick about this trip so far. . . . Miss Yarnell of the office came [backstage] and was more than just pleased. I believe she said that Toscanini didn't have a greater ovation. It was considered most unusual for a Friday afternoon concert in Philadelphia.[54]

All of us might have imagined that my mother's roots were embedded in the compositions of Bach, Chopin, Brahms, Schumann, Scriabin, Dvorak, Scarlatti, and Rachmaninoff, but not until recently have I considered the possibility that, as a child, almost every human root she ever knew had been dug up and shredded, leaving her on her own to fend for herself, or as they say, left to her own devices, expressions traditionally meant to describe the alleged independent, autonomous actions required of young men. The very gift that God presented to her, the talent to which she was entrusted, may also have been related to the wound caused by the early separation from her family and the terror of performing in front of strangers at such an early age. Surely it was related as well to the unhappiness she heard expressed by significant members of her family. Music, obviously, was for her a redemptive force, just as it was a constant reminder of sadness and loneliness, its evocations all too often overwhelming her. Precisely as Freud had theorized, her depression could well have found its origins in the series of losses she sustained at such early ages. Of course every turn in the road, no matter how seemingly innocent, became a frustrating life and death dilemma for her, an evocation of earlier sadness, loneliness, and loss. Screaming, angry, even vengeful people are calling out to be comforted and have their primitive life-affirming roots restored and preserved.

Or these same people may do something else. They attempt to compartmentalize or forget, put whole chapters of their lives out of their minds, or at least separate events from emotions in a manner psychologists call "dissociation," not that anyone is ever completely successful at this. At some level, trauma is always remembered, for emotions sit alongside memories. All of us, presumably, have stories we tell no one, or like my mother, promise to tell at some point but never do. And in this lies a bitter irony for her: On the one hand, the whole point was to forget much of what had happened to her, including perhaps, the constant badgering to return home after she had reached remarkable career milestones. On the other hand, the very thought of forgetting was inconceivable, given her role as artist and concert performer. For her, the very concepts and activities of remembering and forgetting, memorizing and disassociating, were fundamentally charged mental exercises. The poet Rainer Maria Rilke was right: "Murder is but a form of wandering mourning."[55] My mother would have appreciated this line, just as she would have resonated to these words of anthropologist Allan Young: "Anger is pain remembered."[56] Following the earlier discussion of narcissism, I don't know what she would have made of Heinz Kohut's assertion that "narcissistic rage is directed at self-objects who threaten or have damaged the self."[57] In truth, she might well have agreed with the hypothesis that it was this narcissistic rage on both our parts that first ignited and then flamed the fires constituting our skirmishes. The boy in me wishes to proclaim that I wasn't the only one wanting her home.

Whenever I study myself, I see a child surrounded by people and yet depressed by having been abandoned. I see, too, a person whose sense of self, including his sense of masculinity, was profoundly defined not by his father, but by his mother, for it is obvious that boys and girls alike need both parents to make them comfortable with their sex, their gender, their being. Where boys, at times, may differ from girls, as William Pollack has described,[58] is in their conception of a permissible repertoire of public displays of emotion and behavior. It is unclear, generally, how boys are meant to express their responses to normal, much less pathological separation from their mothers. Early on, they learn that expressions of vulnerability, weakness, shyness even, are somehow illegitimate. Encouraged to turn away from their interior worlds, boys characteristically "act out" their sadness, depression, and narcissistic rage, by battling people, screaming at them, and offering up all varieties of bravado as are found in statements like, "Guess what! Willy died!" or, "Maybe everyone would be better off if I simply went away." Strange what a boy or man will do to ward off the ache of emptiness and aloneness, and the enduring sensation that he is the source of other people's misery.

Whenever I studied my mother, I saw a troubled and at times tortured woman, but a deeply faithful woman nonetheless. In the most general terms, I sensed that my mother believed that the greatest failure in life, far worse than forgetting a passage in the middle of a concert or receiving a scathing review, was to be seen as a failure by your family, defined perhaps, as not performing as they want you to do. The ultimate judges for my mother, therefore, were not her musical compatriots, nor even God, but her husband and children and, at an earlier point, her parents as well. All the accomplishments in the world could not possibly compensate for not being a loving, steadfast, loyal, comforting, nurturing member of one's family, the very qualities she always saw in my wife. "Katie's a regular *balabust*," she gushed repeatedly. Whether my wife even knew what the term meant when she first heard it, she came to learn it was the highest praise my mother could give another person. It means someone who is always caring, always working in behalf of others, always there.

Neither my mother nor I ever subscribed to the notion that what public figures do in the privacy of their lives is irrelevant in the ultimate determination of their greatness. I know she harbored troubling thoughts about Volodja's parenting of his daughter, Sonya, who was left in Italy for seven months during her infancy—the baby was one month old—when, together, he and Wanda toured Europe and America. It was as if my mother had read the Greek philosophers, so committed was she to steadfastness and courage. No matter what reviews her family might have accorded her, in the end, no one could possibly doubt her commitment to family and the need to look out especially for the innocent child. When, in my mind's eye, I observe her with sanguinity, I know this to be true. When, on the other hand, I long for something that I feel I never received from her, I wonder whether had I been more innocent as a child I might have been properly looked out for. But given the conflicting directives she received, there was no way she could win.

By the time I reached adolescence, Nathan Milstein had purchased a home in Vermont. Regularly he begged my parents to visit him. In response, my mother revisited her dream of having a home of her own in New England. It was a primitive, almost atavistic vision that she maintained but never acted upon. I feel now as if it symbolized her life: A place that would have been utterly beautiful and tranquil, but one she could never get herself to discover, much less produce. "Folk-tunes," Carl Engel points out, "sing the artist's perpetual nostalgia for his home in the hills of peace."[59] (Interestingly, the word, nostalgia, literally meaning "to return home," implies homesickness, which, one might add, can infer a sickness for home or about home.) But there was something else more profound than this. According to Tobias Matthay:

> Coming back to nature—to the stillness of the country, to sky-expanse and wind-driven cloud, to the magic of the woods and the mystery of the starlit-nights—a fundamental truth is ever insinuatingly and forcibly driven home to us. . . . If we are impressionable—and we cannot be artists unless we are—we find that things in Nature and in Humanity around us impress us strongly, in various ways, and arouse in us vivid feelings, or moods. Now, the purpose of Art, whatever its form, is primarily and mainly the expression of Moods and Feelings, thus engendered. . . . Music is intimate with Nature herself.[60]

I don't know whether my mother ever considered any spot on the earth, with the exception of her artistic gift, her true home. Her romantic spirit, Robert Schumann, may have said it all in his *Aphorisms:* "Music speaks the most universal of languages, that through which the soul finds itself inspired in a free, indefinite manner, and yet *feels itself at home.*"[61] My mother always appeared unsettled to me, unhappy at home yet dreading any upcoming trip, even one to visit her grandchildren. As I say, she could never find a way to win. I wonder whether these words of Liszt, in which he describes his *Préludes,* captured what lay in her heart:

What is our life but a succession of preludes to that unknown song whose first solemn note is sounded by death? Love is the enchanted dawn of every heart, but what mortal is there, over whose first joys and happiness does not break some storm, dispelling with its icy breath his fanciful illusions, and shattering his altar? What soul thus cruelly wounded does not at times try to dream away the recollection of such storms in the solitude of country life?[62]

I wonder whether my decision to settle in New England was unconsciously meant as a way of offering her that ideal homesite, and the restored altar she always craved.

One of the many things I never understood about my mother went beyond psychiatric theories of depression or narcissism. Perhaps there just is a dominating sadness in the lives of some artists. The opera singer Hans Sachs gave the audience the impression he was happy, but he revealed to Henry Finck that he never enjoyed singing.[63] Then there was this sentiment of Tchaikovsky's: "Regretting the past, distrusting the future, and dissatisfied with the present—such is my life,"[64] and Liszt's response to Wagner who perpetually expressed his unhappiness: "Your letters are sad—and your life sadder still. Your greatness constitutes also your misery—the two are united inseparably and must forever harass and torture you."[65]

The nonartist can never completely grasp the evanescent quality of the artistic act, the artistic soul. From deep within one's inner caves arrives these moments of expression that disappear even as they are born. The melody is conceived and written, and although one imagines it lives forever on the printed page, in truth the creative act is completed, and hence, evanescent.

"But don't you feel in your [film making] work," she asked Charles Olin during a 1985 interview, "that you have a chance to remedy certain things? As a film director you can, but as someone who is going to [play music, you can't] do that . . . because in the moment it's gone."[66] Like the composer, a pianist feels precisely the same thing. The moment the key is struck or the pedal released, the note is gone forever. Granted, that same note will be played again and again, but each striking is original and its life momentary, which means that endings, death even, are part of every instant of the creative process. Inevitably, therefore, the act of composing and playing may be experienced as disheartening, for endings are born even as the most human of all acts, the acts of artistic expression and interpretation commence.

Merely Two People

riting these last pages has brought forth two thoughts I either never before entertained, or perhaps never permitted to enter my consciousness. First, granting that my mother struggled with depression, was it possible that her frequent headaches were caused by shock treatments? No one ever said anything about this. No one could afford her any relief. Wanda Horowitz came the closest. Wanda found an Asian aromatherapeutic substance in New York and treated my mother with it. In the days before the burgeoning industry of antidepressant medication, shock treatment was often the therapy of choice, and it did leave patients with intensely painful headaches. A family member on my mother's side, who also had suffered with depression, did indeed undergo a series of shock treatments. They left him noticeably less depressed, but he, too, suffered with the same sort of unrelenting headaches my mother experienced.

Second, was my mother suicidal? To my knowledge, there was never any attempt, although had there been before my birth, I would never have been told. Perhaps all of the derision about the presence of psychoanalysts in the homes of their patients, or allowing their patients to sit on their laps, may be justified, just as it may conceal some fundamental truth: For all I know, Dr. George Wilson kept my mother alive.

What a lack of insight in someone who desires to see himself as insightful. And sensitive! Of course she thought of suicide. Her momentary hatred of me during that fateful utterance, "When you see me in my grave, I'll be smiling," was only one of the roots, one of the parents of the sentiment. The other root had to have been self-hatred, a desire to end her life and silence forever her tormenting demons. In recognizing that by playing or not playing she could make people so unhappy, perhaps she, too, had contemplated the idea of "making it easier for everyone by not being there anymore." I, apparently, was one of the major reasons life held no purpose or joy, or so a young adolescent might well have reasoned. That alone would have been enough to make one feel angry, and morose. More precisely, not even the existence of her two children silenced her anguished wishes. In part, our battles were between two people, two selfobjects, as a certain school of psychology would allege, both of them melancholy beyond recognition, both of them hurt beyond description, each one blaming the other for every unhappiness they ever conjured up even as they recognized that it was the other person who understood them better than anyone. It was the other person who came closest, perhaps, to perceiving their very souls.

At the same time, the battles were between two people who desperately needed to hear from the other that they were good, worthy, without shame, and above all, lovable to the point that no one would ever send them off on their own to New York, or depart Cheyenne, Wyoming, without them, for they were worthy of being alive. No other persons in the world could deliver these messages with the same assurance and authority as my mother. Without her approval, I was destined to believe that successful or not, I was shamefully bad and would bring only pain and suffering to everyone I ever touched, especially those I professed to love. The proof would come in their ultimate rejection or abandonment of me. Only logically, I reasoned, it would be impossible for me ever to father children, or more precisely, dare to contemplate parenting a child.

The night before his grand return to Carnegie Hall, Volodja had been temporarily calmed by my mother's irony, the very irony I had learned from her, along with the deployment of sarcasm, as a technique in our own skirmishes, but which never calmed her demons. They weren't meant to. I indulged her anxieties and insecurities and she indulged mine. We stoked each other's furnaces until they produced an almost atavistic terror that took the form of white hot fury. The unconscious world often acts in a manner that perfectly contradicts the simple wishes and ideals of the conscious world. Desperate for relief, anguished people often tend to torture the very ones from whom they beg for assistance.

If my mother's depression left her at times without energy to comfort or even pleasantly engage me, then perhaps I was special delivering my depression to her. That our respective depressions, moreover, were laced with anger, literally with bile, only confirms

Aristotle's description of a disposition he called *"melaina kole,"* or black bile, from which is derived the common words, "melancholia" and "melancholy," a common characteristic of which is the periodic excessive displays of emotion.[1]

For eight hours I had drawn on all of my resources to perform well at school, with friends, in classes, in sports. I was bolstered, of course, by a supportive environment in which teachers were constantly trying to bring the best out of their students. But when I reached Hawthorne Place at the end of a long school day and athletic practice, I was physically and psychologically exhausted. I was crashing, coming down at the speed of light, and practically itching for a fight. Or was it rather that I, like my mother, was itching for someone merely to hear me and soothe me. One word, one wrong look, the mere image of my mother aggrieved or unkempt, was enough to set me off, which in turn set her off. The costumes alone were enough to tell the actors that once again, there would be no listening, no hearing, no soothing. It was as if we were mutually stigmatized by each other's disorders.

There we were, two delicate mechanisms each totally dependent on the other to maintain normal, not even high-level functioning. On most days the mechanisms managed to keep pumping, my school providing the greatest source of healthy energy. It did this simply in the way it treated me, never once suggesting that I was, somehow, a bad or defective child. Teachers even managed to maintain this therapeutic attitude when they discovered a genuine defect in my ability to read, a classic learning disability. On the bad days, however, the mechanisms collided, and the angry verbal sparring represented the last gasps of psychic energy remaining in our respective reservoirs. In the late afternoons on the second floor landing, we were two people screaming invectives at one another, when really it was our respective demons, our inimitable sense of personal defectiveness that must have driven our despair. It all came down to each telling the other, albeit in convoluted and perverse forms, how defective and pathetic we were. In response, the other proclaimed: "Well, if I am, then you're what made me this way. Dinner's at seven."

I often imagine that in the minds of some people, children become the personification of these very same demons. The children's caretakers then either indulge the children, or ignore them, with remarks of the sort I made to Volodja the evening before his comeback concert. Neither tactic, of course, is what the child requires in those moments. Indulgence and sarcasm hardly calm children, and turning away from them only terrifies and angers them. You don't have to force a child to play the piano in the same way that you don't have to readily agree to curtail lessons the instant a child complains about them. There's a middle road of loving firmness. Erich Fromm theorized that aggressing against children causes them to withdraw, whereas withdrawing from children causes them to become aggressive.[2] If however, one can learn different ways of dealing with one's own demons, which ultimately allow one to discover that middle road, one might do better dealing with children who, in point of fact, do not represent psychic demons at all for those caretakers free of such destructive mental furies, those caretakers my mother would have called *balabusts*.

Why, then, did people like Volodja and my mother fling their furies upon the very people who sought to aid them and offer emotional triage? Is it, perhaps, because at some level they needed someone on the outside to feel a taste of what they lived with every instant of their lives? Granted, their art provided them momentary respite, if not utter glory. Yet unlike the composer, the performer is potentially never free of the demons, because the performance, itself meant to transform the demons into the sources of art, generates anxiety. From Carl Engel:

> Art may be the opposite of nature, but it draws its inspiration from the life within and without us, it holds up to us a mirror that reflects the whole of our interior and exterior world. There we encounter an abundance of what we call ugly, grotesque, cruel, or perverse. And what ugliness life does not suggest, our imagination will invent.[3]

Ultimately, superstition and magical thinking come to be employed, because performers cannot rely solely on their own talent and skills to carry them through the recital; that is, tormented performers cannot. Unpredictable fate may always intervene, leaving the performer vulnerable to any variety of humiliation or catastrophe. What is more, we are, all of us, vulnerable to the assessments of others; to some degree they shape our very selves. If only my mother could have accepted the words of a professional basketball player who, when asked if he was nervous when the money was on the line in a championship game, answered, "What's to be nervous about?

We're just a bunch of guys running up and down the floor in our underwear." But as I've said, every moment for her was a matter of life or death.

Is it, perhaps, that my mother, like Volodja, was constantly experiencing what drowning persons experience? Terrified that they may be going down for the last time, they beg for help but when it arrives, impelled by panic, they practically destroy the lifeguard. In fact, lifeguards are often taught to smack the drowning person if she (or he) is interfering with the rescue, otherwise, and how symbolic this is, both would drown. Unfortunately, as tempting as it may be, a good smack in the face out of the water has never proved a good antidote to panic. Inevitably, in my mother's life, the water proved too deep, the waves too high, the ocean too vast. All of us heard her screams, just as we heard Volodja's, but even the best swimmers among us could not rescue her.

In many ways, I am certain my mother, as did Volodja, felt as though she were drowning. Mundane chores regularly overwhelmed her, which has to mean that earlier in her life she was also overwhelmed by something. She was flung out into the world as *wunderkind* and expected not only to survive, but triumph. Indeed, triumphant results emerged as the only means of survival. There was either grand success or nothing at all, except that even grand success failed to excuse her absences from home. I don't think my mother ever wholly rebounded from those early family separations, wounds, and remonstrations, the early rending of attachments to her family and schoolmates, all of them associated with the piano and performance.

At Hawthorne Place, before any audience, she would play masterfully, wholly free of nerves. (At the home of friends, a cellist invited her to play one sonata with him before an audience consisting of his wife, my father, my wife and me. She happily accepted, but I observed *him* taking a stiff drink to calm his nerves before they began.) Yet one step outside the house, the anxiety and depression returned in full force. As I say, even the mention of a vacation trip to visit her beloved grandchildren unnerved her, for it meant travel, movement away from safe havens, safe environments, predictable routines. And to think that a 1929 photograph of this same woman showed her standing before a two-seater open cockpit airplane, with a caption that read: "Not only Gitta Gradova's fingers fly. The young pianist herself takes to the air as naturally as she does to Bach or Beethoven."[4]

I suspect "healthier" performers might look forward to their concerts feeling that these are times when they truly shine, the times when all the demons are silenced, or transformed, if not awed by the performance, and thus by the performer in whose psyche they reside. Then again, without the demons, can one render great art? Is not the torment part of the beauty emerging from the interior during the performance? Is it not part and parcel of the romantic performer's temperament which essentially forms her deliberations on and interpretations of the composition? After the knowledge and the technique, "all" that is left is the human personality. From Cecil Smith: "Much the most important factor in [musical] success . . . will be the sum total of his personality."[5] "Music begins," Henry Finck noted, "where technic ends."[6]

Volodja and my mother disdained intellectual playing. They admired technique, of course, Horowitz's being world famous. Harold Schonberg, in his book, *Horowitz*, claims Horowitz was one of the most honest technicians in the history of pianism[7]—as was Rachmaninoff, but the real question was what did the performer have to express? Again from Finck:

> The world wants a musician to be different from others, to have individuality, personality; and this must show itself in personal (human) ways as well as in unique "readings" of compositions. You should have something about both your personality and your interpretation that no one else has. . . . Success is possible without personal magnetism (attractiveness, winsomeness,) provided there is a great deal of artistic temperament to compensate for its absence . . ."[8]

The worst thing my mother could say about musicians was that they were "'passionately fond [of music], but not dangerously talented." This meant that despite possessing all the pianistic tools, knowledge, and training, and desire, the pianist, sadly, had nothing to say. Probably he or she required a demon infusion. Magical thinking, therefore, signifies not emotional disturbance, but a logical response to the artist's awareness that personal demons, the atoms of the artistic temperament, never sleep. They rest, perhaps, for a couple of hours late on a Sunday afternoon in Carnegie Hall or Orchestra Hall when neither my mother nor Volodja were playing, but they never truly closed their eyes.

And how did my mother perceive all of this? Given what the young Miss Gradova reported to H. Miller, I fear she would have concluded that all my theories about her are absolute bunk:

> Reading is what gives depth to a musician. One does not have to suffer hunger and vagrancy in an attic to play with feeling. That is the sort of sob-story emotionalism which is too often linked with artists. A much more intellectual kind of suffering is that which grows out of the mental torture of philosophic struggles. I am fond of believing there are two distinct kinds of musical feeling, the personal and impersonal, or the human and aesthetic. As someone has said, "Art should be an expression of the personal particular in terms of the imperial universal." That is what I always try to remember in my interpretations, not to intrude my own personality or intimate feelings upon those which the composer meant to express . . .
>
> Musicians who know nothing about anything except music are not good musicians. . . . One cannot do big things unless one *thinks* big things. Piano playing is not a matter for the heart or the fingertips. It is a mental problem which involves other arts. . . . I only practice three or four hours a day, for I feel that at the end of that time, if one has the ability to concentrate, all has been accomplished that is worthwhile. Another three hours I spend in reading, for, next to my piano, my books are my best friends. . . . I read everything I can lay my hands on from German philosophy to Russian novels. I always feel that an hour with Emerson or Nietzsche, depending on my mood, will do more good for my playing than another hour of practicing. I would far rather put Dostoevsky, Tchekov, or Turgenev into my music than to put myself into it. Balzac, Gauthier and Flaubert are far better food for the fingertips than tedious exercises, accompanied by bitter disappointments. An unread pianist is a cross between a pianola and a "movie musician. . . ."
>
> I am the victim of a sort of Pollyana-Santayana happiness that keeps my spirits up in face of all disappointments. I have developed such a high degree of self-consciousness that I am my best critic. The result is that when I know I ought to be discouraged about something radically wrong in my work, I understand the trouble so quickly that I remedy it before it has time to get hold of my disposition and my heart.[9]

And about her own personal history? Miller claims: "She is as impersonal as she aims to make her work":

> The truth is that there is nothing to tell. My life has been uneventful. I have never been abroad to study. I was never kidnapped by gypsies when I was a little girl. I simply grew up like the average Chicago girl, passed through the horrible "child prodigy" age, received a scattered and spasmodic schooling, and here I am. I swim in the summer, walk in the winter, and read all the year around for recreation. And someday I am going to finish my education. I seriously intend to go to college as soon as my work will allow the time for it. In the meantime I shall continue my self-discipline, invent lovely theories, and then discard them for new ones, for, as Emerson said, "A foolish consistency is the hobgobblin of little minds."[10]

For years I harbored a fear that I would never father children, a belief that was, well, "confirmed" once by a Boston area astrologer. I had to accomplish for people, and perform for them. I had to amuse and charm them, for without achievements and "the act," no love would be forthcoming. As that friend of mine said when I asked him once, how do you explain my unremitting ambition? "You fear you will be sent back." My mother may well have imagined the same thing; a mere being of simple human proportions could never suffice. Perhaps she always wanted to be "sent back," if that implied returning home. (Then again, given the contents of my father's letters, perhaps she wished to be "sent back" to the concert platform.)

In contrast, my mother needed my sister and me to affirm her role as mother, which, through my adolescence, I took special care never to do. That I would tell her nothing about me or anything good that had happened in school from which she could take any pride, was a manifestation of this refusal to let her knew she had worth, or had imparted to me a single strength or virtue. She knew little of my athletic prowess, and had the school not sent my report cards home, she would have known nothing of my academic work either. Telling her of my accomplishments would only have made her happy and confirmed that she was an okay parent after all. It may also have dissipated the emotional independence from her I sought to achieve. I seized every opportunity, therefore, to remind her that as far as I was concerned, she was a dreadful parent, an utter failure, a person possessing not the slightest nurturing bone in her body, an expression I often used, unconscious in those moments of the damage that had been done in the automobile accident to almost every one of her bones.

I recognize now that above all others she must have feared this one assessment of herself; it was the worst review she could ever receive, and it was delivered by a person with more power than the *Chicago Tribune*'s Claudia Cassidy. It was more painful, I am certain, than forgetting a piece of music in the middle of a concert. To the other, each of us was an obscene dance partner, possessing not the slightest redeeming virtue during our battles, but instead, locked together as reminders of our inadequacies and frights, our infantile despair, and the fact that whatever greatness may have breathed within us would never be set free by the other. Alice Miller's notion that parents' unwillingness "to acknowledge their children's pain, anxiety, sadness, or rage, because such feelings would imply their own imperfections as parents, an intolerable possibility,"[11] actually cut both ways, for I never acknowledged her sadness or the foundation of her rage. I was a bad child, she a bad mother, and although I always felt this equation was inherently unjust because I didn't make her the bad mother that she was, she, in fact, had made me (feel that I was) the bad boy, the bad human being that I believed myself to be. Still, I always felt that by dint of our mutual insights and sensibilities, not to mention unwillingness to relieve the other one, we were locked at the soul, and hence, forever connected. No contact with any person has ever shaped the private narratives I will forever maintain more than the lifetime of engagements with my mother.

Stunningly, she was freed from our dance of fury, neediness, and insecurity almost precisely upon the moment of my marriage. She loved my wife, her "*tauchteral*," she called Kay, using the diminutive form of the German word for daughter. My mother despised the concept of in-law. To my mother, my wife was her daughter. But this new daughter did something for my mother that was nothing short of liberating. She allowed my mother to cease mothering, not that I ever communicated to her that I believed her to be particularly distinguished in the role.

How trite is it to say that some people are simply not made to be parents? Freud's provocative dictum, anatomy is destiny, fails in too many ways. Neurology, more likely, is destiny. My mother was an artist, a person by definition, by fate, by genetic magic, absorbed with the various forms her own self could assume. One might have imagined that the demons prodding this art and requiring that the art be made known to others, would have relished the pedestrian chores of managing a house and shopping for food. Sometimes paying bills provides a relief to the burdened creative ego. But it was not this way for her. Without music, she could not get out of her own way, a way that was so memorable when she revealed her art, and what was a genuinely defining facet of her very self.

Music was her gift to all of us, and it goes without saying that she was the music, she was the gift: "Gitta, darling, please play for us, a little nothing, a *schmuntz*, Schumann, the start of the cadenza of the Grieg, ten measures of your beloved Scriabin, just a taste. You know you want to." And I think she always did want to. I, of course, never uttered these words, but I always hoped she would play, anything, even rudimentary finger exercises. Some people long to see their mother smile or hear their mother's voice. We were more than happy to settle for her playing, for playing was her smile, and her voice.

I also think she always wanted to be a mother, indeed a good mother. She may have wanted it just as badly as wanting to be a good artist. She probably wanted it as much as my sister and I wanted it for her, and for us. What she never realized, and until now I could never communicate, was that under the piano, beneath that gold canopy of the Steinway, with Scriabin, Chopin, Bach, and Rachmaninoff soaring over my head, I felt protected by her. I suspect she, too, felt protected by music, although she might have claimed the protection derived from idealized figures like Rachmaninoff and Toscanini. Still, the protection afforded her by music, or musical figures, allowed her, for whatever duration, periods of freedom. The rest of the time, when the music stopped, our early relationship was fraught with threatening sensations and a feeling that at any moment utter calamity would strike. I am convinced she felt the same thing. When an earthquake hits, one is instructed to run to the nearest doorway where, in effect, one is temporarily imprisoned by the power of nature. At all other times she should have run to the nearest piano which would have released her from enduring self-imprisonment. And I could have made a headlong dive underneath the Steinway and be rescued right along with her.

Free from whatever psychological burden motherhood presented, my mother became a sensational friend to all of us, though she never quite allowed herself to perceive the final impact of this transformation from mother to, simply, friend. She never permitted herself to see that it was all right if she allowed us to know the maternal role was not ideally meant for her. Had she been properly and lovingly "daughtered," the story no doubt would have been different. Perhaps she longed for someone to call her *tauchteral*. She did after all, commence her letters to my father with "Dear Daddy."

Grandmothering was more to my mother's liking: the proverbial joy without the responsibility, though decidedly not the consolidation of two generations around a common enemy. She adored her four grandchildren, deriving more pleasure from them than seemed possible, although one saw the outlines of potentially complex relationships starting to form. As she would have said, as she did frequently upon eating a spectacular dessert like a fifteen layer *dobos tort* or a remarkable tiramisu, the grandchildren were better than sex.

In my father's words, the grandchildren were worth the *ganze gelt* (all the money), although I often felt that after a few minutes with them, he was searching for more "interesting" things to do. He would study the newspaper hunting for art shows and concerts, or telephone local physicians involved in the sort of research he was undertaking. I don't think he would ever have thought of moving closer to the grandchildren, but then again, why would he when his work was in Chicago? My mother, on the other hand, might have entertained the possibility of moving to the east coast in order to be near her grandchildren. Well, she might have entertained the thought, but she never acted on it. She simply couldn't leave the familiarity of the world of Chicago. She had known the city for seven decades, the world from which she already had once been ripped away. Still, how many grandmothers in their mid-seventies would do what my mother did one hot August afternoon?

From our living room, I heard our young children shrieking with a degree of delight I had never previously witnessed. What possibly could be going on other than a good old-fashioned water fight, but even this wouldn't generate such squealing. I emerged from the front door to see the lawn sprinkler going full blast, our son and daughter stark naked running through it, followed by my mother who had stripped down to her bra and girdle and was getting completely soaked along with the children. In fact, it was *her* melodramatic squealing I had heard. The children were as ecstatic as they were drenched, not to mention incredulous as, I am sure, anyone passing on a Boston trolley which runs behind our backyard might also have been.

They were equally incredulous that my mother would share with them her inability to say the word, "fart." Sitting in our living room together one afternoon, someone accidentally, and noisily, expelled some gas. Only naturally this caused the children to explode with laughter, which in turn led them to the discovery of my mother's professed inhibition. They were captivated by it and tried every device known to humankind, practically climbing on top of her and physically torturing her, to get her to say the word, but she wouldn't. "I can say poop," she cried out, which only made them laugh harder and try harder still to coerce the magical word out of her.

"Come on, Grammy. Say it. You gotta say it!"

"Say fart, Grammy. You can do it."

And she would go, "fffff . . . . fafafafa . . . farfarfarfar . . . I can't do it. I really can't. Believe me, I'm trying. I want to."

"Pleeeeze, Grammy," they would persist. "Pleeeeze try." They were earnest now."

"fffff . . . fafafafa . . . farfarfarfar . . .

How she would have enjoyed hearing her great-grandson use the word "toot" for this rather ignoble biological process, and how she would have roared with laughter had she heard the following exchange I had will little Luke shortly before his third birthday: "Luke, how does the cow go?"

"Moo," came the answer from the back of the car.

"That's right. And how does the cat go?"

"Meow. Meow."

"Great. And how does the owl go?"

"Who. . . Who. . . Who tooted?"

The Fort Hill astrologer was surprisingly close to being on target. There was no reason in the world for me not to have children. It was my mother who probably should have avoided the whole parenting ordeal and stuck with the music, though she always claimed her children were what she loved the most. I would never have been born, of course, but in some ethereal sense, I might have been happier. She might have been too. This isn't exactly true, as both of us believed that a childless life was as empty an existence as a life without music, although my mother who, we recall, once called the piano her "best friend," would have said: children first, music second.

As I think of it, welded together through our stages of development, my mother and I might together have made one rather formidable person. The final product would have consisted of her childhood with its musical accomplishments, and my adulthood empty of all the squabbles and insecurities of childhood. It would then have been my adulthood that would have dominated the parenting, absent my childhood neuroses, leaving her adulthood to be the continuation of her brilliant pianistic childhood. I would have made the babies, she would have made the music, and many people's lives would have been enriched, and spared. As strange as this calculation must sound, I wonder whether my father, recognizing the profound anguish experienced by his wife, ever engaged in a similar sort of reasoning.

Stated in more realistic terms, my mother and I were welded in more than one way. Our temperaments were inseparable, our insecurities perfectly perverse reinforcements for one another when they weren't openly competing, something we surely learned during our numerous skirmishes. Our sensitivities and perceptions were practically identical, our habits and traits mirror images of one another. Psychologists speak of this complex form of interaction as "twinning." The two of us could happily have lived our entire lives in dirty clothes, rarely combing out hair, and going absolutely nowhere, especially not to parties, the previously cited gossip columns notwithstanding, where we both employed showy performance as a way of hiding. Give us a book or a television show, or let us imagine ourselves in a cozy train berth at night, our heads propped up on several pillows, peering out the window as we speed through little towns, the lights twinkling in the darkness, and hearing the sound of the clanging alarms at the railway crossings. Or perhaps deposit us in a log cabin on a clear blue lake in sight of the mountains, and we would be content. Every decision, every dilemma for both of us became a life or death ordeal that we could barely control. As a result, we bled onto anyone who happened to be close, just as long as that person was someone we loved, or from whom we required love. With strangers, we were always without needs, problem free, and perfectly serene. And always bad things lay just around the corner. No, not bad things: catastrophes wrapped in tragedies themselves bundled up in Armageddon. I, too, on occasion have fretted about sea level and the height of the Alps.

Something else that conjoined us was our belief that our temperaments and narcissism, wounded as it may have been, had the power to destroy or at least damage other souls, not to mention determine the outcome of events. The Cubs won or lost depending on my presence at the game, and given my gloomy Russian legacy, my presence assured their losing. (Then again, apparently, so did my absence.) If my mother and I bought stock the company would go out of business and probably too, the entire New York Stock Exchange would collapse. Either one of us could cause it to rain merely by making plane reservations. One could rest assured that on the day of our flights, ominous thunderstorms would unexpectedly arrive. A friend's mother once made a remark to him that sums up the nihilistic and grandiose outlook my mother and I co-owned: "Jerry," she told her son, "if I bought stock in AT&T, people would stop phoning each other."

We must have made life impossible for my sister and father, and Leah too. Surely we did on the occasion of our first trip to Europe as a family. As it happened, our itinerary was calculated to get us from Milan, Italy, to the port of Le Havre in northern France in time to board the Queen Mary ocean liner for the voyage home. Then, unexpectedly, we were caught in a nationwide French rail strike which meant that the journey from Milan had to be made either by plane or automobile, which in turn meant that either my mother's or my own fatal insecurity would have to be indulged: Terrified, I refused to fly; terrified, she refused to travel by car.

In the end my terror won out and we drove nonstop from Milan to Le Havre, traversing Paris at four in the morning. My father, remembering streets from his childhood, guided us through the city. The car trip over the Alps was unbearable for my mother, each hairpin turn yielding another dazzling view for us, another moment of horrific anxiety for her. We were swooning and cheering, but I remember her seated in the back of the car looking down at her lap and weeping. What a neurotic and pathetic person, I must have thought, but this was far easier than reflecting on my own insecurities and the fact that ultimately she had put her son's concerns ahead of her own. Had she, in fact, done the same thing when she gave up concertizing to raise her children full time? Was it truly the case that she could no longer stand leaving us in Chicago during the winter months to tour? Could she no longer "ignore" the desires of her husband? Come to think of it, had she not done the same thing when she gave up, though not wholly voluntarily, the safety and security of her family to launch her musical training and career? None of these decisions, many of them imposed by others, had ever made her, or any one else for that matter, totally happy, but she had gone along with them all the same. She was there. No matter what she endured, she never left us. She may have been insufferable on occasion and nowhere near as nurturing as I might have needed, but after the first four years of my life she didn't leave me, although some would say the damage had already been done. Still, as unhappy as she so often seemed, divorce, disloyalty, and abandonment were not in her vocabulary, nor in my father's for that matter. Nor apparently, was the idea of returning to her career. My mother read to us, bathed us, and held my head when I had to vomit into the toilet. In fact, this was when she was the most comforting and soothing, adjectives I would normally never attribute to her.

I cannot state that she was at her best when I was sick. There are those people who struggle pathetically with the mundane issues of life, but who, when confronted with genuinely important matters and outright calamities, suddenly become focused and exquisitely rational. There was a modest bit of that in my mother. "Maybe we'll catch a break," she would often say in hopeful tones when something grave loomed, as, for example, my father's failing health. But it wasn't always this way.

I would never tell my mother that I was catching a cold, for example, because I saw how it rankled and distressed her. I could sit at the dinner table, coughing, sneezing, wheezing, mucous practically covering my entire face and totally deny that I was coming down with something. I feared her anger, which was palpable, but which I am certain masked her anxiety. Perhaps she felt my sickness meant that I would have to stay home from school, which would mean that she would have to care for me, which wasn't true because my aunts assumed that responsibility. Perhaps my staying home from school meant that another facet of her motherhood role would be challenged and she feared that she might fail. Perhaps it meant that I would catch a glimpse of how she led her life during the day which, when she was depressed, consisted of not all that much, a great deal of time lying on her bed, a great deal of time watching television, very little if any piano playing. Perhaps my staying home meant that I would be missing school work that would never be made up and ultimately would mean I would do poorly and thus not gain admission to a good college. Perhaps it meant I genuinely was ill and she felt badly for me, and frustrated that she couldn't bring me immediate relief. Perhaps the two or three colds I annually contracted caused her to recognize that she was a source of "my other sickness." Who knows, perhaps my simple running nose evoked the sleeping terror of her hideous automobile accident.

I actually entertained these thoughts lying in bed during the years of my adolescence; the psychoanalytic conversations in the living room had long ago wafted up to my second-floor bedroom. Every movement, every action carried a thick psychological resonance and meaning at Hawthorne Place. A slip of the tongue, a slip of the pen, a slip on the stairs revealed "significant" unconscious underpinnings, whether or not the participants recognized them, and more often than not were a call for psychoanalytic consultation. A friend told me that after not seeing my father for many years, they accidentally bumped into one another. Before any words were even spoken, my father gripped the recently accumulated fat around my friend's waist. "What the hell is this?" he inquired abruptly. "You better come see me at my office tomorrow," which my friend did. Within seconds my father had arranged for him to consult a psychiatrist, which he also did.

Two more examples of this sort of reasoning further illustrate the matter of Hawthorne Place's accentuated emphasis on the psyche.

My Aunt Fanny was occasionally visited by a family from Kansas City. One summer evening they arrived in our Michigan home. Over the course of dinner it was determined by the adults that Tommy would take the visiting family's daughter, Sandy, to the beach for a moonlight swim. Nice of all of these people to make plans. God forbid any one of them should have consulted with us. To show my displeasure at taking a total stranger to the beach on what was actually a brisk July evening, I appeared in the living room wearing my bathing suit and a navy blue windbreaker which I had zipped up to the neck. Everyone got the message. Sandy appeared wearing my father's white silk robe with a fire red dragon stitched on the back. Until that moment, I had never seen anyone else wear that robe.

We descended the stairs to the beach. Sandy commented on the beauty of the dunes and the thousands of little green plants that did their best to protect the dunes from erosion, while I thought about the fact that the American military and its allies may have won World War II, but they had missed one small enclave of Fascism now gathered in a living room in Union Pier, Michigan.

Then, suddenly, Miss Sandy stripped off my father's robe and I observed a magnificent young woman with a stunning figure. One quick and seductive glance at me and she was running toward the water. Maybe the enclave upstairs wasn't so Fascistic after all. Not to be outdone by a girl, I pulled off my windbreaker and raced for the shoreline where I executed that wondrously dolphinesque leap with arched back into the small waves. The first powerful stroke with the left arm as I began the crawl, and then the right arm, and then an explosion of pain as if a piano had been flung against my back.

Standing up in the shallow water, I looked down at where my shoulder used to be. Literally all that was there was an outline of a narrow bone, but sticking out behind appeared to be my shoulder. By this point, Sandy, having heard my screaming, was rushing back to me, an expression of sick dismay formed on her face. Both of us were horrified by the sight, yet somehow I managed to pop the dislocated shoulder back in place. Having reasoned that if it went out with the crawl-like motion, it might return through the reverse motion, which it did.

The adults were surprised that we returned so quickly. Hearing our account, they did not believe that I could possibly have sustained a dislocated shoulder if I had been able to so easily put it back in place. Even Sandy's earnest testimony could not sway them. But here's the point. My thinking in those days, as I "studied" psychoanalysis as a way of defending myself in the house, for it was the only protection one could employ short of all out physical assault, was to conclude that the shoulder separation, that in time became a chronic condition, was wholly psychosomatic. Sandy's obvious sexuality had caused me, unconsciously of course, to become terrified of what the future minutes with her might portend. How to maintain one's seemingly secure masculinity when being terrified by sexuality? It is all very simple. Dislocating my shoulder was a perfect symbolic representation of castration. In the end, hospitalization substitutes for fornication.

It all made perfect sense. Why, after all, did it take Sandy's appearance in a bathing suit on an isolated moonlit beach to trigger any recognition of her attractiveness? The denial of her sexuality had taken place, presumably, at the moment of our meeting, a denial indicating the existence of some unconscious anxiety. The solution to the terror had to be performed, the ego must have determined, through a somatic symptom. How creative to "think" of a separation, a provocative term at best. It surely beat amputation. It all made perfect sense in the same way that the smack in the nose I received in a pick up basketball game one afternoon at school was also psychosomatic. That a fine athlete who had never once been injured

even slightly in a basketball game, or a practice, should suddenly retire with a bloody nose—the organ that had become my father's
medical specialty—on the very day my mother underwent hysterec-
tomy surgery could not be coincidence. The athletic injury was
proof of all of us being Oedipally conjoined in a fashion that surely
would have delighted Sophocles himself.

There was no such thing at Hawthorne Place as mere coincidence. There were always reasons for human actions, all of them
housed in the unconscious, and all of them accessible only through
the study of psychoanalysis and actual treatment. Psychoanalysis
was to my psyche what the hundred pounds of armor were to the
medieval knight, a necessary protection during battle as well as pro-
hibiting burden. Armor does indeed keep outside armies from in-
vading one's personal fortress. Unfortunately, it also keeps the
interior from finding its way to freedom.

The battles that took place during my adolescence never completely receded. Years after her grandchildren were born, my mother,
ever sensitive, heard my sadness on the phone one evening when she
called to "check up" on us. As always, the conversation concluded
with her saying in wistful tones, "I know there was something else I
wanted to ask you." Whatever it was, she never remembered, although I often felt this expression was merely a way of holding on to
me a moment longer, almost as if she feared I wouldn't have much
interest in communicating with her unless I knew something portentous was about to be disclosed. Then again, perhaps she wanted to
know whether I loved her, something I cannot recall ever telling her.

On the occasion of this one particular call, I described to her having received several rejection slips that week from different editors
and how this writing business of mine was doomed to fail. "Some
people," I said, "just have to recognize they don't have it. You can't
keep saying the world isn't ready for this; you have to face the facts of
your life." By that point in my life, I had come to understand that rejection notes from unknown editors crushed me because they meant
that my mother had been right all along: I was unworthy of respect
and unlovable, not to mention unpublishable. I suppose I wanted to
make certain she knew the role she had played in these rejection slips
forty years after giving birth to me. One of my mother's favorite expressions went: "You should take a good, long look at yourself in the
mirror." There's truth in the admonition, and I might have done it

sooner had her words not been uttered in such angry disapproval, and her counsel not evoked such intense self-blame.

"You know," came the voice, strong and assured over the phone, "for someone who's as smart as you are, who has accomplished more than any ten people I know ever will in their entire lives, I don't see why you just can't relax and enjoy all that you've done."

"Mother," I responded, and we might just as well have been standing on that second-floor landing outside my parents' bedroom, "of all the people in the world to make that statement, with all those years of analysis, I cannot for the life of me believe you just said what you said. *You* of all people don't know why I can't just relax and enjoy my life? Unbelievable! Here's Kay, she wants to say hello," I said as I walked away from the phone feeling precisely what I felt as a teenager. I always headed to my bedroom after one of our skirmishes. In this comfortable place, I would lick my wounds, shake my head, as she, too, always did, feel some strange and sudden sexual arousal, and at the same time feel like I wanted to kill someone, or go somewhere and disappear. Sometimes, I might amble across the street and find Naomi in the Weiss's kitchen. It was all a barely disguised sense of desiring to destroy myself, making it easier for everyone by not being there anymore.

The thought has never fully dissipated. It probably never did for her as well. The blend of Freud's alleged life and death wishes, *Eros and Thanatos*, married as one, just as the psyches of a mother and son might be married, and all of it expressing itself in verbal battles of narcissistic and erotic proportions that ultimately brought not a single instant of gratification, nor any form of genuine intimacy. We were merely two people who never felt secure in their identities, never confident in the roles thrust upon them, nor the expectations others maintained for them, and surely hurting from the judgments made of them, especially by people who had pledged undying love to them.

9

Giant Shadows

A seemingly endless list of biographies of luminaries may be found, many of them authored by their children. Not surprisingly, one discovers numerous performers happy when, as the expression goes, they "are on," then turning sad when opportunities for performance or creative expression disappear. Psychological theory would predict that the children of these luminescent figures would feel inadequate not only because their meager childhood accomplishments cannot hold a candle to the achievements of the adults they and others idealize, but also because they, the children, cannot produce the same degree of happiness in their parents as their parents derive from their own creative activities. Complicating these matters, moreover, is the comparison children make between their own contemporaries and the famous folk who parade through their parents' living room. Whatever the child does, whatever the child is, simply falls short.

It is probably the case that some of the gratification derived from performance is compensatory. Onstage or off, performers are merely doing what they have always done to capture the recognition they themselves craved when they were children. So, whereas the momentary applause seems all and all, its nourishment lasts only as long as the public adoration pours forth. Once the concert halls and living rooms are empty of their audiences, the depression, caused in some measure by the absence of love shown these persons early in their lives, returns. For all one knows, the performance is a childlike seduction, an act of urging people to attach themselves to the performer, and ultimately to fall in love with her, not to mention remain with her forever.

If these notions are valid, then nothing would seem more hurtful to the performing adult than the arrival into adolescence of her own children, for now these young offspring are publicly announcing that the time is right to embark on their own lives. It is now *their* moment. As young people seek an albeit compromised form of independence, their parents only logically interpret this natural evolution as a rebellion against them. Strange as it may seem, normal development can be interpreted by parents as rejection or repudiation, the very acts that so damaged the performing adult in the first place. Said differently, the art form may be forever tinged with childhood hurt or unhappiness. Thus, no matter how old the performer, the sadness and pain travel with her, along with the moments of rapture.

There was little question that my arrival into adolescence triggered a mutually reinforcing rage, fright, and sadness in my mother and me. If the present weren't being sufficiently churned up, then the dust of the past filled Hawthorne Place; it took more than chamber music to wash it away. Simply by my reaching "that" age, my mother was obliged to once again revisit the hurts she had known during her truncated adolescence, a period of time fraught with separations and decouplings. She was obliged, moreover, to revisit the joys of her own adolescence. These were the years, after all, of her own great freedom, her own great flights into significant work and public success. As she herself said, "this piano business wasn't all it was cracked up to be. But it wasn't all that bad either."

Valid or not, these notions represent examples of so-called psychodynamic constructs being employed to explain human behavior. This same behavior, however, may be explained in terms of cognitive or family system constructs. One might consider, for example, Howard Gardner's research on human intelligence as an illustration of a cognitive construct.[1]

It is Gardner's contention that all people are born with innate intelligences that arrive in varying degrees with the newborn as part of the genetic wiring. That is, some people seem to possess "higher" intelligences here, "lower" intelligences there. Not so incidentally, Gardner defines intelligence in part as the ability to solve a problem or create something the culture deems worthwhile. What happens to these various intelligences, of course, remains a function of the degree to which a person cultivates them, or more likely, has someone encouraging this cultivation. Which brings us to an important matter.

Exercising a talent is not something a child necessarily undertakes eagerly on her own. In the beginning, especially, no part of the exercise seems fun. It requires encouragement, even forceful prodding. This is especially true in the prodigy's development of her artistic skills. "Mechanical training," Adolph Kullak said, "is the primary and indispensable condition of pianoforte-playing. To the spirit of the same it stands in just the same relation, as the form to the substance . . ."[2] In observing the extraordinary technical skills of the students graduating from the Russian Conservatory, James Francis Cooke noted that "the student is examined first upon technic. If he fails to pass the technical examination he is not even asked to perform his pieces."[3]

Interestingly, the technical examination represents an examination of the quality of habits the performer has cultivated, in Gardner's terms, regarding her intelligences. A Dr. Carpenter, cited in a volume written by E. F. Bartholomew, states that "our nervous systems have grown to the way in which they have been exercised."[4] Habit, in other words, reflects the manner in which we relate to or manage our intelligences, but it also possesses a power captured by Montaigne:

> Habit is a violent and treacherous schoolmistress. . . .
> She, by little and little, slyly and unperceived, slips in the
> foot of her authority, but having by this gentle and humble
> beginning, with the aid of time, fixed and established it, she
> then unmasks a furious and tyrannic countenance, against
> which we have no more the courage nor the power so much
> as to lift up our eyes.[5]

Earl Woods and Richard Williams, the fathers, respectively, of golfer Tiger Woods and the tennis playing sisters, Venus and Serena Williams, are prominent examples of authoritative fathers who insisted their children establish the "proper" habits of mind and performance, and thereby exercise their unique intelligences. Neither man was an accomplished athlete. Mr. Williams learned tennis in his thirties for the sole purpose, he claims, of developing his daughters into champions. My grandfather could not have pushed my mother to a tenth of the degree these men pushed their children, literally determining their destinies for them, as the fathers of Mischa Elman and Jascha Heifetz had done for their sons, acts that some allege may damage the souls of young people. Yet, perhaps too much emphasis is placed on this concern. Perhaps some families would do better insisting that their children develop their intelligences as far as humanly possible. Perhaps parents would do better requiring their children to play a musical instrument in the same way they require regular medical and dental examinations.

Where my grandfather may have made his biggest mistake was not in demanding that his daughter become a world-class performer, but in shipping her out of her home before she was psychologically prepared, a mistake not made by Mr. Woods or Mr. Williams. In fact, these fathers may have responded only too well to a fundamental need of children. It is impossible to imagine that Tiger Woods, Venus or Serena Williams will ever utter the words so many of my generation have uttered: "I wish I had spent more time with my father."

Gardner employs eight different criteria for establishing the existence of each of the alleged innate intelligences—the notion of a single IQ test emerging inadequate for the task—one of them being that the intelligence can be ablated by neurological accident or surgery. Verbal skills, for example, may disappear because of a stroke, a phenomenon known as *aphasia*. Musical intelligence, another of Gardner's intelligences, along with intelligences he calls logical-mathematical, linguistic, spatial, kinesthetic, interpersonal, intrapersonal, and naturalistic, can also be eradicated by stroke, the result labeled *amusia*.

Theoretically, we each possess these intelligences, although some of us exhibit distinguished levels of one or more of them. At the highest level of intelligence is the prodigy, the *wunderkind* athlete, mathematician, poet, musician. But prodigy or not, the development of any intelligence requires the support of parents, teachers, perhaps an entire culture. Girls traditionally were discouraged, for example, from pursuing athletic careers, or even developing their intrinsic mathematical intelligence.

Each of Gardner's intelligences is unique, with music, perhaps, being the most unusual of the litter. From Daniel Gregory Mason:

> Music is always fatally handicapped by association with words. In the first place, words impose upon it a concrete meaning immeasurably more trite, prosaic, and limited than that abstract and indefinable meaning to the heart and mind which is its proper prerogative; the expressive power of music really begins where that of poetry fails and ceases.[6]

Simply put, there are neither words nor pictures with music. When interpretation of notes commences, it is no longer a purely musical intelligence that is at work. Knowing this, musicians often speak in terms of "musical meaning," a term defined by Aaron Copland in this way: "What they (musicians) really mean is that no appropriate word can be found to express the music's meaning and that, even if it could, they do not feel the need of finding it."[7] Similarly, there is no music that accurately coincides with or describes a physical entity. According to Anthony Storr: ". . . music is neither propositional, nor does it usually imitate phenomena. It does not put forward theories or inform us about the world."[8] And finally there is composer Igor Stravinsky's observation:

> Musical compositions, one product of the musical intelligence, exist in their own right. Compositions represent *not* "a communication of the composer's feelings to his audience, but rather a communication about how he makes sense of his feelings . . . transforms them from raw emotion into art.[9]

One thing more about the musical intelligence seems relevant to the lives of people like Horowitz and my mother. As obvious as it is to state, music is essentially an auditory experience, although clearly it can be "heard" in the head without the use of the ears. When listening to, or most especially composing and playing music, the outside world is removed, if not walled off altogether. On the surface, it would appear that involvement with music is a form of retreat from external reality, what psychoanalysts might call "a regression" to an earlier and more primitive moment of existence, but this is hardly the case. Horowitz playing Liszt, or Stravinsky composing the *Firebird* are hardly primitive acts or manifestations of regression. They are in no way "escapes from reality," though they may be invitations to join another person's "momentary reality." In fact, Edward Hirsch[10] observes they are the creations that make us fall in love with life, or perhaps fall in love with hating life.

At very least, the musical intelligence allows the performer to create a reality that is shared with others, no matter how this reality comes to be construed or articulated. Not only that, the performer's work refreshes us, inspires us, transforms us. Even as a teenager raging against my mother, I was becalmed by her playing. I loved coming home and discovering her at the keyboard. Normally I would either go for my graham crackers and milk or rush directly to my bedroom. But on those occasions when I found her practicing, I would sit on the stairs, away from her vision, of course, for long, long minutes.

The worlds of the musician and her listeners are indeed transformed by the music and the performance which remain inseparable. In this manner, Gitta Gradova the pianist legitimately imposed her will on her listeners. Her playing demanded they pay attention not only to her, but to the music as well. In these instants, her own world was properly in order, just as in some degree this order affected the order of the world of the listeners. More than the need to be recognized was at play here. When she played, her audience heard pure Chopin, Scarlatti, or Scriabin, not my grandfather's scoldings of his daughter, nor my mother's terror of being in the world alone. Playing by herself in the music room, unaware that a single soul may be listening, proved this to be the case. She was communing with composers, and being driven by needs and motives that cannot be accounted for merely as narcissistic pleasure or compensation. She was playing the piano, and I know that just as she could not elaborately describe the nature of the technique she employed, neither could she put into words the sensations she derived from the playing, and that which constituted the work in the first place.

In the world of music, apparently, my mother operated relatively free of anxiety and sadness, her emotions and intellect forming the foundation of the interpretive act. In this world, she was never overwhelmed. Every problem had its solution, every new experience became a challenge to be addressed, as opposed to a threat from which she had to flee. In the world of the auditory, she succumbed to the structure and beauty of the music, never to the profane obligations of the culture. I was overwhelmed by the majesty of the sounds she conceived and rendered, not by the tasks and routines of everyday life, but by her musical strength. I am convinced that in these moments at the keyboard, my mother felt neither terror nor sorrow. Oh, she claimed she was terrified of that passage at the bottom of page eleven, but this was only a challenge she embraced, a mountain ridge to be traversed. Not only would she eventually navigate those dreaded octaves or those beastly thirds, she believed she was invincible. As she herself said, ". . . when I know I ought to be discouraged about something radically wrong in my work, I understand the trouble so quickly that I remedy it before it has time to get hold of my disposition and my heart . . ."[11]

I suspect, too, that rising from the piano stool after an arduous workout, she felt healthy, happy to have experienced moments away from her inner torment. Perhaps she even enjoyed being herself. These were the transcendent moments when she turned herself over to higher powers. Not to God, but rather to Bach, Chopin, Brahms, Schubert, and all the other deities of her private pantheon. She did on more than one occasion speak of them as Gods.

I believe that no great talent can ever properly explain what it is they do, or how they do it. When they find themselves transported by their own endeavors, when they attain those glorious moments of self-transcendence where an exquisite freedom resides—what athletes call "the zone"—they are liberated and unaware of what it is they are doing to keep themselves there. Before our eyes, and ears, they employ their God-given intelligences and fall back on thousands of hours of training in order to reach a point in the creative firmament that is made possible by their own talents and sensibilities, as well as the talents and sensibilities of composers whose own self-transcendence lives in the lines and dots propped up on the music stands in front of them, or indelibly etched in their memories.

Just as miraculously, their audience feels this same sensation of having been transported. Absent, for the instant, of anguish and terror, the listeners are free and immortal right along with the artist, equally unaware of what is happening, or how they got there, when all they are doing is sitting quietly in a darkened concert hall. But the inexplicable transcendence is palpable. My mother made me want to kill her and made me want to kill myself. My mother also made me feel this self-transcendence through music. I never told her, but she made me feel the soaring power of music, its literal flesh, and how, because of a composition *and* an interpreter of a particular composition, I literally rose above myself and felt nothing short of a surging life-force rarely experienced in normal, everyday routines. For this genuine life-force, we require artists.

I suppose our pains make us special in some way; they are part not of our baggage, really, but of our identity. We even imagine that pain draws others to us when in fact we are unable often to recognize that it is others who have drawn the pain to us, or out of us. We are our relationships, our histories, our joys, our anguish. I suppose, too, that some of us fear ridding ourselves of these pains, as though an emptiness would replace them that would forever cause us to feel bereft. We know that patients in psychotherapy are loath to relinquish the very injuries they claim brought them to a therapist in the first place. The story of narcissism is one in which magnificent acts of character and personality continue to be tinged with suffering. Only logically a person fears that relinquishing their suffering means forfeiting the act or, more likely, the intelligence that generates it. Quite possibly, the phenomenon of magical thinking begins to take over and a person imagines that if she gives up the pain, she'll lose the talent, thus she cannot afford to release it no matter how liberating it might be. If she stops leaning against the brick wall, it will fall upon her.

Music makes possible a reordering of the world, an opportunity to adapt to it, or more precisely re-adapt to it in ways that ideally improve the world and aid in making oneself (and others) feel sane and whole, and for a moment without pain. There is no more retreat from "reality" in performing *The Paganini Variations*, or Liszt's *Fantasia After Dante* than there is in solving mathematical problems. In the home of a musician, there is nothing more real than music. As ironic as it must sound, my mother's playing made me feel safe. It was the most delicious part of my reality. It was magnificent in and of itself, just as it was the most glorious and essential part of her I would ever receive. It stood for something on its own, that flesh of art again, just as it stood in place of something else that was not to be. Her music was not an escape from reality. Her music transported me to a serene reality that I continue to enter whenever I wish, a reality, moreover, that does not always contain her.

My mother, clearly, was born with an extraordinary musical intelligence. She happened to possess as well exceptional linguistic and interpersonal and intrapersonal intelligences. Those around her saw early on that it was her musical intelligence that had to be nurtured, a task her father assigned to himself. Clearly, her parents influenced her development, as did her teachers and colleagues, and later on her husband and children as well. Yet in many respects, the first thirty-seven years of her life revealed her identity being constructed in greatest measure from this one inborn gift and all the activity, soothing and hurtful, that swarmed about it. Sadly, it was the lack of a rich development in what Gardner calls the "logical-mathematical intelligence" that caused her to believe she wasn't smart. Somewhere along the line she determined that aesthetic or empathetic intelligence was inferior to scientific and abstract intelligence.

To not possess this heightened degree of an intelligence, what most of us non-prodigies everyday endure, is to not be able to fully appreciate the role the highlighted intelligence plays in the emergence of the personality, much less what a person experiences if that intelligence is stripped away, unused, or heaven forbid, lost forever, as it is in the case of a dancer becoming paralyzed.

Said simply, beyond the problems confronting any biographer, we non-prodigies cannot possibly approximate the phenomenology of the prodigy, much less the meaning of that prodigy retiring. So we either reduce complexities to banalities, retreat almost instinctively to the familiar theories we always conjure up when faced with inexplicable psychological questions, or listen to talk show hosts lamely ask an artist, "What is that like?" Not even knowing the proper questions to ask, how possibly could we non-prodigies begin to approximate what the loss of one's art might produce, a loss akin to the loss of a parent's love or respect, or the permanent loss of a job or loved one. "I'll never see my mother again," is transformed into, "I'll never run again, or perform again." The words of Paul Valéry capture the essence of this notion:

> One forgets too often that art exists only in the act; art is action; it is this action whose goal is to excite and modify the sensibilities of man and to obtain those developments that make themselves indefinitely desired. . . . Thus, the virtuoso is the one who, par excellence, gives life and reality to what was only writing, available to any comer, to the ignorance, the clumsiness, the insufficient comprehension of any comer. The virtuoso renders the work incarnate.[12]

If this were not enough, then consider the notion of loss inherent in what Paul Rosenfeld called the "romantic ironists," people like Carlo Gozzi, whose writing Prokofiev transformed into *The Love of Three Oranges*, Prokofiev himself, and perhaps my mother as well:

> All have been left dry by life, and felt with some bitterness their dryness, and seen the world an empty nurse's tale, a ridiculous self-deception of the dreaming ego. . . . For one moment, at least, these men must have escaped from their subjectivity, and seen it impersonally. And in that moment of release they must have conceived, and been enabled to snatch a pleasure out of the void, and sculpt their nothing into solid form.[13]

Although during my youth I harangued my mother and matched her denunciation for denunciation, I cannot imagine the experience of retiring the most critical cognitive skill in one's repertoire and, in Valéry's words, forfeit the act and the action, not to mention the modifier of sensibilities. What does one feel when one can no longer "snatch pleasure out of the void," but knows, perhaps, only that void?

Surely my mother lived with fear, a sentiment for which, as a boy, I had nothing but contempt, and which probably masked not only my own fears, but the fears I felt from seeing her so fearful. Children, after all, learn fear. Something happens to them and they look to their mother to see what reaction they are meant to experience. When the mother appears courageous, the child mimics the mood. In contrast, when the mother becomes hysterical, so, too, does the child. In time the reactions come to form the nature of the relationship between mother and child, hysterical reactions yielding anxious couplings.

If a child is pulled away from her parents and sent to live on her own in a place where nothing about the physical and human community seems familiar, much less sustaining or comforting, it is only natural that the child will become fearful. Even more, practicing for concerts in which one's talent is put on display for public assessment only intensifies the fear, although many performers are at their least fearful at the moment of their appearance; they long for these public displays. Which causes one to conclude that perhaps my mother's early experiences of learning the piano were fraught with fear caused by my grandfather or heaven only knows what else. If Oakeshott is right, and we are what we have learned, then my mother learned that piano playing and fear go hand in hand.

But there is also the matter of that void to which Paul Rosenfeld alluded. A classical pianist hardly composes the music. However, she surely faces the terror of forgetting it in the middle of a concert. She can also face the terror of remembering every note, rest, and tempo, but having her fingers fail her, even during slow movements where technical skill is not on display. The void is the cavern in which interpretation lives; it is the region of the mind to which the performer must travel to make music, and no one knows what lurks in this region. Only logically, therefore, any performer wonders, when I go to snare it, will it be there? And what precisely is "it," and where precisely is "there?" The great ones know that playing all the notes correctly is merely the foundation of the work; the construction of music is far more mysterious and evanescent. It is enough to make the strongest person frail. But no child knows about these matters, and even if he did, all he can see is a frightened mother who turns her fright into anger and sadness, just as the little boy ultimately learns to do.

With this as background, I once again reflect on the self-imposed loss of one's supreme talent. One can only speculate on the additional distress caused by the self-imposition of the loss. Surely the loss puts one in a constant state of frustration, as well as induces a sense of personal incompleteness and mourning. A part of one's being, after all, has been amputated. The analogy of going on a diet and giving up the foods one adores—a sort of musical anorexia—comes close to describing the experience, but eventually it fails inasmuch as no diet requires the permanent cessation of eating. Giving up one's genius may well be like giving up all foods.

A better analogy, perhaps, is to imagine losing one's speech. I recall a telephone conversation with my late mother-in-law during the very moments she was experiencing a cerebral shock. Bab had suddenly become aphasic, her speech, normally so acute, sounded like a tape recording of human speech played backward. Yet periodically, in the midst of her gibberish, this intelligent and artistic woman uttered one perfectly coherent word: "DRAT!" she would say, obviously recognizing her own incoherence. A self-appraising portion of herself, what psychologists call the "observing ego," was listening and commenting. Later on, Bab exhibited an uncharacteristic sadness that surely was caused in part by a recognition of her compromised neurological capacities.

My mother's observing ego also spent a great deal of time watching, listening, and commenting, to herself as well as to others. In leading a life without musical performance, she too, uttered a form of "DRAT!" on numerous occasions, often in those notorious skirmishes with me that so disturbed my father. Yet she continued playing; there was never anything resembling an amusia. So why the consternation? Why the histrionics? She practiced at home by herself, she played with colleagues, she played for family, friends, and strangers at the soirées. Why wasn't this sufficient?

I shall never know for certain the answers to these questions, and herein a dilemma I cannot resolve. On the one hand, the answer would seem to be that self-imposed amusia can only be cured by public performance in the legitimate concert halls of the world. But now, have we not returned to our original starting point? Does this not imply that my mother required public approval and affirmation to compensate for the early losses, rejections, and schisms of childhood? Perhaps so. On the other hand, being neither a prodigy nor a virtuoso, I am not certain whether practice sessions, musical soirées, and concerts at private gatherings can ever compensate for the "real thing." As much joy as they generate, practice sessions in worn-out clothes or playing at elegantly catered soirées may inevitably end up as *faux* performances.

The virtuoso requires a full and complete public display, in Town Hall, Orchestra Hall, or Carnegie Hall, no less! How many thoughtful, gifted people, after all, refuse to call themselves writers until their words appear in print? How many children, knowing full well that their parents veritably worship them, require the presence of those same parents in the front rows for every one of their school plays, recitals, and poetry readings, or on the sidelines for every athletic contest? In these moments, it is the public display of these various intelligences that defines the person. It is the dancing and mathematics, the baseball pitching, the logical reasoning and piano playing that allow people to stand before the world beyond their families and say at last, "Here I Am!" When my sister sang for our parents, which she did on the little make-shift stage in the basement at Hawthorne Place before it was turned into a research laboratory, it was my job to announce: "Ladies and Gentlemen, my sister, Judy Cottle." But this is merely a formal way of proclaiming: "Here She Is!"

But "HERE SHE IS!" in my mother's case seemed always to be conjoined with, "When are you coming home?" "Why haven't you written or wired?" "Why," in other words, "have you been a bad girl?" For every public appearance, every public expression of herself, there seems to be a counterforce coming from her family clearly in the form of a communication that her place is not on the road performing, but in the home. "Here She Is!" therefore, becomes defined in most literal terms: "Here She Is!" at home, with her family, where she is *meant* to be.

Drawing an analogy to actors may prove illustrative. Do actors perform merely for public accolades and adulation, awards, and fame? Are they driven solely by a need for affirmation from an audience because they didn't receive sufficient affirmation when they were small? Is everything they (and we) do about self-love, self-esteem, narcissism? I think not. I imagine that many people who act have to, in the same way that people who write, sing, dance, and play the piano, simply have to. Their public performance as well as their internal narratives, in some measure, are dictated by their in-born wiring. Think of the actor who, for the while, has no part to play and hence, cannot act. What does she do? Forget the problems associated with earning a living; my mother didn't need to earn a living, just as she didn't need to perform household duties. Without a legitimate part, however, without a stage, the actor must feel dead inside. Her singularly most powerful cognitive defining force has been unplugged. Truly this is a Ferrari caged in a garage!

Although actors find ways to make ends meet, they forever struggle with the problem of having their very soul, of which their intelligences are fundamental components, temporarily crippled or even permanently damaged by not finding acting work. Even more, the out-of-work actor represents each one of us who senses there is some inborn gift that has never seen the light of day. Do we not counsel young people: "If you don't try now, you'll never know?" And does this mean that more parents might do well following the leads of Mr. Woods and Mr. Williams?

My mother knew all too well what she could have been, what she could have accomplished. She was a concert pianist, a famous, well-loved, child prodigy, and adult performer whom critics and audiences adored. After more than thirty years of successful concertizing there can be no turning back. Granted, her self-imposed exile, not merely from the stage but from her most cherished intelligence, was related to her resisting, perhaps, her father's insistence that she hone her skill and achieve stardom. Granted too, he needed her success, for her and for himself. In a telegram she received from him in Detroit in 1924—she would have been nineteen at the time—he wrote: "May your success today be the greatest in the world." (Predictably, the telegram concluded with a familiar criticism, and request: "Why don't you let us hear from you. Please wire immediately.") Perhaps too, she fell victim to an unconscious desire to stay home, first to be near her mother and sisters, then later her husband and children. One cannot forget that she always lived with her mother and sisters, even ones who were married and with children. Yet I suspect our entire family may have symbolized for her the quieting of the magic, the unplugging of an entire chunk of her brain, no matter how intense her love for us may have been. We were all calling for her to come home, and stay there. And be happy there, moreover.

I suspect, too, that her intrapersonal intelligence only made her feel more conflicted and her entire life less harmonious, often to the point of complete discordance. Which means that even in the midst of her most tortured hours or screaming at her son, she understood it all. At least I imagine she did. In every verbal battle I had with her, it seemed, she would blurt out, "You just don't know the half of it." And I, with bitter sarcasm, responded, "Well, why don't you just take a few months off from whatever you do around here and tell me the half of it." As I have stated, I imagined there were some palpable events about which I needed to learn. But it may also be that what she sought to describe for me was the complexity of her anguish, her daily ruminations, the trips back and forth to that void, and significantly, her attempts to interpret what indeed she was experiencing and feeling.

Inasmuch as nobody knew viscerally better than she that children require their mothers, and fathers, my mother may well have gone to her grave believing the decision to quit her career for the sake of her family, or because of a need to "return home," in all senses of the phrase, was indisputably correct. I, however, shall go to my grave—and I shall not be smiling—insisting that she who leaves a Ferrari in a garage, or just as bad, uses it only to go to Mannie Stockenberg's butcher shop on Broadway, fails to employ the God-given wiring that ultimately defines her, not to mention nourishes her soul. And that's the point she never let me get across to her.

She *was* nourished by music, but not by me, and that fact troubled both of us, and locked us together in the most pitiful of ways. I needed her love as she needed mine, but we both knew that music was a better and more enduring partner. Scriabin and Chopin put forth monstrously difficult challenges to the pianist, but they didn't sass her from the second-floor landing. What I don't know is whether my father felt the same thing. An ambitious man, he would never have uttered the familiar phrase of the present generation of performers: "I'm quitting to spend more time with my family." Ambitious or not, perhaps he knew that if my mother's true romance was with music, the tortuous moments notwithstanding, his true romance would have to be with medicine. Heaven only knows the hurt felt by the physician, but it cannot compete with what he must have known when, supporting her as publicly as he clearly did, she often could respond only with depressed resignation. He, too, after all, saw her star shine brilliantly when music was in the air, and then witness it fall to the ground when it stopped. He, too, knew that with all his accomplishments and generosity, he couldn't budge her personality. He couldn't make her feel secure. He couldn't help her get through the anguish she appeared to drag to everyday activities, as well as to those who waited on her, and looked to her for affection. Whether or not he felt culpable for his role in her decision to quit playing is something I shall never know. For he may well have lived with some guilt for drawing her home from the concert stage.

One finds in my father's letters to his young fiancée and later his wife not one occurrence of the word, depression. But it is evident that this sensitive physician is more than troubled by what he is observing and hearing:

> Relax and you'll regale—if you don't relax—regrets . . . please don't be unhappy. . . . Leaving from Northwestern [train station]. Is anything wrong? (1926) . . . Hope you are well and your spirits [are] rising. . . . Your unhappiness at departure was today more than ever most regrettable and sad. It grieves more than I can say (February, 1926) . . . Please don't worry or fear. Just go right along without too much meditation . . . I beg you not to be upset by anything or anybody. . . . You are discouraged and disappointed in New York. I am sure that when you see it in retrospect you will be much happier and very probably pleased with what you experienced. Please cheer up. . . . I hope you have been well—your unrest just makes me worry and fret . . . Your loneliness makes me very unhappy, but I share it with you for the good of our beautiful and peaceful future. Our loneliness is a product of our efforts to do something constructive and beautiful and in the near future only happiness can result, I am sure. So hold tight my dear lover, we'll be on top together. . . . Could I but impress on you that you must not become downhearted. Of course one can't go around smugly contented—on the contrary one must kick like hell to get something—but self-discouragement and depreciation lead only to endless moodiness and morbidity— and that can't happen. . . . And as always, it is not so much that your success is big—but that we hope it might please you a little that makes us rejoice when you wire your success.[14]

I want to believe that my mother eventually saw it my way, and that at the end of her life she was finally released from her self-imposed, indeed, self-indulgent exile partly because of the words I spoke to her, sometimes in love, although more likely in fury. Is it possible that she recognized that, as much as anyone, I understood her struggle? Could it be that, even as an obnoxious budding little psychoanalyst, the closer I hit home with the truths of her life, the more ambivalently attached she became to me, or to my own intrapersonal intelligence? Is it possible that she wished she might have heard my plea to her to return to her career earlier in her life?

At the same time, might this recognition also have caused her to feel resentment toward the boy who carried her father's name? Together we shared the knowledge that throughout my lifetime she mourned the deaths of her parents. I was the one who insisted that she also mourned the death, by murder or suicide, of her most exceptional intelligence, her virtuosity. I was also the one who most loudly revealed an emptiness that was meant to be filled by her, an emptiness which, as an adolescent, I presented as rage and a sense of desolation. I never let her overlook this. We both longed for people, for comfort, for a quieting of minds. In the end, our skirmishes may well have been our own mutually destructive "acts of wandering mourning." Then again, all of this may be pure fabrication meant to convince myself of my importance to her.

If children are born with their cognitive wiring which, like computer hardware, arrives in the package upon purchase, they are also born with temperament. Some babies emerge from the womb curious about what awaits them, whereas others emerge ostensibly angry about a host of things, and offering indications that the resolution of their consternation may require, say, eighty years. This, too, is part of what psychologists refer to as "innate wiring."

In the psychological shorthand of the day, the personality is that with which we are left after dealing with those who raised us and lived among us. If personality has something to do with the unique ways we perceive the world and ourselves, as well as feel about the world and ourselves, all related, of course, to our temperaments, then clearly our parents, or significant childhood figures, have influenced these deeply personal elements. My own personal computer contains my mother's temperament, prominent features of which are impatience, ambition, impulsiveness, an abiding toughness on myself, (what I jokingly refer to as "Microhard Word"), and a commitment to never feeling good enough, as if every personal narrative will devolve to some degree of disapproval.

It is the construct of personality that captivated Freud as he constructed a theory of the mind, the ego, id, and superego, as well as the concept of defense mechanisms, emerging as major ingredients of his groundbreaking attempts to formulate a systematic theory of personality. Parents, naturally, played major roles in his theory. The ego and superego, in some respects, were derived from family functions and gender related demands of traditional mothers and fathers.

In the eyes of contemporary family system theorists, however, Freud never fully acknowledged the drama that is the family itself, what Augustus Napier and Carl Whitaker call "the family crucible,"[15] namely, the allocation of power and recognition, the various roles members are required to perform, the alliances made between and among individual members, the manner in which the world of one person ramifies in the worlds of all the other family members, and the various degrees of closeness or separation established by individual members. For family system therapists, family members behave primarily as a function of their interactions, not necessarily their individual personalities. Psychoanalytic thinking, in contrast, urged observers of families, or more specifically, observers of children like me who were pushed into psychotherapy at early ages, to see little more than the unconscious secrets and instinctual forces that theoretically dominate one's actions and emotions, thereby implicitly teaching us that no one but we ourselves contribute to our unhappiness.

Less concerned with *why* people acted in a certain manner and more concerned with *what* people did in their families, various family system theorists suggested that it was precisely in the ordinary operations of everyday life that families are seen to unravel, or, conversely, reveal their greatest strengths. The way I announced William Kapell's death to my mother is raw meat for the family therapist. Of course individual personalities and temperaments play their part in the family crucible, but they are hardly the only part. They may be the piano soloist, but they are neither the entire orchestra nor ultimately the completed composition.

Personalities aside, what was the role played by my maternal grandmother in the life of her youngest daughter? How did she deal with her husband who clearly saw my mother as the person to garner the international acclaim he may well have desired for himself, although I do not know this last to be true? What was the effect on my mother of my grandmother's constant fretting about my mother always being away from home? How did she treat her other children, lovely to be sure, but leading lives nowhere near as thrilling as her youngest? And what of my grandfather? Is it possible that as a performing artist himself—his 1920 business card reads, "Yiddish Character Performer"—he understood intuitively the ultimate value and necessity of concertizing?

How did my mother treat her mother and father once stardom had been achieved? Did she bring them the happiness of her career? The misery of it? Did she make them proud, or constantly remind them of her unhappiness despite her acclaim? Why, as a child, did she telephone her mother but not, apparently, her father? Why in the telegram in which her father alludes to international stardom, did he have to remind her to contact her parents? How, moreover, did she treat her siblings? Who did she favor? What happened with the other siblings as a result of my mother's success? What lay at the bottom of her destructive tirades against Leah, her only unmarried sister? Who in that relationship was depending on whom? Was my mother envious of Leah's being single and hence, free to do whatever she wished? Imprisonment, after all, can take many forms. How does one explain the treatment of my parents by their siblings, one of whom telephoned me for the sole purpose of disparaging my mother within two weeks of her being buried? As insightful as I thought I was as an adolescent social worker, I had no idea how much resentment swirled around our family, much of it surfacing after both my parents had died. It was as though some people couldn't wait to express their bitterness.

My mother's actions in the house clearly contributed to the very consternation that so bedeviled her. Her treatment of all of us, and our reactions to it, bring the family system construct into full view. My mother raised me to be a successful man, perhaps even a star, although she would have fervently denied this. Whatever motives, or ambivalence, that may have lurked behind this intention, she reveals her disappointments every time I appear as though I may be wandering "off course," which I did in her eyes, for example, when I got sick. In turn, I, perhaps, resent what I only sense she wants but never hear clearly articulated.

When I was applying to colleges and feeling anxious about the process of getting accepted, my mother claimed she could not understand my uneasiness. "Who cares about those fancy schools," she always said. "My choice for you would be The University of Illinois. That way you'd be close to home." But she was lying. For later on she would say, in her inimitable joking manner of course, "If you do get into Harvard, do you think just once you could do your old mother a favor? Maybe write me a letter, it doesn't matter what it says, like you could say, 'Dear Mother, please drop dead,' but just write it on Harvard stationery so when I go to the beauty shop I could maybe drop it on the floor and then bend over and say, 'Oh, dear, I just dropped my letter from my son at HARVARD. . . .'"

Here is where family system therapists would have helped us. To begin, we needed coaching on how to deal with one another. We really couldn't speak a language that the other could fully comprehend and respond to in kind. It was always performer and audience, lecturer and student, the *schreirer* (shrieker) and the assailed victim. Our conversations were forever competitive and combative. We needed someone to say to my mother, "Don't be worried if Tommy gets a cold; all children get colds. When Tommy sees you angry he won't tell you he has a cold, as if you didn't know already." Some of the issues were just this rudimentary. My mother and I fell apart over matters as mundane as empty jelly jars. As well-intentioned as it was, the psychoanalytic work only drove us back upon ourselves. Each of us was instructed to once and for all exorcise the demons, the unconscious rubble generating our outbursts and sadness, rubble that affirmed our being defective. If only one of my therapists had suggested inviting my parents to our sessions, I would have been terrified, but exhilarated. I needed a coach and an advocate as well as an interpreter, but one who could get us to alter our dance, not one to enlighten me on the hidden significance of my personal dance of pathology for which, not surprisingly, I wanted to blame my parents. Eventually, however, I learned to hold myself responsible for all the household's sadness and turmoil, and I suspect, as I said earlier, that my mother did the same. Clearly, I needed someone to assure me that a desire to just go away and disappear was not only symptomatic of my depression, but also a disingenuous message to my parents, and a hurtful one at that.

Let me linger one moment on the notion of depression. Although we know significantly more now about the disorder, it was Freud's contention that much of depression was due to the loss of an important figure, rejection, or even emotional coldness. Freud's use of the term anaclitic depression—the word anaclitic meaning to lean—suggests the image of the child leaning on his mother, depending upon her because emotionally he cannot stand fully upright without her. We regularly see this image of a child leaning against his parent as she strokes his face, an experience of which I have no personal recollection.

The irony of anaclitic depression, however, is that when the parent moves away, the child not only topples over, but in some instances feels the parent falling on top of him. Thus, he not only is psychologically bruised by the fall, but he also feels crushed by the weight of the force lying on top of him in the form of control, guilt, resentment, narcissistic rage, and outright abuse. When Wilhelm Stekel counseled that the purpose of psychoanalysis was to help one transcend the weight of the past, he may have considered that much of the weight came not only in the form of our memories, but in the form of people treating us in ways we cannot uphold. We say we cannot tolerate particular behavior, but often it feels as if an unbearable weight keeps us from moving. Which may be the point. If I weigh you down, I assure myself that you will never move away from me, for apparently I require your presence to make me feel safe, and whole. Funny that the common expression laying a "guilt trip" on someone carries this notion of an unbearable weight. The problem is that with intense guilt we find ourselves unable to undertake any trip.

I needed someone in my mother's presence to tell me that my mother genuinely loved me and believed she was demonstrating this love when she pushed me to perform and become everything good she perceived in me. I needed someone in my mother's presence to tell me that my mother loved me so much she actually grew frightened when I revealed the slightest physical symptoms. Then I needed that person to tell my mother, in my presence, how to communicate messages so that I wouldn't automatically repudiate them and hence, renounce her. Moreover, I needed them to tell my mother that her performing in public had not the slightest connection to her love for her family, unless of course she was willing to accept the notion that everyone might have been more loving had she continued concertizing, although this is a sticking point since some of them had already told her that they might have loved her more if she stayed home. In a family systems context, when one person is desperately unhappy, all the other family members feel her weight. Thus, I needed someone to tell my mother, "Mrs. Cottle, I want you to look at your son and speak these words: 'I love you, Tommy, with all my heart.' And incidentally, Mrs. Cottle, if you think your son is coming down with a cold, move into a hotel somewhere, preferably in a city five hundred miles from Chicago. And keep in mind when you're sitting in that hotel room that not all colds are psychosomatic. Children get sick for reasons other than wanting to stick it to their mothers, or just lean on them."

Similarly, I required someone to instruct me how to speak to her, tell her who I was, what I was doing, what I was thinking. Apart from the normal aspects of an adolescent's life that he chooses to keep from his parents, I wanted to share much more with both my parents than I ever did, especially since so much of me is them. Parents' selves are intimately tied up with the selves of their children, as anyone who has ever attended a parent-teacher conference knows all too well. Even as I reach the end of my days, I'm still leaning, or at least wishing to. Thus, I too, needed instruction: "Tommy, I want you to look at your mother and speak these words: 'I love you, Mom, with all my heart.'" In truth, I never uttered this phrase. Moreover, just as my father never said the name "Gitta" in my mother's presence, I could never call her "Mom."

A family therapist would have pointed out to my parents that when I flunked that college biology course, the last place in the world for the fateful meeting with my father should have been the hospital, *his* turf, *his* site of grand success. Unconsciously, the selection of that location may have represented his expression of disappointment. A failure in biology meant that I was unconsciously resisting becoming a doctor and only psychoanalysis could lift the resistance. But someone needed to tell him, "Go to Tommy's room where *he* feels safe, and observe how personalities are influenced by the ascents and, alas, descents of individual family members." As I say, all of the counseling I received resulted in making me believe I, alone, was the source not merely of my own unhappiness, but everyone else's unhappiness as well; *I* was the family pathology. As my mother often repeated in defending her actions to my father, "If I did something bad, I learned it from a master!"

As it happened, I won some awards at summer camp. My parents determined I would enjoy the Silver Spur Ranch in Woodland Park, Colorado, in the foothills of Pikes Peak. I'm not completely certain why they believed this inasmuch as the only time I had ever ridden a horse, I had fallen off even with my Uncle Charley holding me.

Still I went, crying so profusely, at age twelve, my mother had to buy me a pair of sunglasses in the train station.

That I won any award is amazing. For in the first week of camp a horseback riding test was administered to all campers, the results posted outside the mess hall. I and another boy were tied for dead last, the two worst riders at the Silver Spur Ranch in Woodland Park, Colorado. Let the record be noted, however, that a counselor confided in me that the other boy was actually a better rider.

Walking on the Colorado Springs station platform at the end of the summer prior to boarding the train to Chicago, the wife of the camp's director put her arm around my shoulder and told me that I must not let the awards go to my head. I must be modest at all times. I promised to honor her words. I hid the trophies from my parents and told them nothing of the awards.

I recount this experience in the context of needing a family counselor to teach me how to tell my parents of the good things that occurred, how grateful I was for the Colorado experience, for it taught me a new competence, horseback riding, and how much I wanted their recognition. But that brand of coaching never arrived. A family counselor would have recognized that the alliance inherent in the skirmishes between my mother and me, however grotesque and perverse, noticeably excluded my father and sister. A family counselor might not only have transformed our destructive Oedipal tango into a loving one, but also made it so that others could dance with us. The counselor may also have recognized that given the relationships she had with her own father and husband, I may have been the only male with whom she could allow herself to be openly furious. Surely the counselor could have taught us how to ask for the nourishment we required from the others, and how to deal with us when, in hunger, we became especially crabby, frightened, impetuous, and raging. A family counselor could have helped us formulate requests rather than believe that performance, artful or perverse, was the only way anyone could ever garner recognition. The counselor could have taught us how to move toward each other rather than run away in anger or, conversely, become so enmeshed with one another we couldn't even detect where one person's neurosis or wiring ended and the other's began. I would happily have settled for sole ownership of my anger and depression.

In helping us to establish healthy physical and emotional boundaries, ones that protect not only individual narratives and individual integrity but interpersonal relationships and narratives as well, the counselor may have removed an invisible boundary that kept my father from entering my bedroom. Miss Yarnell, a stately woman who taught us as grade school children how to ballroom dance and whose voice I can still hear singing out in the school's gymnasium, "Not too close, not too close," might have helped us as much as many of those highly skilled psychoanalysts. After several months of work, Miss Yarnell might have changed her chant to, "Not close enough. Not close enough." Gitta and Tommy could have danced a whole lot closer and nobody's toes would have been stepped on. Maurie and Tommy could have danced now and again as well, and no one would have looked twice.

Finally, Tommy would have enjoyed seeing his mother and father dance together, just dance, not perform. For their dance, like his dances with each of them individually, would have strengthened him and made him feel more confident in managing not only the problems of his little world, but also the inevitable problems inherent in both his software and hardware. It would have helped him to recognize that not everything one experiences is a matter of life or death; some things can remain, merely, a matter of life. A little screwy wiring needn't be destructive if one knows it is properly encased and safeguarded by family. That is, if family members are genuinely allowing and encouraging others in the family to be the people they are "meant" to be, and not the people these family members need other people to be. And heaven knows, we all needed my mother to be someone, apparently, she was not meant to be, or not meant to be full time.

How to summarize these constructs regularly used to explain the nature of families? On the one hand, the best way, perhaps, is to offer up the words heard by every human being who ever inquired about his or her parents, the very words my Aunt Leah spoke a thousand times to me: "They did the best they could." On the other hand, an irony remains: The very tools of psychology I prematurely, and inexactly, employed to battle my mother and protect myself from external assault or internal eruption, are the ones to which I presently turn in order to allow myself to imagine that I understand her, and was loved by her.

As I look back upon my mother's life, I feel more than ever the giant shadow cast by her father, one that both ennobled and troubled her. Sadly, her family could never help her completely step away from that shadow, nor apparently, could all the psychoanalysis she underwent. Similarly, all my life I, too, felt caught in a shadow, this one, ironically, cast by her, a shadow that, during my adolescence, injured and diminished me. I, too, felt that neither psychotherapy nor my father served to extricate me. I'm sure my father would have, if only he knew how. Then again, he led a life dictated in part by the seeds he carried from prior generations. Accordingly, he chose not to focus on the turmoil that surrounded him, turmoil that may have been avoided had he insisted my mother continue concertizing. He, too, cast a rather formidable shadow, on me and his wife as well. Still, making one's life about someone else is the most noble task of all. Jokingly, we say it is the reason God created mothers. I like to think it's the reason God created adults.

Having made an effort not to forgive my mother, exactly, but only to recognize who and what she was, I feel for the first time comforted by that very same shadow, proud of it, and her, and grateful that it, and she, are forever lodged in my soul as my very being, along with my father's shadow as well. But shadows come with a price. There is always a lingering sadness. Ultimately I am the cause of my parents' unhappiness. Not surprisingly, one of family therapist Murray Bowen's provocative criteria for a healthy family remains etched in my brain: "The healthy family," Bowen claimed, "allows each of its members their own emptiness."[16] I take his words to mean that I wasn't the cause of *all* my family's struggles, maybe just the significant ones.

And herein lies another insidious irony that silently passes on to the next generation. I brought this same attitude to parenting. All too frequently I communicated to our children precisely what my mother always claimed. I was a master teacher of badness. If our children struggled with something, it inevitably had to be because of me. How fascinating, and, as I say, insidious, this role of narcissism, broken love, and broken spirits, this need to have others reassure one that it is all right to remain alive.

Bad enough that one should be so self-preoccupied there is no room for anyone else in his life, unless, of course, they want to serve him in some fashion. Add to this the notion that the narcissist cannot permit another person to create his or her own allusions and neuroses. He or she is always there to claim the patent for any neurosis anyone establishes. Claiming the patent and insisting that one is the source of the problem remains anything but an affirmation of the other self. It is dis-affirmation of the worst order, because it constantly forces the other person into the posture of granting mercy rather than allowing the other person to discover his/her own life, much less come to terms with his/her own anger at the narcissist. If I regularly cause you to engage in rituals of forgiveness of me, then you can never get angry at me. This, for certain, I have precluded. I have kept the raging wolves away from my door. Which means not only have I prevented you from claiming your own legitimate emptiness, but I have prevented you from expressing whatever emotions you wish to express and designing whatever life you wish to design. Apparently I don't have the courage to let you go. At least I hope you're there, for I am still leaning.

Final Concert

*O*n the occasion of their fiftieth wedding anniversary, June 8, 1976, my parents, along with my sister and her family joined us for a weeklong celebration in London where we were living at the time. Kay and I arranged for a week of spectacles: a ballet with Rudolf Nureyev, a Sunday afternoon concert featuring pianist Daniel Barenboim, and a play starring Paul Scofield. The celebration commenced with dinner at the posh Belvedere Restaurant in Hyde Park, capped off with bowls of raspberries and cream, extra helpings of which I took when the waiters weren't looking. We even arranged to spend an evening outside of London at Ye Olde Belle, one of England's oldest inns, where at breakfast my father ate kippers, a food he had adored since childhood.

In his late seventies, it was evident that my father was viewing England for the last time. Ironically, on the afternoon of my parents' arrival on our way to Louie's, the Hampstead sweet shop we frequented with our children, my father discovered he had lost his wallet. In it was every piece of identification he owned, his credit cards, driver's and medical licenses, and perhaps a hundred dollars in cash. Such an experience would have driven my mother and me crazy. I would immediately feel that there was no reason to continue living. Already someone would have charged eight million dollars on my credit cards and begun practicing clinical psychology, which would mean I would be brought before the Massachusetts board of examiners.

Not so my father. He was perfectly unruffled, may I say, characteristically British. "There's no problem," he announced quietly. "This is England. It will be returned to me, and nothing will be taken. There is still honor here." On occasions of this sort, I would notice his speech retreating ever so slightly back to his original British accent. The pronunciation of a word like garage became softer, the emphasis falling on the first syllable, *gare*-ahge, and peppermint became peppa-mint.

My father was as loyal to Great Britain as he was antagonistic to its monarchy. He abhorred the idea of a monarchy doing nothing while living off the taxes of the working class, the stratum in which he had been raised. The idea of ascriptive success, generally, troubled him: The more wealth into which one was born, the more one had to *prove* one's worth. The Kennedy children were for him perfect examples of an admirable work ethic. There was nothing more noble than disciplined labor, whatever the field, especially when one had no financial incentive. Still, I found his prediction of the wallet's return as naive as his romanticization of his homeland. Then again, he was a man two years shy of his eightieth birthday, and this may have been his final journey home.

Toward the end of the anniversary celebration, my father earnestly suggested that I would love to see the two seaside towns where he spent vacations as a child. This was his characteristic tone. My father told rather than requested. We rented a car and headed off to the seaside villages of Ramsgate and Margate on England's east coast. While there, my father pointed out the little buildings a few turnings from the seashore where he and his family had resided some seventy years before. He was amazed at how little had changed, and how beautiful the towns still looked. In contrast, I was amazed at how unattractive I found both towns. Evidently, he had maintained an idealized vision, and version, of the past. I am not alone, at least, in this one narrative endeavor.

That my father located places where he had stayed during the summers stood in sharp contrast to our first sojourn in England twenty-three years earlier. On the occasion of that trip, the one concluding with the treacherous car ride over the Alps, my father wanted me to see the neighborhood east of St. Paul's Cathedral where he had grown up. The year was 1953. As we walked the streets of London's East End where few tourists would have reason to explore, my father spoke of Hitler's vengeful plan to bomb the communities of London inhabited by Jewish families. How ironic that because of their proximity to St. Paul's, no targets could have more infuriated the British. He spoke of his relatives who, cramped together in the deep tube stations, survived the shelling of London. Every street now was familiar to him. At each corner, he would announce the name of the street we were about to encounter.

Arriving at Philpott Street, his excitement grew palpable. "We lived at 27 . . . which would be . . . on the other side . . . right there!" And together we looked across the street where the house was meant to be, but there was nothing to be seen, nothing, that is, but a bomb crater around which a shabby wooden fence had been erected. My father was stunned. I could barely look at the site, he could barely take his eyes off it. We stood silent for minutes. Finally, he said simply, "It's time to go now."

My parents' anniversary visit with us lasted one week. Upon returning to his office, my father found a small package awaiting him. It contained his wallet with all its contents, money included, intact, precisely as he had foreseen, along with the professional business card of the sender.

Given my father's history, it would appear that by fiat he accepted the role of family protector no matter what the context. Late in the evening, with people of all ages gathered in the living room at Hawthorne Place, he would announce, "Well, children, it's time for bed." It wasn't precisely that he was controlling us, although I often felt as if he were; he was merely looking out for people, making certain they would get their rest. Probably too, somewhere in the recesses of his mind, he was re-experiencing the bedtime rituals of his own childhood when he helped his mother get his six siblings into their two or three beds. He was protecting people even then, and he never lost the sense that this was his central purpose in life. When my mother would look disdainfully at me at the dinner table, flare her nostrils and announce, "If I have done anything bad I learned it from a master: HIM!" my father would smack the table and shout: "NOW STOP IT!" And, like children chastised by their father, we would.

My father worked six full days a week and a half day on Sunday. He left the house before seven in the morning, typically driving my sister and me to school. From there he went to the hospital, then to his downtown office, returning around six in the evening whereupon entering the house he whistled for us. Ambitious, intellectually curious, and committed to medicine and his patients, I also believe that at least two other factors shaped his work patterns, which in turn shaped the role he necessarily played with me.

First, he clearly did not appreciate the tension that, like tea, perpetually brewed in his house. He could take only so much bickering.

I know he hated the notion of his wife blaming his son for the brewing, but he never knew how to deal with it other than to slam his hand down on the table and state with old world male authority: "NOW STOP IT!" I am sure that he, too, longed for the nights of the soirées, for they guaranteed that his wife, for a while anyway, would appear not only beautiful, but full of joy and confidence as well. He was free to delight in it all.

I imagine he also disliked the tension because it hurled him back to his childhood days when much of his life revolved around family dilemmas, which meant that he had to solve the problems of other family members in the manner of the traditional mother or, in his case, mother's aide. Psychologists refer to children like my father as "parentified children." I believe, moreover, that he brought to our family a heightened sense of personal responsibility and morality often laced with resentment for having to play the paternal role by the time he was ten years old. Perfectly happy to be our father, I think parenting for him always evoked a sense of time being lost, time that might better be devoted to work. Or was it that he thought of the time that had been taken away during his youth by dint of his own father not owning up to his paternal responsibilities? Perhaps this meant that acting as father evoked his own longing for a father. No one ever took care of my father. He never even appreciated the nature of hospital care until the end of his life when he became a patient. He took care of everything, and everyone. I recognize that some people resented this quality in him, feeling perhaps that he was patronizing or even infantilizing them, but he had never been taught another way. His culture instructed precisely this orientation of protecting and providing. His wife did not always offer him a full partnership in this caring business, and it troubled him.

Television's Mr. Rogers came to Hawthorne Place one Saturday afternoon, along with a camera crew, to interview my parents, about me, actually. That Fred was himself an accomplished pianist and his wife a concertizing pianist only enhanced the glow of that one experience. My mother even played for him. Fred's thank you note, dated March 5, 1980, revealed how charmed by them he had been. He even used the magical Hawthorne Place word, "sensitive:"

> You must have sensed (because you're such sensitive
> people) how much your warm welcome meant to all of us
> who came to be with you this past weekend. . . . I felt that

we had been friends forever. . . . After meeting Tom, I had the feeling that his mother and dad had to be very special persons.

Fred's genuine sweetness allowed my father, sitting on the little couch where Jofe always sat, to go on record about this matter of proper parenting. Looking first at Fred, then glancing quickly at my mother, he said, "It was not easy for Tommy growing up in this house." It was not easy at times for my father either.

In one of the most complicated tricks of generational succession, my father gave me everything his father failed to give him, save one. I didn't have to work, I didn't have to sleep on the floor cushioned by the cuttings of fabrics, and I never had to concern myself with the well-being of siblings. But like many sons I wanted more of him, and not understanding the ways of culture, much less the personal dynamics of a man who, by sheer chance, was my father, I blamed myself for his seeming lack of interest in me or the decisions he made regarding his daily activities. In the psychoanalytic sense, I internalized all of this information and patted it into shape so that it would fit neatly into my own developing sense of identity, that, not so incidentally, contained rather large amounts of loneliness.

Even as he was dying, in a state of incoherence that could not have been more unlike this articulate man who spoke several languages—he was tutored in Spanish so that he might deliver a lecture in Mexico City in the native language—he was consumed with obligations. Lying in a hospital bed, his dying breaths punctuated by a squeaky sound that rose at the end almost in the tone of a question, he appeared to reveal an agitated concern. I bent over and assured him that everything was taken care of. All he had to do now was rest comfortably. His responsibilities were finally over. His concern was with a bill owed to Simon Drugs, a neighborhood pharmacy that had closed its doors more than fifteen years before.

My father succumbed to multiple myeloma. A dreadful illness of the bone marrow, it plays a series of cruel jokes on those who suffer with it. Often living free of any symptoms, people are shocked to learn on routine examinations that they are gravely ill, although my father did experience a foreshadowing in the form of bouts of extreme fatigue. For long periods of time, multiple myeloma patients appear to be perfectly healthy. Then, without warning, these stretches of remission recede and it appears as though the patients now surely will die. Hospitalization, of course, is required, and visitors may believe they are witnessing their loved ones perishing in front of them.

On one such occasion, my father, appearing to have been in a coma for several days, awakened and magically his strength began to return. In response, I decided to transport his favorite foods to the hospital, notably stuffed cabbage which Leah always served to him in a huge tureen. The food, coupled, no doubt, with the natural cycle of the illness and the effects of the medication and blood transfusions, brought him back to life. This vacillation between impending tragedy and normality, the very scene that seemed to characterize my mother's daily mood swings, actually occurred several times. The re- coveries were such that he resumed his medical practice, actually performing surgery into his eighties.

As the months went on, however, his body lost its capacity to fight the disease, and he was spending longer periods of time falling asleep in front of the television set in an ugly gray flannel easy boy chair in my parents' bedroom. I visited him several times during these months, seeing now a very old man. On one trip I was accom- panied by our son, then eight years old, who, recognizing my sad- ness, offered to travel to Chicago merely to be with me. I explained to Jason that this was not going to be a fun excursion, but he trav- eled with me nonetheless. I remember thinking how much my fa- ther would have appreciated this boy's sensitive gesture. My obvious sadness was also not lost on our two daughters, the youngest, not quite three at the time, making the following pronouncement upon hearing my wife and me speak of my father's illness: "Well," she began portentously, "life is mysterious and shitty."

After several days in the hospital, my mother, sister, and I keeping watch on him, it was evident that the end was at hand. Sit- ting in a chair in the dimmest corner of the hospital room, my mother revealed none of the emotions we all recognized lived within her, and offered few words. No longer was she uttering her wishful sentiment: "Who knows, maybe we'll catch a break." Finally, the doctors approached us regarding the futility of the platelet transfu- sions. Should we, perhaps, pull the plug? Rightly, my sister said yes, but I couldn't get myself to agree, or disagree. "I abstain," I told the doctors, which essentially meant I passively concurred. My mother took no part in the voting.

We were in the dining room at Hawthorne Place, in sight of the breakfront which housed my father's Asian treasures, when Dr.

Braun, my father's old friend and colleague, telephoned to say that my father had died. Dr. Braun, too, was heartbroken.

We went at once to the hospital but there was little for us to do. We were merely visiting with him for the last time. Each of us in turn kissed him goodbye. My mother leaned over him, kissed his forehead, and said softly, but with measured certainty, "I shall join you soon." Reflecting on this moment, I am reminded of Ignaz Friedmann asking her, "How sure are you before you walk on the concert stage?" And her reply, "Sure enough."

Then, in the midst of our sadness and confusion, I was notified that there was a phone call for me. It was an emergency. What could be so pressing? The call turned out to be from one of my father's brothers who insisted that my father be buried in a mausoleum with his late wife. The man was well-intentioned, but I have always thought this was God's way of offering a moment of levity. My sister and mother actually grinned at the incongruity of my father lying eternally next to his sister-in-law. I just know my father would have laughed out loud at the prospect.

Even from the grave my father protected and provided for people. On the day following his death, I accompanied my mother to a funeral home on Chicago's north side where we selected a simple wooden casket and arranged for services and burial. The man across the desk from us could not have been more officious, or insensitive. He, of course, had no idea that the broken woman sitting with me was once a glorious figure in Chicago's music and social worlds. After burying his head in some papers, he looked up at me with a quizzical expression as a sardonic laugh started to form, He said: "Your father was one peculiar man. It says here he owns *eight* graves at Westlawn Cemetery. Can you explain to me, I wonder, why any man would need *eight* plots?"

I completely lost it; my mother, however, was silent. Years before she would have strangled the man with words just as the critics had used to describe her New York debut: "Splendidly virile attack . . . admirably controlled temperament from persuasive lyricism to brittle hardness, and when she lashes out, tigerlike. . . ."[1]

Now, in the shabby office of the funeral home director, words that well may have been uttered by her were coming from my own mouth. "Strange?" I began, matching the funeral director's sardonic tones with my own, and showing him not a scintilla of respect. Little did he know that Hawthorne Place was the site of the university one attended if one sought a doctorate in sarcasm. "What the hell's so Goddamn strange about a man buying all these graves? Might it have dawned on you that he bought graves for relatives who might not have had the money to buy their own? Or for his wife and children? Can you understand *that*? Because if you can't, here's something you *would* understand. How much do you think he paid for those plots fifty years ago? And what do you think they're worth now? How 'bout *that* for a wise business deal, huh?"

I was infuriated. This nobody was insulting a man we were about to bury? I heard my mother say very quietly: "Tommy." She never looked up. Her face was buried in a black cloth coat that she wore on a sunny May morning in Chicago. Only recently have I learned that the older one gets, the more layers of clothes one wears. Then quietly I heard her utter the Yiddish word she always used to describe someone of this sort: "*Yutz.*"

My father's death, the funeral arrangements that had to be made, the act of buying a coffin and steel coffin liner, something I had never heard of, yielded a perfectly surreal few days. Having given in to my sister's insistence that I deliver a eulogy, I went to my father's second-floor study and sat at his desk peering at the objects upon it as if magically they would yield up the proper sentiments and words. It was in this very spot that my father remarked to Judy: "If you can't keep up with the times, you don't deserve to live *in* the times." Instinctively, I turned to what my father would have turned to: the books. I decided that my remembrances of him would be laced with passages from the volumes that obviously had meaning for him. Why else would they now be resting on his personal desk?

The books I discovered, many of them with scraps of paper marking important passages, made the task relatively easy. Predictably, there were volumes of poetry and letters, the correspondence between Freud and the surgeon Wilhelm Fleiss, history, philosophy, psychology, and medicine. I read bits from almost all of them recalling, in particular, a passage from Francis Collingwood where my father had underscored the writer's notion that the most important profession was human conduct.

Following the eulogy, I received the condolences of his many friends and surviving family members, one of whom congratulated me saying I spoke beautifully given my speech impediment. I thanked her profusely. All these years and no one had ever told me I had a speech impediment. Was this something else I could lay at the feet of my parents? Not only had they *caused* me to have a speech impediment, they never got around to telling me I had one. "You could tell me," I began diffidently, "what is my speech impediment?"

"Well, surely, you must know."

"I guess I don't." What I wanted to say was, "I used to know but I forgot."

"You have a sibilant "s" which you cover up very nicely. My daughter and I both noticed it. You know, you can have therapy for it."

"I'll have to look into that."

"They can help you. Sorry about your dad."

Automatically, I glanced at my mother who had heard the entire exchange. Once again, I heard her utter "yutz" in that inimitable tone.

Then, out of the corner of my eye, I spied Elaine Hacker making her way down the aisle in my direction. When I was young and she was Elaine Sampson, the daughter of Sophie and Sam, our Passover seder hosts, she was my personally adopted oldest sister. Elaine was the person who chauffeured me to the Michigan City, Indiana, bookstore when I was too young to drive so that I might purchase a copy of *The Castle* by Franz Kafka. The saleswoman had not heard of the book and wondered about it. "It's a novel," we told her.

"Oh," she said, looking suddenly glum, "we have fiction and nonfiction but no novels."

By now my personal driver was Dr. Elaine Hacker, psychiatrist, and as she walked toward me I thought of evenings at Hawthorne Place with all those psychoanalysts present, and the role psychoanalysis had played in my own life, people interpreting every remark and gesture and finding them all of supreme significance. What would Elaine, now steeped in all that psychiatric literature, say to me in this moment? She moved close to me, put her arms around me and just held me. Then at last I heard her whisper, "I love you."

Returning from the funeral, I wasn't in the house on Hawthorne Place two minutes when I heard a neighbor advising my mother: "Gitta, you've got to get out of this house. Why on earth would you want to stay in such a barn all by yourself?" On the spot I intervened, telling my mother in front of that presumptuous woman, "Don't do anything you don't want to do. You want to stay here, you stay here. You have years, the rest of your life, to make any decisions. Have some students move in to look after things if you want. Don't listen to anyone but yourself." In the very entrance hall, the scene of some of our most vicious verbal encounters, I had become her protector. I, the person who, as an adolescent, would have given anything if she had moved out of the house if only for a few days to give us all a moment of peace, was assuring her she could remain within these rooms forever. I don't know whether she even heard me.

I was speaking, moreover, in behalf of a woman who, but a few days before, had leant down to kiss the forehead of her dead husband and whispered the words: "I shall join you soon." Not once in my life did I ever hear him call her by her name, Gitta, only "Dear," or "Lovey." She used the same terms with him, but his name as well—Maurie. He may not have been a part of the Horowitz menage, but she was proud of him, and he was her anchor. He knew it, she knew it, we all knew it. Indeed, he protected us from her at times. He protected her as well, for there were moments when I saw her turn to him as a father figure and in a child's voice call him "Pappy." On June 8, 1979, the occasion of their fifty-third wedding anniversary, she offered this inscription to him on a handsome card:

> This is such a precious day for us—we are blessed people to have had a long, beautiful life together. By now you know—I live for your love! If it is possible I love you more than ever. I cherish every moment with you and will always be deeply grateful for your love and devotion, and your sensitive response to my silent thoughts. G—

I imagined she viewed Rachmaninoff and Frederick Stock, the conductor of the Chicago Symphony, as father figures as well. She seemed comfortable with Dr. Stock, as if she knew he would never let anything untoward happen to her during a performance. This in contrast, perhaps, to the sort of fright her own father had created by his well-intentioned insistence that she develop her talent and launch a career (too) early in life. My father, conversely, never publicly turned to her as a mother figure. His own mother, presumably, represented the only substantial maternal object he would ever require.

Standing next to my mother in the crowded living room, the site of all the soirées, where people were beginning to sit *Shiva* for my father, I was advised that there was a telephone call for me from one of my father's friends. The voice was unfamiliar but it was kindly and filled with expressions of sympathy. "Your father was a great man," he began, "I'm sure you will miss him."

"Yes, we will," I replied, still unable to believe that my father was really gone. I honestly imagined that at any moment he would enter the living room with a tray of drinks and offer up some statement in which he referred to everyone present as children.

"Now then," the man went on, "several weeks ago, actually, your dad bought your mom a diamond ring as a surprise. She wouldn't know about any of this. Anyway, he put about 10 percent of the cost down and unfortunately I now must ask you for the rest. It amounts to three thousand dollars. I really hate bothering you at this particular moment, but I'm sure you can understand my position."

"Absolutely," I responded. "My father was a man of his word, ethical to the core." During income tax season, my father actually hunted longer for income receipts to send on to his accountant than receipts documenting legitimate deductions. "I would be totally remiss not to fulfill every outstanding obligation."

"I know that he was. As I say, he was a great man."

"Look, I don't know who you are, but if you'd like to come by the house right now I'd be happy to give you the money. Personal check be all right?"

"That'd be fine."

"Of course," I continued, "you don't know what I look like, so let me describe myself. I'm about six feet one inch, and have curly brown hair. I'll be the one standing next to the vice officer."

With that, I heard the phone go dead.

What a scam some people run, reading the names of the deceased in the morning's obituary pages and then pulling numbers from the phone book on the days of funerals. Apparently the scheme proves successful often enough that it gets repeated. This scam, however, was dead on arrival. My father putting down short money and paying the remainder on time? My father buying anything on margin? My father invented the phrase: "If you don't have the money in your pocket to buy a car you can't afford it!" As for the diamond ring, this man didn't know Gitta Gradova. Oh, she swooned over many a diamond necklace and earring set in her time, but she wouldn't have worn a diamond ring, as she herself would have said, if she could have seen her mother one more time.

My father, the grand knight and protector, was gone. As trite as it sounds, a part of all of our lives died with his passing and the eventual sale of the Hawthorne Place house. The people and the house were inextricable, and during the Saturday evening soirées they were all nothing short of spectacular. If any one of those guests listens intently, and, of course, sensitively, the echoes of those evenings can still be heard.

"Darling, Gitta, how do we thank you for such a precious night? I'm calling you first thing in the morning."

"Thanking me is easier than you think. Don't call me in the morning!"

With the days of the soirées officially over, my mother, now in her mid-seventies, undertook the superhuman effort of moving from a huge house to a lovely but considerably smaller apartment, one block away, actually, from Madame Herz's studio on Grand Boulevard, now Bellevue Place. The physical ordeal of moving, not to mention the psychological cost, assuredly cut her days short. I know she did it for her children. She didn't want us to face all the objects and even more, the emotionally wrenching decisions. The biggest burden of my childhood, she wished to spare me of every life burden.

Seeing her in her new home was as unsettling as it was incongruous. It would have been less bizarre to see my mother walking around Hawthorne Place in a thong bikini. This was not the way she was meant to live, although she had grown up in relative poverty on Chicago's southwest side, a neighborhood one could almost discern from the windows in her new bedroom looking out on Chicago's "backyard." For all I know, she may have been able to pinpoint South Avers Avenue from which she had been wrenched more than sixty-five years before.

My mother living in this apartment seemed perfectly incongruous. Despite the strange sensation of sitting in a small handsome kitchen on a black bench I had never met—it now sits in our entrance hall—at a narrow shiny black kitchen table, which we also possess, it was good to see the old friends, the Steinways, in her new living room. Still, this new setting was never right, somehow, no matter how elegant the appointments. Only the bathrooms in the new apartment were superior to Hawthorne Place, though noticeably smaller—ultramodern fixtures, marble tile on the walls and floors, and lights hidden beneath the vanity in the guest bath. By now, all her siblings and many of her cherished in-laws and friends were gone.

For her eightieth birthday, my sister and I decided to throw my mother a surprise party in a Chicago eatery. My sister, without any signs of fretting, did all of the planning. Notwithstanding her hatred of surprise parties, my mother of course attended it, putting on a good face, just as she did in her new home, even though it was evident she would never be happy there. I always felt the new apartment would kill her; however, I knew she would never move closer to her children. A widow who now rarely socialized, dreaded spending money on herself for she feared that her money would run out. She regularly called her nephews who looked out for her financial concerns, convinced that her money was quickly ebbing away. Everyone told her to treat herself. She did buy, however, for everyone but herself.

As it turned out, the party's surprise that one August afternoon was on us. For, after the toasts and celebrations with people who had attended the soirées and dinner parties years before, it was my mother's turn. As I say, show me a gathering of three hundred and fifty people ranging in age from two to a hundred and they will all remember best that one fabulous storytelling woman.

Indeed she did have a story for us. My mother was returning to the concert stage, Ravinia Park no less, the summer music festival site located in Highland Park, one of Chicago's northern suburbs. Ironically, it was at Ravinia that she had played one of her last concerts before retiring. She would be playing the Rachmaninoff Piano Concerto no. 1 with the Chicago Symphony Orchestra under the direction of guest conductor James Levine, whom she called Jimmy; she often referred to him as the "kingpin of Ravinia Park." I wouldn't play with anyone else," she said. "Rach One," as she affectionately referred to the piece, was the one concerto of Rachmaninoff's she had never publicly performed. Decades before, she had promised Sergei Vassilievich that she would play his First Concerto before she died. Enrico Caruso was right: "When you hear that an artist intends to retire," he once remarked, "don't you believe it, for as long as he keeps his voice he will sing. You may depend upon that."[2]

The Ravinia concert was scheduled for the following summer, July 5, 1985, forty-four years from the date of her last Ravinia appearance when she had played Rachmaninoff's *Rhapsody on a Theme of Paganini*, forty-three years from the date of her last performances in Carnegie Hall with the New York Philharmonic with Sir John Barbirolli conducting. The Ravinia concert would also include Wagner's Overture, *The Flying Dutchman*, and Gershwin's *The Cuban Overture* and *American in Paris*. Gershwin and Rachmaninoff together, precisely as she had arranged decades before. A contract had been signed. She would be receiving five thousand dollars.

At age eighty, with nerves of freshly forged steel and a strength that returned from heaven knows where, my mother practiced in her new apartment every day. To help her prepare, the young Russian pianist, Vladimir Ashkenazy, told her he would be willing to come to Chicago and play second piano for her. I could only imagine the two slender wedding rings being removed and placed on the piano shelf. I could only imagine the pedaling, the finger exercises, the occasional retreats to Czerny and Bach, and the Rachmaninoff-like passages of the extemporaneous concerto that comprised her daily lyrical warmup. I always hoped she would get a dog to keep her company—Patsy had died many years before—if only to sleep on the floor beneath the piano, its head resting on the pedals.

As the months wore on and the anticipation began building, to say the least, Chicago friends reported that her playing was beautiful, and powerful. That she was even willing to rehearse in their presence represented a colossal step. This was going to be neither a joke nor a freak show. "Not too bad for an old broad, if I have to say so myself," she would tell me on the phone when I inquired of her progress. Steven Heliotes, a young man who visited her from time to time, marveled at her playing. He later sent a tape recording he had made. She was going to do it, by God! And there would be no music on the music stand either. Whether undertaking the concert terrified her or not, "Rach One" would be memorized!

In an effort to record history accurately, even if it diminishes the drama of the narrative somewhat, it must be reported that the Ravinia concert would not be the first time the public would hear my mother since her retirement, aside, of course, from the soirées. There had actually been one small concert several years before her surprise party announcement.

Like most urban centers, Chicago is home to a variety of clubs, many of them rather exclusive. My parents were never ones to belong to country clubs. They detested the notion that religion and race might be employed for membership selection. They did, however, belong to The Arts Club which was housed in a handsome building on Ohio Street, a few blocks east of Dr. Mohr's office.

Hardly without its own brand of exclusivity, The Arts Club, as the name suggests, required that candidates for admission be practicing artists. Money may have played a role in one's candidacy, but only artists and their spouses could join. The Weisses also were members of the club. Ed Weiss was not only one of Chicago's preeminent advertising executives, but a professional portrait artist as well.

Over the years, my mother became a member of the Club's music committee which periodically arranged concerts for members and their guests in a lovely open space, followed by an elegant dinner in the equally elegant dining room. I attended a few of these events, particularly when my mother had been responsible for booking a performing artist, one of whom was a young South American marimba player. I was certain this man would conclude his performance by looking out at the opulent audience and saying something like: "Well, rich folks, what'd you think of that? Too far out for you?" Of course, the man said nothing, but these words could well have been spoken by my mother who feared her fellow members would not appreciate this sort of evening. They did enjoy it, however, but not as enthusiastically as they did the night my mother and her friend, the cellist Raya Garbousova, played the Rachmaninoff Cello Sonata in the small Arts Club concert hall.

Raya and her husband Kurt Biss, a scientist with a curious and organized mind, were regulars at the Hawthorne Place soirées. A short woman with small hands that one would never associate with cello playing, Raya regularly called me "Joseph," and never came to the house when she didn't speak about her own son. It was clear that she liked me, but I always felt frustrated not knowing what to say when she listed her son's recent accomplishments. It always made me think that my parents and their friends belonged to a generation who were no less proud of their children than my own generation of parents. The only difference is that we tell our children directly of our pride in them, whereas my parents' generation, probably overeducated with psychoanalytic theory, told everyone *but* their children. Someone, perhaps the inventor of those clear plastic mitts for children, came up with the misguided notion that one didn't tell one's child good things for fear that it would only give the child a swelled head. I imagine these parents confused Freud's notion of transference and the alleged nondirective silence of the psychoanalyst with proper parenting. What else *does* one want to communicate to a child other than that their head, and hence their being, is perfectly swell?

The thought of my mother playing a concert at The Arts Club sent a wave of excitement and dread across Hawthorne Place. If something was bound to derail Volodja the night before the momentous

Carnegie Hall "Grand Return Concert," then inevitably something had to backfire to prevent the concert with Raya Garbousova from occurring. No question but that a wizard and a Cyclops would hit Chicago on that fateful Sunday spring evening.

Predictably, the rehearsals with Raya caused my mother to feel anxiety. It wasn't going to work out well. Frankly, upon hearing the initial rehearsals, I doubt that anyone could have predicted the final form of the concert. The rehearsals were uneven, beautiful in some spots, but precarious at best at other spots. I remember feeling this concert was going to be like traveling across an immaculately engineered suspension bridge which, from a distance, appears to be in perfect condition. Then, when one is already halfway across its span, it gives way and one falls to his death thousands of feet below. Perhaps it would be best if my wife and I had something unexpectedly come up that Sunday so we could miss the bridge completely. Perhaps my back could conveniently go out. Many years later, I learned that my mother had asked Kay to turn pages for her, but my mother's apprehension had become so contagious, my wife, a person of exquisite equanimity, politely declined.

The anxiety grew exponentially as the days to the concert counted down. The mood around Hawthorne Place during the final countdown hours was probably not too different than the mood in any regular old death row facility prior to an execution. My mother vacillated between barely reasonable calm and a form of chaotic, tremulous distress that I could not remember ever having observed. It was as if her conscious and unconscious had traded places. I remember asking my father whether the concert venue might be shifted to a locked ward in a mental hospital? He thought my attempt at a joke vulgar, but my mother's frantic pacing and her desperation at the sudden loss of mundane lists and bills, telephone messages, or items of clothing, all of which, of course, turned up, were driving everyone mad. I could not believe that a human being could work themselves into such a frenzied state and still remain alive. Human hearts, brains, and intestines have exploded at far less provocation.[3]

Sunday finally arrived. It was only hours now before the execution. The scene at Hawthorne Place truly had become death row central with time itself totally altered. The stretch from 9:00 A.M. until noon took precisely eleven hours. Every second of the afternoon was experienced as an hour. Finally, it was time to leave for

The Arts Club. My mother and Raya were going to meet for a quick last minute run-through before the audience arrived. I was certain I had begun to hear the sounds of the bridge cables cracking.

Then, upon reaching The Arts Club, like an ominous storm turning into the clearest day of one's entire life, my mother was overtaken by calmness, every pore of her soul, seemingly, filled with serenity. She sat peacefully in a high-backed chair in the club's entry hall looking elegant, fashionable, gorgeous, exactly as Constance Keene had appeared during the hours before her Chicago performance years before. The bridge was going to hold after all. Not only would no one fall to their death, The Arts Club audience would be treated to a soaring rendition of the Rachmaninoff Cello Sonata played by two confident artists. For that one performance, I heard not one note of the cello line. Gitta Gradova was back, and the entire audience loved it! More importantly, so did she.

The post-concert appreciation went on for hours. My mother played the role of a distinctly modest but distinctly captivating celebrity. Afterwards, she ate like a horse, for she had carefully watched her diet over the prior weeks. She enjoyed every instant of an evening where not only did time resume its normal tempo, but seemed to go noticeably faster than usual. I had to admit I was stunned by the transformation of her personality and, of course, her glorious playing. The blend of accompanist and soloist in such a sonata is difficult to achieve, but as always her taste, lyricism, and interpretations were impeccable, as was her ability to conjoin individual and ensemble playing. Rachmaninoff, I am certain, would have smiled had he heard the performance, in the same way that he smiled at hearing my mother play his *Paganini Variations*, if Abram Chasins' account is to be believed.[4] I thought my mother made Raya look even better, but I am certain that Raya and Kurt drove home that evening feeling that the cellist had clearly carried the pianist.

So this was what it was once like. This was how it might have been had she not retired. This was how it was when that antic, delightful, magnetic, desperate, neurotic powerhouse of a dynamo was turned on and the volume pumped up full blast! When her energy came through her fingers and onto the keyboard it was nothing short of miraculous. And to know that she possessed this gift and held it inside all those decades was enough to make one weep, which I did at The Arts Club that Sunday night when I was absolutely certain no one would see me.

It appeared that all was going perfectly on schedule. She was practicing regularly, training as a boxer might, the Ravinia event drawing closer and closer. We all surely sensed her nervousness, but it was Charles Olin, in an interview conducted late in the winter of 1985, who heard her true feelings about the impending concert. His interview, conducted, really, as a rich conversation between two thoughtful people, afforded her an opportunity to reflect on her entire life. Listening to it, I like to imagine that because he was my college roommate and lifelong friend, she was, perhaps, speaking to me as well during these minutes. The centerpiece of the discussion, naturally, was the Ravinia concert, an event to which my mother continually returned.

> [The Ravinia concert] is very difficult to do. This is very dangerous. The manager said, "Is one rehearsal enough?" I'm not going to be a dilettante and say no. Well, we shall see what we shall see.
>
> If [I] were to play the beginning of the piece for you, for example, it goes with such a bang. A friend was here one day, he asked, "When you start, do you gather up speed?" I said, "No, no. The orchestra introduces the tempo for me. The orchestra starts . . . and the tempo that Levine takes is the tempo that I will take. If it's too fast, it's too bad." But he said, "Maybe you can start gathering momentum." And I said, "No I don't play that way. I don't gather momentum. It's either I've got it or I don't!" The playing is there. But how does one know what happens at the crucial moment? You're right, there are many facets, the least of which is exhibiting yourself.[5]

Later in the conversation, she reflected on the topic of self-esteem and self-acceptance, and the role the impending concert played in these contexts. Lurking in her reflections, moreover, was the question of whether she had made a wise decision to retire prematurely from the concert platform.

> If you're successful, you begin to have a little more respect for yourself, and a little more self-esteem. The lower depths are not pleasant, especially when you're all alone. When you've lost your spouse . . . you make some friends, some beautiful ones, but when you go home you go home

alone. You go home to your own thoughts, your lonely thoughts. . . . You know, when I talk to a good friend like you, [Charles Olin] and I don't talk to many people because I won't let people come here. I don't have many people come here, which may be a big mistake. Don't ask me why. . . . That doesn't mean that playing will compensate for it. It only helps you for yourself, not in the loneliness as much as the fear of getting so old that you don't know what you're doing, losing control, not having full memory control, not the recall that you used to have. It might give me a little more self-esteem. There's more pressure. But I've had that pressure [to perform well] all my life, because I enjoy very much not being a second-class pianist. I don't even have any conceit about it. I never was a conceited kid. I wasn't a conceited adult. I'm very grateful for what I can do. I was one of the great pianists of the day. I had royal receptions, but I'm lonely. I confess to that . . .

You come to face this [concert] raw. I wish I had a good day for everyone in the hall who thinks I'm going to fall flat on my face. I'm sure of it. Lots of kids who haven't made it, you know. One young pianist who was starting out and never made it, was introduced to me: "This is Madam Gradova." And she said, "Madam Gradova? I thought you were dead." It's understandable. I was forty-five. That doesn't bother me. It's the old colleagues like Milstein and Horowitz and Firkusny and Rudi Serkin, and that bunch, a lot of them are alive and I feel close to them. The ones who know I'm going to play—I haven't told Serkin yet—but the ones like Milstein and Horowitz, I told a couple of people, Ashkenazy, who's a wonderful colleague. . . . I talked to Ashkenazy and told him I was going to play. And he said, "Really?" He said how difficult it was. "Oi, is that [concerto] difficult." I told him, "You had to tell me that?" I just got a card from Switzerland that worried me a little bit, because there's a kid missing on the picture, and they all look so sad. He had a lot of kids.

[Tom and Judy] think it's Hallelujah. They think it's the smartest thing I ever did. It's courageous. Tom called, "Why, it's the best thing you ever did, mother!" I wonder how they're going to feel about it when they're in the hall. I'm sure they know the risks. The day it comes you pace the floors, you wonder whether you're going to get through it, and of course one always has the fear that when nervousness gets to be so extreme, what does it do to the brain? You're playing at a terrific speed, you're not sure what's coming next, and all of a sudden you don't know where the hell you are.

If I were talking intimately with you without [the tape recorder] and I had free associations to certain thoughts and enlighten my own concerns, (sic), such as, is this something I'm doing for self-esteem? I can't say that I miss the concert stage. I would not consider a tour. I wouldn't mind playing with five or six orchestras a year. That's all I want to do; leave my card in a few places, and have the sound in my ears . . . how far am I from . . . the other thing at this age? The only thing wrong with it . . . anybody with a more profound mind would say, "*Why* are you doing this?" instead of what's *wrong* with doing this? You're right to ask it that way because you can question my psyche and say, why are you doing that? What's making you come back? No, I just question myself if down in the lower depths, without reading Gorky, you wonder why. Should there be a time of peace because you have accomplished something? I was in good company. I had to fight against Myra Hess and Guiomar Novaes; they were all great friends. I was lucky with the press. I don't know, Rachmaninoff thought I was a good pianist, Hofmann thought I was a good pianist. Those are very encouraging things to hear. They all tried to talk me into coming back. But so many years have elapsed, but why now?

You have to be so sure of yourself, but you have to have a lot of performances behind you. But there are a lot of places where you can play with major orchestras. I'd be delighted to play summer time concerts. I can't back out. And with one rehearsal . . . I think it will be impossible for me to get through a mediocre performance without stumbling. I would be grateful for that. It would be horrible to get into a horrible spot where you can't get out of it. I couldn't live with it. I couldn't. I say to myself, "what am I getting myself into?" I would love to play Boston because Tommy is there. And I love Seiji Ozawa. I would love to play certain towns where my friends are. I'd love to play Los Angeles. I'd love to play some concerts and then say, farewell! If I can do this one well, I'll go back.

And it's interesting, I never played this. I have six or eight concerti that I have played. Schumann was a triumph, *Paganini Variations* of Rachmaninoff, Beethoven One which I had success with. Give me about six or seven. Now I want to see how they go with me now. I can learn the Schumann

concerto in no time. In one week I could play it; I am ready
to go. And I can do the same with the Beethoven One, and
the Beethoven Four. But the fact that I have never played
[Rachmaninoff One] . . . With the Rachmaninoff, I can play
brilliantly for about eight pages, then I think, what happens
here? Where am I? What am I supposed to do?[6]

There is little doubt of her anxiety as well as her hope that just
maybe the years of performing will have formed a sufficiently secure
foundation upon which to rest this one performance. But predictably,
she returns to the theme of the rescuing father figure, the conductor,
James Levine in this instance, Horowitz in the past, who will smooth
over the present and save her from any dangerous mishap.

> . . . But you learn years ago that playing in public is dif-
> ferent. It comes back to you like a lovely waterfall. I could al-
> most say, "I'm not going to do number one." I could play the
> [*Paganini*] *Variations* because that was my piece. Or maybe
> I'll do the Schumann for you, which is very difficult. It's ro-
> mantic, it's classic, and it isn't just a bunch of tricks I have to
> do. [Rachmaninoff One] is a tightrope walk, and if the hands
> start to get clammy, and the heart starts to beat . . . You know
> what Josef Hofmann said to me? He was always the dean of
> pianists, the greatest pianist in the world. He said, "Who do
> you think you are that you can stay in your house and pre-
> pare the *Paganini Variations*? And you go straight from your
> house to Carnegie Hall? We go to New Jersey. We go to Flush-
> ing, we play five or six concerts. But you went straight from
> your house to Carnegie Hall. You could have had a heart at-
> tack and dropped dead on the stage," which is what one pi-
> anist did. He did the Grieg Concerto, he started to play and
> he died. So I don't know. I haven't had much talk with
> Horowitz lately. He hasn't been too well. I thought, should I
> tell him or shouldn't I tell him? I didn't tell him . . .
> What do your inferiorities have to do with it? What do
> they. . . . Suddenly they come from way down and they sur-
> face at the very top and they hit you right between the eyes.
> Every little obstacle becomes a gigantic thing. The fact that
> the hands aren't steady. You fall over one phrase and you're
> finished. And if its finished, it's a suicide. If I could be doing
> it in *Carkavascheiss*, as we say in Russian, in some small
> town, or in Lakeside, Michigan, with the bowling alley

orchestra, then it would be great. I'd have a chance to hear how it sounds. Don't forget, I sat on the [Leventritt] jury while other kids went through it. [Rachmaninoff One] sounded good to me. . . . I know how it is supposed to sound. It's a gorgeous piece. You just have to learn to play it.

One thing about James Levine is that he knows every note of every score. He will know that piece better than I. When he does opera he knows every word. He sings right with the singer's mouth. In German, Italian, and French. If a conductor can, he can help you from drowning. Stock could do this with the Chicago Symphony. Prokofiev lost thirty-two bars the night I was in the hall. He forgot it. And the first violinist, Mischa Mischakoff, who spoke with such a funny accent, said, "I didn't know what he was doing there." Mr. Stock had a way of letting you know that you would meet at a certain place. I had a rehearsal with him in the Beethoven, and I lost it in the rehearsal, and that night in the performance he looked at me right at that bar as if to say, "you're never going to lose it again" . . .

Well I come away now with one fear that I tasted that I shall never forget. When I was engaged with the [New York] Philharmonic, just a baby, twenty years old, you know, [there was only] one rehearsal in the morning for the performance Thursday night, and then a performance Friday afternoon. So [on] Thursday morning, I'd already been warned by some great musicians interested in my career that the famous von Mengelberg, who had two big red pomps (*sic*) and looked like Mephistopheles and [who] scared everybody to death, . . . could be hard on me, because he had been very hard on a famous soloist who was his senior when he said, "I feel like I have pots and pans and nobody to cook with." So [the pianist] left the stage and never came back.

I was not even known except for two recitals. Wonderful press, and right away we made it. You either make it or you die. You come with recital management and you go home with concert management. When they think you're good, they sign you up. I was so frightened when I started the Rachmaninoff, [Mengelberg] stepped down and said, "Rachmaninoff would kill you for this." And since a lot of friends had said to me just sit quietly because you can't say anything, I looked at him and he said, "Start over again and pick up that tempo." I started over and picked up the tempo and we went ahead and we didn't stop anymore and I knew I couldn't play it. I knew I couldn't go out. I looked at the stage door as a death trap. There was nobody with me.

You're supposed to go, by tradition, to the conductor's [dressing] room to meet him there; he waits for you. He doesn't make it easier for you. I walked out to where the famous [Carnegie Hall] door is and I knew I couldn't go. So look what happens to you in a moment of frenzy. I looked up at him—I weighed all of seventy-nine pounds—I said, "Maestro." He didn't even bend down to look, just stood and stared ahead. "Could you pretend that you're my father, and I was your child, and help me get through this piece?" That made some impression on him. He didn't talk to me and we walked out on the stage. I never had a better accompaniment in my life. I fell on my face on the first page, picked myself up and went on.

The next afternoon it was great. Well, it wasn't great, but at least I wasn't throwing up all over the place. It wasn't courage, it was absolute frenzy. Suddenly I made a transference to him; he was my father. He'd either kill me or help me. Who else is going to help you? They open the door and shove you out. Other people will handle [the anxiety] in a more mature fashion. I was a little child then. Scared to death. Papa help me. I'm drowning. And I would have drowned sure as anything. But to this day, I can taste that fear.

Then I go home after I played and in 1928 we had the automobile accident and that was the end of everything. Everything. So when I did come back after that long silence, it was Horowitz who made me come back. He didn't say go try it in New Jersey like people do, he said, "You're playing with the Philharmonic. This time you'll do the *Paganini Variations.* You'll have my piano, [and] you'll have a good rehearsal. [Sir John] Barbirolli is conducting, leave it to me." So I played Saturday night, I think, and Sunday afternoon a national broadcast. We used to always listen to the New York Philharmonic on the air Sunday afternoons. So the rehearsal was not so aye, aye, aye, but if the rehearsal is too good, don't come back for the concert. Horowitz came back stage and he said [to Barbirolli], "I don't like that you played too loud." He listened to Horowitz. After all he was a great musician and the son-in-law of the great Toscanini. "You're drowning her out. You have to hold back a little bit." Anyway, we had not too bad a time at the first performance. But on the second, you can hear it on the recording, because there comes a time in the last variation where I have a moment to pause and then I'm supposed to go right into it, and suddenly the timpani player makes a crack with his pair of cymbals, and Rachmaninoff is in the hall, nice, and I jumped, and everybody started to laugh. Where did that sound come from way in the back? But you take a breath and you go, that's all. You plunge in. With the last variation you're off to the races and you have a good time.

Going in the car with Mr. Horowitz, who had tremendous humor, I wish I could tell the story, he said to me, "You're going to get very nervous tonight. Whatever you do, and if you do lose your memory, don't stop, play anything [any] old thing you know." It was a nice way to say goodbye. I left a good record the first time and then again with the Philharmonic. And everybody thought I was going to come back.[7]

Eventually she reflected on that old nemesis, memory, and the utter unacceptability of a performer bringing music onto the stage. But it is not about memory, really, that she is so concerned. Once again, it is about the mind sabotaging one's greatest gift.

. . . I talked with Tom about it recently. Tom said, "If your memory is what's bothering you,"—and I had a remarkable memory. I could memorize a concerto in a week when I was a kid—"then why don't you play with a musical score. You don't think they won't respect you at the age of eighty if you use a score?" But for me, that is already a confession of weakness. I would feel it is a three quarter job done. I would feel badly about it. You're disrobed without the music. You come out naked. Your bad technique is showing, and everything else is showing. One clinker at the beginning of the thing, and oh, Christ! [The Rachmaninoff First] starts with such a tremendous amount of force, you don't know how you're going to get through it. I'd rather do that then start slowly, because it's very hard to get the sweat . . . glands going. If you hit the piano with a pounce, very dramatically, and you begin to sweat, that's much better . . .

I think the psyche plays havoc with pianists. There's no question about it. I don't think it does it in the area of dexterity. I don't think so. Where we fail is where we are not properly educated; we are not properly trained, otherwise we would not enter the hall with such stage fright. Somebody told me about a woman pianist who was supposed to play Carnegie Hall and she never showed up. She just left and was gone for a week. That's all I had to hear. So I was thinking, so where can I go? At Ravinia Park, I could go to the lake and drown myself someplace. My kids will be here. They're going to be sitting there. And my friends are all going to be there. I don't know the answer. This white paper with the black dots on it is very frightening. I would not be able to handle [a failure] because I never flopped like that. I remember when Tommy went to Harvard, he went to the Widener Library, and he went to get a copy of *The Nation* magazine. There was a critic [Henrietta Strauss] who wouldn't review me. She said, "Gradova doesn't interest me. I won't review her." And Mr. Oswald something who was the editor and owner of *The Nation* said, "Yes you will, because she's great. You'll go there!" And she heard me and she gave me a whole page. Well, we'll see. Maybe we can get a second rehearsal . . .

Then you have to question: What have I done? Why do I have to exhibit myself? I am so lonely, so discouraged, so bereft; *that* I am. All of those things, I am. And the time is close to the end chronologically, there's no question about it . . . this is my last chance. Is it a need to be accepted? Is it a need to . . . maybe I hate being forgotten. I don't think I am. Not in our field I'm not. Even the young pianists know who I am. That isn't it; that's too superficial an explanation. I don't know what it is. It's a disturbed psyche and a very old slob's loss of self-esteem. I'm positively frightened; I'm positively old. I can't speak to Jimmy Levine as a father. I have to see him as an equal now. The worse that can happen is that at the rehearsal, which is usually the morning of the concert—a bad rehearsal is a good performance—a good rehearsal is no good. If I can't control myself [with Levine] I'll just have to go some place. I don't know how could I face anyone. That's harder than making a jackass of yourself on the stage. How do you face *yourself* is more important.

Sarah Zelzer announced [my return] at the party. I knew it would give her pleasure to say it and for people to know that at eighty I'm coming back. Yes, you're proud of a person who has to fight that horrible, horrible nervousness. That is a ghastly thing and I can still remember it. . . . When they gave me the menorah at Maurie's funeral, my eyes filled with tears and I pointed to Tommy for help. He was sitting there in the second row. And he came up and he simply explained what a menorah was, how it shed light. It was poignantly said, beautifully said. I couldn't do that. That's his exchange with friends. It's his métier; his words are him. He just gets to you in a very nice, quiet way. And his language is his music. He's gifted, and he had a father to live up to who was not only gifted but extraordinary. He knew more about music than I did. I learned all my chamber music from him. He opened the whole world of chamber music for me. I knew a little about it, but I was an idiot. An absolute idiot. Stage people are very superstitious. They worry about things that go on before the performance. I might walk on the stage and have to go directly to the hospital . . .

No, there's nothing sudden about it. It's a slow developing deliverancy (sic). When you get depressed and you think, maybe this compensates for that . . . and you have not such a good picture of yourself. There are other things. Lots of your colleagues are playing and you're not. And there may be a touch of identification with them, or a little envy. As I say, you lose a little self-esteem; there but for the grace of God go I, you know. There's a lot of people [who] used to say, "Why don't you come back? Why don't you come back?"[8]

Turning briefly to the topic of old age, a topic spurred, no doubt, by my mother's reflections on memory loss, she reminisced on a conversation with her most prized father figure, who, like her own father, insisted that she remain a concert pianist. Rachmaninoff, in this one vignette, reveals no appreciation of what possibly could have caused her to retire from the platform.

When one says old age it's abbreviated, it's putting something in a tight category with crowds of people and thousands of different emotions and variations of anxiety and self-esteem loss, a loneliness and a grievance (sic). I have friends, and I don't have friends. What's happened to my brain? Why don't I have the inspiration to improvise? There are thousands of ideas [about old age] so how can you bring yourself down to one thing? One sits in an atmosphere. I can't call [this apartment] home because it isn't. Not after forty-seven years of living in a beautiful old house. But that's beside the point, [for] those are material concepts. I think it a very difficult thing to put us all into one group. The only thing we have in common is the loss of memory. Total recall is not there anymore.

. . . I can go back to wonderfully touching conversations I had with Stravinsky. Better than that was Rachmaninoff who wrote me a nasty letter once. He said, "I heard something very unkind about you." I have the letter some place. Did I have enough sensitivity to put it away? No, it went in the drawer with everything else. "Now, I'm coming to Chicago and I should like to talk with you." Everything very formal. Signed, "Sergei Vassilievich Rachmaninoff," and that's it. Several weeks later he calls me to say, "I'm coming into town this week and I'll be at the Palmer House [Hotel]. Do you wish to hear what I have to say?"

I made a date—I'll make it very short—and he invited me, and his wife, Natasha, was with him, which she always was, and of course all eyes were on him, and he sat there and he looked at me . . . and it wasn't a good look; he looked like Rasputin anyhow. And before the dessert he said, "Do you want me to tell you now why I wanted to talk to you, or would you rather continue your lunch?" I said, "I would rather continue my lunch because I have a feeling if you get talking to me I won't have dessert and since dessert is my favorite course I'd prefer to wait." In the middle of the chocolate thing, "Is it true," says he, "that you actually cancel concerts?" I said, "Yes." He said, "After you've signed and given your word that you will come and you still don't come?" I said, "If I don't feel well I don't go." I can't say I was as superficial about it, as casual about it. It's not that if I don't feel like playing I don't go. I'd rather stay home. It's so much more attractive to me than going to Duluth on a cold night, or is it Wisconsin, or wherever the hell you have to go. In short, I said to him, "Sergei Vassilievich, I don't want to play at all." He looks at me. "In your twenties you're ready to quit already?" "Yes, I prefer to stay home. I have great gratification staying home. I can play chamber music once or twice a week; that appeases my appetite, and I'm tired. I have to play here, and play there."

I started in New York and played two recitals and within five weeks I had a Steinway contract and I was already contracted for an entire season. I looked around, I was only nineteen years old. When I was [in New York] at fourteen I didn't have the price for a sandwich. I lived on thirty-five cents a day. That's when I met Prokofiev. My father arranged for him to listen to me, this great genius. And he was impressed; he helped me with the Grieg Concerto. Can you imagine, of all things, Prokofiev coaching me in the Grieg Concerto? What did I know who Prokofiev was? So I was told that I could come to his apartment [in New York] and report to him what I'm learning. So that went on for a year and a half. It was wasted on me. Absolutely wasted on me. Fine intellect who also gave me no. 1 Prokofiev that I also never played.

So there were lovely episodes. It's easier for me to go back. Then I got this lecture from Rachmaninoff: "Why don't you come and tell me this in about fifteen years from now, when you're thirty-five, forty. If you don't want to play anymore then I can go along with that, but not now. You'll regret it."[9]

Inevitably, Olin turned the discussion back to the theme of regret. To anyone who knew my mother, there was no more obvious concern, no more obvious source of unhappiness.

Do you regret certain things? Yes. The invitation that [Rachmaninoff] gave me to spend three to three and [a] half months with him and his wife in Switzerland—we used to go there every summer. It took me one week to cry that one out. I went to Maurie to help me make a decision. He said, "This time I can't help. This is up to you." One morning I said, "Yes, I'm staying. Who gives up an opportunity to work with Rachmaninoff!" The next day I changed my mind, and I finally went home. Things might have been different; who knows? I was always a professional procrastinator. I always say, don't do today what you can put off to tomorrow. I've done research on that already . . . Now, when you ask me, and I'm sure you will do so, do you regret it? Isn't that your next question? The answer is "Yes. I regret that I stopped."

[My life] now is nothing. Nothing. It's walking briskly so that you can save a leg. I don't know as we get closer what's going to happen. I really don't know. I know the score, but I never played it in my life.[10]

In April, 1985, less than three months before the scheduled Ravinia concert, my mother was admitted to the hospital. I was assured by her physician that it was nothing serious. There was no reason for me to come to Chicago. A visit from me, moreover, would have caused her to believe she was more ill than the doctors had let on. Several years earlier she had experienced cardiac congestion and a valve had been inserted in her heart. This same valve, apparently, was the cause of some minor discomfort. My phone conversations with her at the hospital convinced me she was fine. On the afternoon of April 25, I called her and learned that she would be leaving the hospital the next day. She felt she ought not talk with me, however, because she was being visited by the pianist, Shura Cherkassky, with whom she was joking and talking music, which meant her feeling happy. Decades before, they had recorded piano rolls which today safeguard many of the pieces for which they gained fame. I heard Mr. Cherkassky in the background roaring with laughter over something my mother had said. As my father would have said, "Is good." I promised to call her back in a few hours.

Thank God all was well. I could attend the Spring high school musical, *The Pajama Game*, in which our oldest daughter was appearing. At six o'clock, I was starting to prepare to leave for the school when I received a call from the hospital. My mother had arrested and the doctors were deeply concerned. I was advised that I probably shouldn't stray too far from the phone. I decided at once to do two things. First, attend the play and then fly to Chicago first thing the next morning. I know that my mother would have said, "There's no decision to be made between going to your sick old mother and seeing your gorgeous child in a play. You belong with your daughter. Stay there!" Once again, I know that she put the happiness of my children before any need she might have had, or that I might have had.

I remember her talking to me when, after a year of living in London, my wife and I debated whether staying a second year would be as good for the children as it appeared it would be for us; we were in some consternation over the decision. "Listen to me," she counseled over the phone, acting sternly but gently in a manner I found as compelling as it was uncharacteristic. "As long as your children are with you and feeling secure, they'll be fine. You can do this for yourself; your children aren't going to suffer one iota. They don't need to see their grandmother all that much. Take it from someone who knows, they'll be just fine!" No matter how ingenuous her words, I never dealt with her without feeling some shard of guilt, and then the sadness that was her sadness: "As long as your children are with you and feeling secure, they'll be fine. Take it from someone who knows . . ."

I remember my mind flashing on a scene of a little girl with dark hair, all alone, curled up with her precious books on a bench in the New York Public Library.

I recalled as well her numerous tales of that same era, traveling to wealthy homes on Long Island where, in her party dress and shiny black shoes, she would sit alone for hours in an upstairs bedroom until it was time to perform. Then she would play for small audiences who would be dazzled, I imagine, by this powerful but romantic child, who, as that one critic would write, looked "like a combination of Peter Pan and Lord Byron . . ." and who, within a few years, would be making her Town Hall debut recital. Then, after being offered some food, she would once again, alone, return to the city. So many stories of my mother involved people all by themselves, frightened in crowded situations, with no one to comfort them, or even accompany them. No wonder she always wanted to telephone her mother from Prokofiev's home.

A few minutes before leaving for my daughter's school, the telephone rang again. It was the same doctor. My mother was dead. The details from that point on are insignificant, although it may be said that several years later, when we learned that her death had been caused by a defective valve and that people in the country were suing the valve's manufacturer, my sister and I chose to obey our father's admonition: "You don't make money suing people, you earn it. Of course, if someone wants to offer you an interesting stock tip . . ."

Our family did attend the play, my chest feeling as though a Steinway was sitting on it, two Steinways actually. It was appropriate that once again in a momentous hour I was seated in a concert auditorium, an important woman, my wife, to my left.

After the play, I drove our daughter home, my wife and our other children having left earlier. In the car my daughter said, "You didn't like it, did you? I peeked out from the side and saw your face. You were unhappy." I told her I did like it, I loved it in fact, and I loved her, and that she was great! Then I said, "Grammy died tonight, that's why I looked unhappy." She began to cry. I never did cry, actually, until the moment I wrote these words.

Only years after her death did I discover two letters written by Shura Cherkassky, the last person outside of medical personnel to see my mother alive. The letters were addressed to a man named Steven living in London's Regents Park. April 30, 1985:

Just now I heard the news of dear Gitta. I am so shattered and sad that I can not think of anything else . . . two short visits with her [in the hospital] more than confirmed my feelings about her—a rare, deep, genuine person, direct. I will miss her forever.[11]

In his second letter, dated May 8, 1985, Cherkassky reveals that he had been requested to substitute for my mother and perform the Rachmaninoff First Piano Concerto at Ravinia Park, but he had declined. "I strongly feel and believe it is my duty to learn Rachmaninoff's First Concerto. I believe Gitta would have liked me to do it. I will play it in public later on when it is completely in my system." Earlier in that same letter, Cherkassky had written: "Gitta's death made a stronger impression on me than I can possibly think of; it was just as though she left a message for the rest of my life."[12]

These last words, apparently, were more portentous than our family at first recognized, for it was only later that I discovered the second page of his April 30 letter and the postscript it contained: "I remember so well, almost last words (*sic*) of Gitta: "'I don't know if I could play July 5. Play this concerto for me.'"[13] Years later I would learn that she had expressed this same fear to my niece, her firstborn grandchild.

The funeral took place in Chicago. The night before the actual service her casket lay in wait in the same north side funeral home where my father, too, had been eulogized. The funeral home directors, none of whom remarked on the remaining number of gravesites owned by my late father, had suggested that my sister and I and our families arrive at the establishment one-half hour before the commencement of the official visitation. The casket would be left open if we wished. We could view my mother one last time, alone.

To say that this sort of ritual was hardly my mother's cup of tea is a bit like saying that the Pope doesn't always find the time to say *Kaddish* (the Hebrew prayer for the dead) every morning for his parents. She hated open caskets, although she did observe that some people actually looked better in death than in life. "Throw me in the lake," she counseled me once when the subject of her death came up. "What do you want all that *dreck* for? Save your money. If someone doesn't like being seen in a bathrobe, why would they want people to stare at them in their casket?"

As instructed, we arrived early and from the main hall of the funeral home I could look into the room, bland and uninteresting, where, at the far end, my mother's casket rested on a metal stand with wheels. The casket was open. I stood absolutely still. Then I said to the funeral director, "When we are finished viewing, can we close the casket, please? It was not something my mother wanted." He was only happy to comply. My sister was already moving into the room. My son remained with me. "Jason," I told him, "I don't feel like going in just now. Do you want to go in and see Grammy?" He did, and I watched him approach the mahogany casket where, for a few seconds, he peered inside. I will always see him walking away from me toward her. After twenty minutes or so, the first guests arrived and I motioned to the funeral director to close the casket. It was only then that I stepped into the room where my mother's body lay forever hidden from view. Now, for the first time, my desperate wailing on that Cheyenne train station platform came true: "I'll never see my mother again."

Several months later I asked the question of my son I so much desired to address. "Jason," I began without the slightest trace of emotion, "do you remember seeing Grammy in her casket?" He, of course, did. "Did that bother you in any way? I mean, you know, make you sort of upset or anything?" It hadn't. "Did you look at her face?" He had. "Tell me, you're sensitive about these sorts of things, was there any sort of expression on her face? I mean, for example, would you say she looked peaceful?" She did. And at last, "Was she smiling?"

My sister insisted that I deliver the eulogy for our mother just as she had urged on the occasion of our father's funeral. She always claims that she sings, I talk. What to say? Perhaps everything I have said above. I spoke a bit about her life. I know I used words like passion, strength, power, and sensitivity. I recall mentioning my antipathy, her antipathy, toward the notion of her playing like a man.

Finally, I read a review of her concert at Ravinia, the concert of July 5, 1985, that, of course, never took place, "Rach One" with the Chicago Symphony Orchestra with guest conductor James Levine whom she called Jimmy, the concert, I choose to believe, only the angels heard, and adored, as they did her. Not only that, but when she walked on stage the entire orchestra stood in appreciation and the horns played her a *touche*.

Notes

Preface

1. In the references and citations found in the book, I have given all the information available. Unfortunately, many of the articles, reviews, and notices taken from photocopies discovered in my mother's memorabilia lack complete information. Given the age of these documents, moreover, magazine and newspaper offices were unable to retrieve original material from their archives. In the case of personal letters, I offer all available information, but again, exact dates are often missing.

Chapter 1

1. James Francis Cooke, *Great Pianists on Piano Playing* (Philadelphia: Philadelphia Press, 1917; Mineola, NY: Dover, 1999), p. 15.

2. *Musical Leader*, Boston, 18 December 1924, p. 65.

3. Cecil Smith, *Worlds of Music* (Philadelphia: Lippincott, 1952), p. 124.

4. Carl Engel, "Harking Back and Looking Forward," in *From Bach to Stravinsky: The History of Music by Its Foremost Critics*, ed. David Ewen (New York: W. W. Norton, 1933), p. 352.

5. Josef Hofmann, *Piano Playing* (New York: The McClure Company, 1908), pp. 40 and 52.

6. John Redfield, *Music: A Science and an Art* (New York: Tudor Publishing Company, 1949), p. 154.

7. Adolph Kullak, *The Aesthetics of Pianoforte-Playing* (New York: Schirmer, 1893), p. 7.

8. Michelle Krisel, "Speak Memory," in *Los Angeles Times Book Review*, 9 July 2000, p. 7.

9. James Francis Cooke, *Great Pianists*, p. 116.

10. Daniel Gregory Mason, "The Periods of Musical History," in *From Bach to Stravinsky*, ed. David Ewen (New York: W. W. Norton, 1933), p. 18.

11. Neville Cardus, *Talking of Music* (London: Collins, 1957), p. 214.

12. From an interview with H. Miller, "Study of Literature The Ideal Tonic for the Pianist, Says Gitta Gradova," New York, *Musical America*, 31 January 1925, p. 37.

13. Eugene Stinson, "Sees Specialization Fatal to Artistic Growth," New York, *Musical America*, 9 August 1924, p. 8.

14. "Concert Pianist Visiting S.L. Praises Western Hospitality," *Salt Lake Telegram*, 1937.

Chapter 2

1. I am grateful to the Library of *The Boston Globe* for this reference.

2. M. Montagu Nathan, "Russian Musical History in Kaleidoscope," in *From Bach to Stravinsky: The History of Music by Its Foremost Critics*, ed. David Ewen (New York: W. W. Norton, 1933), pp. 253, and 254.

3. A photograph of my mother in graduation attire is dedicated: "To the woman Esther Harris who has made me what I am, Gertrude Weinstock. August 12, 1919."

4. Review of musical performance of Gitta Gradova. Photocopy of document with no visible sources.

5. Review of performance of Gitta Gradova. Photocopy of document with no visible sources.

6. Review of performance of Gitta Gradova. Photocopy of document with no visible sources.

7. Ruth Crawford, "Letter to My Mother," 1 November 1921. Cited in Matilda Gaume, *Ruth Crawford Seeger: Memoirs, Memory, Music* (Metuchen, NJ: The Scarecrow Press, 1986), p. 36.

8. Ernest Hutcheson, *The Literature of the Piano: A Guide for Amateur and Student* (New York: Knopf, 1965), p. 332.

9. Hugo Leichtentritt, *Music, History and Ideas* (Cambridge, MA: Harvard University Press, 1941), p. 262.

10. Harold C. Schonberg, *The Lives of the Great Composers* (New York: W. W. Norton, 1997), pp. 523, and 524.

11. George Upton and Felix Borowski, *The Standard Concert Guide* (New York: Blue Ribbon, 1940), p. 446.

12. In Ernest Hutcheson, *The Literature of the Piano*, p. 333.

13. Eugene Stinson, "Sees Specialization Fatal to Artistic Growth," p. 8.

14. Gitta Gradova, *Contemporary American Musicians*, 11 November 1925.

15. In Eugene Stinson, "Sees Specialization Fatal to Artistic Growth," New York, *Musical America*, 9 August 1924, p. 8.

16. Matilda Gaume, *Ruth Crawford Seeger: Memoirs, Memories, Music* (Metuchen, NJ: The Scarecrow Press, 1986), p. 36.

17. "Gradova Answers Three Vital Questions Regarding Modern Music," *Music News*, 17 October 1924, p. 21.

18. H. Miller, "Study of Literature the Ideal Tonic for the Pianist Says Gitta Gradova," 31 January 1925, p. 37.

19. H. Miller, "Study of Literature," p. 37.

20. I am grateful to Judith Tick for bringing this passage to my attention.

21. Letter to my mother, 2 February 1922. Cited in Matilda Gaume, *Ruth Crawford Seeger: Memoirs, Memories, Music* (Metuchen, NJ: The Scarecrow Press, 1986), p. 39.

22. Judith Tick, *Ruth Crawford Seeger: A Composer's Search for American Music* (New York: Oxford Press, 1997).

23. "Gradova Answers Three Vital Questions Regarding Modern Music," *Music News*, 17 October 1924, p. 21.

24. I wonder whether my mother ever came across Erik Satie's wry remark: "What I love about jazz is that it's 'blue' and you don't care." In Richard Lewis, ed., *Praise of Music* (New York: Orion Press, 1963), p. 73.

25. Cecil Smith, *Worlds of Music*, (Philadelpia: Lippincott, 1952) p. 116.

26. "Gradova—An Example of American Training." November 7, 1924.

27. Edward Barry, "Gitta Gradova Acclaimed for Rare Artistry." Chicago, *Chicago Daily Tribune*, 17 January 1941.

28. Romain Rolland, *Some Musicians of Former Days*, trans. Mary Blaiklock, 4th ed. (London: Kegan Paul, Trench, n.d.), p. 327.

29. Judith Tick, *Ruth Crawford Seeger*, p. 45.

30. Josef Hofmann, *Piano Playing* (New York: The McClure Company, 1908), p. 51.

31. Neville Cardus, *Talking of Music* (London: Collins, 1957), p. 214.

32. Cited in Anthony Storr, *Music and the Mind* (New York: Ballantine, 1992), p. 17.

33. Interview of Gitta Gradova with Steven Heliotes, Chicago, 1984.

34. Interview with Steven Heliotes, Chicago, 1984.

35. See Daniel Jaffé, *Sergey Prokofiev* (London: Phaidon, 1998).

36. Interview with Steven Heliotes, Chicago, 1984.

37. Interview with Steven Heliotes, Chicago, 1984.

38. Letter from Maurice H. Cottle to Gitta Gradova, Chicago, undated.

39. Interview with Steven Heliotes, Chicago, 1984.

40. Interview with Steven Heliotes, Chicago, 1984.

41. Interview with Steven Heliotes, Chicago, 1984.

42. Cecil Smith, *Worlds of Music* (Philadelphia: Lippincott 1952), p. 103.

43. Frank H. Warren, review of concert performance of Gitta Gradova, New York, recital, *Evening World*, 1924.

44. Review of concert performance of Gitta Gradova, New York, recital, *New York American*, 1924.

45. Review of concert performance of Gitta Gradova, New York, recital, *New York Times*, 1924.

46. W. J. Henderson, review of concert performance of Gitta Gradova, New York, recital, *New York Herald*, 1924.

47. In Abraham Veinus, *The Concerto* (Garden City, NJ: Doubleday, 1944) p. 162.

48. New York, *New York Staats Zeitung*, 1924.

49. F. D. Perkins, review of concert performance of Gitta Gradova, New York, recital, *New York Tribune*, 1924.

50. G. W. Gabriel, review of concert performance of Gitta Gradova, New York, recital, *New York Sun*, 1924.

51. "Gitta Gradova," New York, *Musical Courier*, 29 November 1923.

52. Esther Harris to *Musical Courier*, Chicago, 17 January 1924.

53. Maurice H. Cottle to Gitta Gradova, Chicago, 1926.

54. Maurice H. Cottle to Gitta Gradova, Chicago, April 1926.

55. Review of recital of Gitta Gradova at New York's Aeolian Hall, *New York Times*, November 1924.

56. "Gitta Gradova, Pianist, Fascinates," *New York Times*, 27 November 1924.

57. Alfred J. Swan, *Scriabin* (London: John Lane, The Bodley Head, LTD, 1922), p. 93.

58. Review of recital of Gitta Gradova at The Women's Musical Club of Toronto, 2 January 1925.

59. Henrietta Straus, "Gitta Gradova," *The Nation* 118, no. 3059 (20 February 1924).

60. See Harold C. Schonberg, *The Great Pianists: From Mozart to the Present* (New York: Simon and Schuster, 1987), chap. 25.

61. Herman Devries, "Gradova Master of Her Instrument, Music in Review," review of concert performance of Gitta Gradova, New York, *Musical Courier*, 20 December 1928.

62. Herman Devries, "Gitta Gradova is Sensation with Symphony," Chicago, "Music in Review," 14 January 1928.

63. Herman Devries, "Music in Review," review of concert performance of Gitta Gradova, *Musical Courier*, 14 January 1928.

64. Herman Devries, "Music in Review," review of concert performance of Gitta Gradova, Chicago, Chicago Symphony, *Musical Courier*, 17 February 1939.

65. Rutheda L. Pretzel, "Praises Gradova's Amazing Artistry," Music News and Events, *Winnetka Talk*, 11 February 1928.

66. Letter from Maurice H. Cottle to Gitta Gradova.

67. Robert M. Taylor, "People: An Afternoon with Gitta Gradova," *Amica International*, July, 1983, volume 20, p. 142ff.

68. Letter from Wilfrid Van Wyck to Gitta Gradova, London, 1 July 1935.

69. "Chicago Pianist Triumphs," author and source unknown.

70. Critic Hans Rosenwald, source unknown (p. 59).

71. Olin Downes, review of concert performance of Gitta Gradova, New York, Beethoven Symphony Orchestra, *New York Times*, 3 February 1927.

72. Richard L. Stokes, review of concert performance of Gitta Gradova, New York, St. Louis Symphony Orchestra, Rachmaninoff C-Minor Concerto, *New York World*, November 1927. Cited in *St. Louis Post-Dispatch*, 20 November 1927, p. 2A.

73. Claudia Cassidy, "Gradova Brilliant with Symphony," concert performance of Gitta Gradova, Chicago, *Chicago Tribune*, 10 February 1932.

74. Claudia Cassidy, "On the Aisle," review of concert performance of Gitta Gradova, Chicago, Chicago Symphony Orchestra, Moszkowski Concerto, *Chicago Tribune*, 14 February 1936. Five years later in 1941, another critic, Robert Pollak, also observed a cerain similarity of style to that of Horowitz: "Her command of the small crescendo and diminuendo resembles that of her good friend, Horowitz." In *Chicago Daily Times*, 1941.

75. Claudia Cassidy, "On the Aisle," "Gitta Gradova Scores Triumph with Stock and the Chicago Symphony Orchestra," review of concert performance of Gitta Gradova, Chicago, *Chicago Tribune*, 17 February 1939.

76. C. E. W., "Gitta Gradova Takes Evanston By Storm," review of concert performance of Gitta Gradova, Chicago, *Music News*, 7 November 1924.

77. Albert Cotsworth, review of concert performance of Gitta Gradova, Chicago, *Music News*, 22 May 1925.

78. "Heard By the Concert Goers," *Musical Leader*, 21 December 1925.

79. Lenott Field, "Breezin' Round," review of concert performance of Gitta Gradova, Chicago, Chicago Symphony, 20 January 1941.

80. Robert Pollak, "All-Russian Program Wins Ravinia Crowd," review of concert performance of Gitta Gradova, Chicago, Chicago Symphony, *Chicago Daily News*, 18 July 1941.

81. Eugene Stinson, review of concert performance of Gitta Gradova, Chicago, Chicago Symphony, *Music Views*, *Chicago Daily News*, undated.

82. "Chicago Pianist Is Soloist with Chicago Symphony Orchestra—Plays Rachmaninoff Concerto—New Russian Work Received Favorably," citation unavailable.

83. "Gradova Answers Three Vital Questions Regarding Modern Music," *Music News*, 17 October 1924, pp. 20–21.

84. Eugene Stinson, review of concert performance of Gitta Gradova, *Chicago Daily News*, Chicago Symphony Orchestra, Ravinia Park with conductor Nicolai Malko, *Music Views*, 18 July 1941.

85. Eugene Stinson, "Tumult of Acclaim Greets Gitta Gradova's Concert," review of concert performance of Gitta Gradova, Rachmaninoff's Concerto in C Minor, Chicago Symphony Orchestra, *Chicago Daily News*, *Music Views*.

86. *Chicago Daily News*, review of concert performance of Gitta Gradova, Chicago, March 1935.

87. Uncited source, 7 March 1931.

88. Edward Moore, review of concert performance of Gitta Gradova, *Chicago Daily Tribune*, 9 December 1932.

89. Review of concert, *Chicago Daily News*, 14 January 1928.

90. "Gitta Gradova Gets Ovation for Moszkowsky Piano Concerto," *Chicago Daily News*, 14 February 1936, p. 36.

91. "Chicago Symphony Orchestra—Mischakoff—Serkin—Gradova Soloists—Hageman Conducts Own Work—"review of concert performance of Gitta Gradova, Chicago, Chicago Symphony Orchestra, 29 February 1936.

92. Edward Moore, "Stock Returns and Orchestra Plays Welcome. Gitta Gradova Helps Make Concert an Event," review of concert performance of Gitta Gradova, *Chicago Daily Tribune*, undated.

93. Gary Graffman, *I Really Should Be Practicing* (Garden City, NY: Doubleday, 1981), pp. 144–145.

94. Francis D. Perkins, review of concert performance of Gitta Gradova, New York, New York Philharmonic Orchestra, 5 December 1940.

95. Review of concert performance of Gitta Gradova, New York, New York Philharmonic Orchestra, Brooklyn, N.Y., December 1940.

96. Review of concert performance of Gitta Gradova, New York, New York Philharmonic Orchestra, *World Telegram*, December 1940.

97. In fact, my mother had earlier, in 1928, broadcast a concert from the Hotel Barbizon in which she performed alone as well as with the violinist Ruth Breton in Grieg's G-minor sonata. This fact is reported in *New York Times*, 1 March 1928.

98. Emanuel Feurermann to Maurice H. Cottle, from Salt Lake City, 8 December 1940.

99. Ania Dorfmann, telegram to Gitta Gradova, New York, 8 December 1940.

100. Rudolf Serkin to Gitta Gradova, Crescent Hotel, New York Riverside Drive, 8 December 1940.

101. Howard to Aunt Gitta Gradova, University of Illinois, Urbana, Illinois, 13 December 1940.

102. In Neville Cardus, *Talking of Music*, p. 216.

103. Cited in Henry T. Finck, *Success in Music: And How It Is Won* (New York: Charles Scribner's Sons, 1913), p. 21.

104. Tobias Matthay, *Musical Interpretation: Its Laws and Principles, and Their Application in Teaching and Performing* (Boston: The Boston Music Company, G. Schirmer, 1913), pp. 152 and 153.

105. Richard Lewis, *Praise of Music*, p. 15.

Chapter 3

1. Ernest Hutcheson, *The Literature of the Piano: A Guide for Amateur and Student* (New York: Knopf, 1964) p. 336.

2. Harold C. Schonberg, *The Lives of the Great Composers* (New York: W. W. Norton, 1997) p. 390.

3. Interview with Steven Heliotes, Chicago, 1984.

4. Interview with Steven Heliotes. Chicago, 1984.

5. Romain Rolland, *Some Musicians of Former Days*, trans. Mary Blaiklock (London: Trench Kegan Paul, n.d.) p. 22.

6. Interview with Steven Heliotes. Chicago, 1984.

7. Interview with Steven Heliotes. Chicago, 1984.

8. In Romain Rolland, *Some Musicians*, p. 17.

9. Paul Robeson, Jr., *Paul Robeson Speaks to America* (New Brunswick, NJ: Rutgers University Press, 1993).

Chapter 4

1. I am grateful to Professor Richard Warren Cottle for this information.

2. Aaron Copland, *What to Listen for in Music* (New York: New American Library, 1957), p. 163.

3. *A Folha Médica*, August, 1986, vol. 93, no. 2, (1986): p. 136.

4. Ibid., p. 136.

5. Willard Marmelszadt, *Musical Sons of Aesculapius* (New York: Frohen Press, 1946), p. 112.

6. Homer Ulrich, *Chamber Music: The Growth and Practice of an Intimate Art* (New York: Columbia University Press, 1948), p. 5.

7. Ernest Hutcheson, *The Literature of the Piano: A Guide for Amateur and Student* (New York: Knopf, 1964), p. 6.

8. Homer Ulrich, *Chamber Music*, p. 8.

9. Willard Marmelszadt, *Musical Sons of Aesculapius*, p. 74.

10. Interview with Steven Heliotes, Chicago, 1984.

Chapter 5

1. Gregor Piatigorsky, *Cellist* (New York: Doubleday, 1965), pp. 194–95.

2. "Sauce for the Goose," *Chicago Sunday Tribune*, 16 April 1933.

3. June Provines, *This Gala World*, Chicago, *Chicago Tribune*, 7 April 1933.

4. Mrs. Henry Field, "The Social Whirl," Chicago, 22 January 1934.

5. Mrs. Henry Field, "The Social Whirl," Chicago, 9 April 1933.

6. Glenn Dillard Dunn, *Chicago Tribune*, March 1932.

7. See Max Schoen and Esther L. Gatewood, "Problems Related to the Mood Effects of Music," in *The Effects of Music: A Series of Essays*, ed. Max Schoen (New York: Harcourt, Brace and Company, 1927), p. 152.

8. Cited in H. Miller, "Study of Literature the Ideal Tonic for the Pianist, says Gitta Gradova," *Musical America*, 31 January 1925, p. 37.

9. Edward Moore, *Chicago Tribune*, 7 March 1931.

10. Henrietta Straus, "Gitta Gradova." *The Nation*, 20 February 1924, vol. 118, no. 3059.

11. "Next Symphony Concerts, with Gradova as Soloist, Are Oberhoffer's Farewell," *St. Louis Post-Dispatch*, 20 November 1927, p. 2A.

12. H. T. Parker, *Boston Transcript*, 8 December 1924.

13. Interview with Steven Heliotes, Chicago 1984.

14. Harold C. Schonberg, *The Lives of the Great Composers* (New York: W. W. Norton, 1997), p. 520.

15. Hugo Leichtentritt, *Music, History and Ideas* (Cambridge, MA: Harvard University Press, 1941), p. 262.

16. Edward Moore, "Stock Returns and Orchestra Plays Welcome. Gitta Gradova Helps Make Concert an Event." *Chicago Daily Tribune*, Undated.

17. Willi Apel, *Masters of the Keyboard: A Brief Survey of Pianoforte Music* (Cambridge, MA: Harvard University Press, 1947), p. 231.

18. Abraham Veinus, *The Concerto* (Garden City, NJ: Doubleday, 1944), p. 220.

19. Hugo Leichtentritt, *Music, History and Ideas*, p. 206.

20. Ibid., pp. 196, 198, and 219.

21. James Francis Cooke, *Great Pianists on Piano Playing* (Mineola, NY: Dover, 1999), p. 14.

Chapter 6

1. See Marc Pincherle, *The World of the Virtuoso*, trans. Lucille H. Brockway (New York: W. W. Norton, 1963), p. 19.

2. In Glenn Plaskin, *Horowitz: A Biography of Vladimir Horowitz* (New York: William Morrow, 1983).

3. June Provines, "Front Views and Profiles," *Chicago Tribune*, 23 October 1940.

4. Ned Rorem, "Beyond Playing," in *The Lives of the Piano* ed. James R. Gaines (New York: Holt, Rinehart and Winston, 1981), p. 137.

5. Ernest Hutcheson, *The Literature of the Piano: A Guide for Amateur and Student* (New York: Knopf, 1964), p. 5.

6. Robert Pollak, *Chicago Daily News*, 18 July 1941.

7. Aaron Copland, *What to Listen for in Music* (New York: New American Library, 1957), p. vii.

8. Francis Cooke, *Great Pianists on Piano Playing* (Philadelphia: Philadelphia Press, 1917; Mineola, NY: Dover, 1999), pp. 6–7.

9. See David Dubal, editor, *Remembering Horowitz: 125 Pianists Recall a Legend* (New York: Schirmer, 1993), pp. 58, and 333; and Harold C. Schonberg, *Horowitz* (New York: Simon and Schuster, 1992), p. 195.

10. Glenn Plaskin, *Horowitz*, p. 443.

11. Interview with Charles Olin, Chicago, January 1985.

12. Cited in Arthur Elson, *The Book of Musical Knowledge* (Boston: Houghton Mifflin, 1927), p. 471.

13. Arthur Elson, *The Book of Musical Knowledge*, p. 383.

14. Carl Engel, "Harking Back and Looking Forward," in *From Bach to Stravinsky: The History of Music by its Foremost Critics*, ed. David Ewen (New York: W. W. Norton, 1933), p. 357.

15. Interview with Steven Heliotes. Chicago, 1984.

16. Tobias Matthay, *Musical Interpretation: Its Laws and Principles, and their Application in Teaching and Performing* (Boston: The Boston Music Company, G. Schirmer, 1913), p. 151.

17. Cited in Richard Lewis, *In Praise of Music* (New York: Orion Press, 1963), p. 31.

18. In Richard Lewis, *In Praise of Music*, p. 72.

19. Paul Bekker, *The Story of Music: An Historical Sketch of the Changes in Musical Form* (New York: W. W. Norton, 1927), p. 196.

20. Ibid, pp. 196 and 199.

21. Ibid, p. 200.

22. Interview with Steven Heliotes. Chicago, 1984.

23. Interview with Steven Heliotes. Chicago, 1984.

24. Interview with Steven Heliotes. Chicago, 1984.

25. Interview with Steven Heliotes. Chicago, 1984.

26. Interview with Steven Heliotes. Chicago, 1984.

27. Interview with Steven Heliotes. Chicago, 1984.

28. Glenn Plaskin, *Horowitz*, p. 350.

29. Cited in Neville Cardus, *Talking of Music* (London: Collins, 1957), p. 16.

30. In Neville Cardus, *Talking of Music*, p. 215.

Chapter 7

1. "Concert Pianist Visiting S.L. Praises Western Hospitality," *Salt Lake Telegram*, 1937.

2. Paul Rosenfeld, *Musical Chronicle: 1917–1923* (New York: Harcourt Brace, 1923), p. 62.

3. Maurice H. Cottle to Gitta Gradova, Chicago, letter undated.

4. Maurice H. Cottle to Gitta Gradova, Chicago, letter undated.

5. Harold Schonberg, *Horowitz* (New York: Simon and Schuster, 1992), pp. 122–123.

6. Edmund White, "The Past Recaptured," *Los Angeles Times Book Review*, 6 August 2000, p. 7.

7. See, for example, M. F. Basch, *Doing Psychotherapy* (New York: Basic Books, 1980; and *Understanding Psychotherapy: The Science Behind the Art* (New York: Basic Books, 1988).

8. Michael Oakeshott, "A Place of Learning," in *The Voice of Liberal Learning: Michael Oakeshott on Education* (New Haven: Yale University Press, 1989).

9. Felton Earls and Mary Carlson, "Towards Sustainable Development for American Families," *Daedalus* 1, 122 (Winter 1993): 93–122.

10. Alice Miller, *The Drama of the Gifted Child*, trans., Ruth Ward (New York: Basic Books, 1981); Heinz Kohut, *Search for the Self*, ed., Paul Ornstein, vol. 2 (New York: International Universities Press, 1978).

11. Sue Erikson Bloland, "Fame: The Power and Cost of a Fantasy," *Atlantic* (November 1999): 51–60.

12. Rollo May, *The Discovery of Being* (New York: W. W. Norton, 1983).

13. Cited in Vivian Gornick, "Fatal Attraction," *Los Angeles Times Book Review*, 16 September 2001, pp. 1–2.

14. Abraham Veinus, *The Concerto* (Garden City, NJ: Doubleday, 1944), p. 152.

15. Henry T. Finck, *Success in Music: And How it is Won* (New York: Charles Scribner's Sons, 1913), p. 22.

16. Romain Rolland, *Jean-Christophe*, vol. 4, no. 41, cited in Marc Pincherle, *The World of the Virtuoso*, trans., Lucille H. Brockway (New York: W. W. Norton, 1963), pp. 16–17.

17. Cited in Richard Sennett, "Pianists in their Time: A Memoir," in *The Lives of the Piano*, ed., James R. Gaines (New York: Holt, Rinehart and Winston, 1981), p. 194.

18. In Henry T. Finck, *Success in Music*, pp. 19–20.

19. Cited in Josef Hofmann, *Piano Playing* (New York: The McClure Company, 1908), p. 54.

20. Cited in Robert Charles Marsh, *Toscanini and the Art of Orchestral Performance* (New York: Lippincott, 1954), p. 58.

21. Interview with Charles Olin, January 1985.

22. John Redfield, *Music: A Science and an Art* (New York: Tudor Publishing Company, 1949), p. 155.

23. Adolph Kullak, *The Aesthetics of Pianoforte-Playing* (New York: Schirmer, 1893), p. 32.

24. Neville Cardus, *Talking of Music* (London: Collins, 1957), p. 16.

25. In Josef Hofmann, *Piano Playing*, p. 55.

26. Ibid., p. 55.

27. Anthony Storr, *Music and the Mind* (New York: Ballantine, 1992), p. 66.

28. Cited in Arthur Loesser, *Men, Women and Pianos: A Social History* (New York: Dover Publications, 1954), p. 607.

29. Interview with Steven Heliotes, 1984

30. Cited in Arthur Elson, *The Book of Musical Knowledge* (Boston: Houghton Mifflin, 1927), p. 469.

31. Abram Chasins, *Speaking of Pianists* (New York: Knopf, 1961), p. 257.

32. Cecil Smith, *Worlds of Music* (Philadelphia: Lippincott, 1952), p. 111.

33. Jack Goodman, "Genius Quest: The Lively Arts," *Salt Lake Telegram*, 4 January 1947.

34. Reported in *New York Times*, 27 November 1947.

35. Reported in *New York Times*, 13 May 1949.

36. Reported in *New York Times*, 28 March 1962, and 19 May 1962.

37. See Helen Epstein, "The Exquisite Agony of a Musical Olympics," *New York Times*, 6 June 1976, sect. 2, p. 1ff.

38. Ibid., p. 19.

39. Gary Graffman, *I Really Should Be Practicing* (Garden City, NY: Doubleday, 1981), p. 144.

40. Joan Last, *Interpretation for the Piano Student* (New York: Oxford University Press, 1960), p. 1.

41. Cited in Leon Wieseltier, "Get Smart: Lionel Trilling's Exhilarating Pursuit of Moral Realism," *Los Angeles Times Book Review*, 11 June 2000, pp. 4–5.

42. Henry T. Finck, *Success in Music*, pp. 423–424.

43. Interview with Charles Olin, January 1985.

44. E. F. Bartholomew, *Relation of Psychology to Music* (Rock Island, IL: The New Era Publishing Company, 1902), pp. 26–27.

45. In Henry T. Finck, *Success in Music*, p. 24.

46. Neville Cardus, *Talking of Music*, p. 231.

47. Romain Rolland, *Some Musicians of Former Days*, trans., Mary Blaiklock (London: Kegan Paul, Trench, n.d.), p. 21.

48. Harold C. Schonberg, *The Great Pianists: From Mozart to the Present* (New York: Simon and Schuster, 1987), p. 35.

49. *The Etude,* 36, no. 112 (November 1918): 689.

50. See for example, Michael Gurian, *The Wonder of Girls: Understanding the Hidden Nature of Our Daughters* (New York: Pocket Books, 2002).

51. Letter from Maurice H. Cottle to Gitta Gradova, Chicago, undated.

52. Letter from Maurice H. Cottle to Gitta Gradova, Chicago, undated.

53. Letter from Maurice H. Cottle to Gitta Gradova, Chicago, undated.

54. Gitta Gradova to Maurice H. Cottle, undated.

55. See also David B. Morris, "About Suffering: Voice, Genre, and Moral Community," *Daedalus,* Winter, 1996, vol. 125, number 1, pp. 25–46.

56. Allan Young, "Suffering and the Origins of Traumatic Memory," *Daedalus* 125, no. 1 (Winter 1996): 258.

57. Cited in Ernest Wolf, *Treating the Self: Elements of Clinical Self Psychology* (New York: Guilford, 1988), p. 78.

58. William Pollock, *Real Boys* (New York: Henry Holt, 1998).

59. Carl Engel, "Harking Back and Looking Forward," in *From Bach to Stravinsky: The History of Music by its Foremost Critics,* Ed., David Ewen (New York: W. W. Norton, 1933), p. 356.

60. Tobias Matthay, *Musical Interpretation: Its Laws and Principles, and their Application in Teaching and Performing* (Boston: The Boston Music Company, G. Schirmer, 1913), pp. 148 and 151.

61. In Richard Lewis, ed., *In Praise of Music* (New York: Orion Press, 1963), p. 68.

62. In George Upton and Felix Borowski, *The Standard Concert Guide* (New York: Blue Ribbon, 1940), pp. 350–306.

63. Henry T. Finck, *Success in Music,* p. 19.

64. Ibid., p. 20.

65. Ibid., p. 18.

66. Interview with Charles Olin, January 1985.

Chapter 8

1. See for example, Robert Burton, *The Anatomy of Melancholy* (New York: New York Review of Books, Classic Series, 2001).

2. Erich Fromm, *Escape from Freedom* (New York: Farrar and Rinehart, 1941).

3. Carl Engel, "Harking Back and Looking Forward," in *From Bach to Stravinsky: The History of Music by its Foremost Critics,* ed., David Ewen (New York: W. W. Norton, 1933), pp. 350–351.

4. "The Bulletin," *Concert Management Arthur Judson, Inc.,* New York, 1 May 1929, p. 4.

5. Cecil Smith, *Worlds of Music* (Philadelphia: Lippincott, 1952), p. 101.

6. Henry T. Finck, *Success in Music And How it is Won* (New York: Charles Scribner's Sons, 1913), p. 424.

7. Harold C. Schonberg, *Horowitz* (New York: Simon and Schuster, 1992).

8. Henry T. Finck, *Success in Music*, p. 423.

9. H. Miller, "Study of Literature The Ideal Tonic for the Pianist, Says Gitta Gradova," *Musical America*, 31 January 1925, p. 37.

10. Ibid., p. 37.

11. Cited in Sophie Freud, *My Three Mothers and Other Passions* (New York: New York University Press, 1988), p. 177. The reference to Alice Miller is to *The Drama of the Gifted Child*, trans., Ruth Ward (New York: Basic Books, 1981).

Chapter 9

1. Howard Gardner, *Frames of Mind: The Theory of Multiple Intelligences* (New York: Basic Books, 1983).

2. Adolph Kullak, *The Aesthetics of Pianoforte-Playing* (New York: Schirmer, 1898), p. 99.

3. James Francis Cooke, *Great Pianists on Piano Playing* (Philadelphia: Philadelphia Press, 1917; Mineola, NY: Dover Press, 1999), p. 176.

4. E. F. Bartholomew, *Relation of Psychology to Music* (Rock Island, IL: The New Era Publishing Company, 1902), p. 77.

5. Ibid., p. 77.

6. Daniel Gregory Mason, "The Periods of Musical History," in *From Bach to Stravinsky: The History of Music by its Foremost Critics*, ed., David Ewen (New York: W. W. Norton, 1933), p. 17.

7. Aaron Copland, *What to Listen for in Music* (New York: New American Library, 1957), p. 20.

8. Anthony Storr, *Music and the Mind* (New York: Ballantine, 1992), pp. 133–134.

9. Ibid, p. 100.

10. Edward Hirsch, *The Demon and the Angel: Searching for the Source of Artistic Expression* (New York: Harcourt, Brace and World, 2002).

11. H. Miller, "Study of Literature The Ideal Tonic for the Pianist, Says Gitta Gradova," *Musical America*, 31 January 1925, p. 37.

12. Paul Valéry, "Sketch for a Eulogy on Virtuosity," speech delivered in commemoration of the death of Niccolò Paganini, May 27, 1940. Cited in Marc Pincherle, *The World of the Virtuoso*, trans., Lucille H. Brockway (New York: W. W. Norton, 1963), p. 36.

13. Paul Rosenfeld, *Musical Chronicle: 1917–1923* (New York: Harcourt, Brace and Company, 1923), pp. 236–237.

14. Letter from Maurice H. Cottle to Gitta Gradova. Chicago, 1926.

15. Augustus Y. Napier and Carl A. Whitaker, *The Family Crucible* (New York: Harper and Row, 1978).

16. Murray Bowen, *Family Therapy in Clinical Practice* (New York: Jason Aronson, 1978).

Chapter 10

1. New York, *New York American*, November 1923.

2. In Henry T. Finck, *Success in Music and How it is Won* (New York: Charles Scribner's Sons, 1913), p. 23.

3. In contrast, see Dr. Annie W. Patterson, "Preparing for a Recital," *The Etude* 17, no. 9 (September, 1925): 624.

4. Abram Chasins, *Speaking of Pianists* (New York: Knopf, 1961).

5. Interview with Charles Olin, Chicago, 1985.

6. Interview with Charles Olin, Chicago, 1985.

7. Interview with Charles Olin, Chicago, 1985.

8. Interview with Charles Olin, Chicago, 1985.

9. Interview with Charles Olin, Chicago, 1985.

10. Interview with Charles Olin, Chicago, 1985.

11. Letter from Shura Cherkassky to a man named Steven. Regent's Park, London, 30 April 1985.

12. Letter from Shura Cherkassky to a man named Steven. Regent's Park, London, 8 May 1985.

13. Letter from Shura Cherkassky to a man named Steven. Regent's Park, London, 30 April 1985.

About the Author

$$\sim\sim\infty\sim\sim$$

Thomas J. Cottle is professor of education at Boston University. He has written 30 books, published in several languages, and more than 550 essays and reviews, which have appeared in professional, literary, and religious journals as well as in publications such as the *New York Times*, the *London Times*, the *Washington Post*, the *Boston Globe*, the *Atlantic Monthly*, *Harper's*, the *New Republic*, and *Psychology Today*. He has appeared on *Good Morning America*, *Today*, *Face the Nation*, and the *Charlie Rose Show*, and he has hosted his own shows on PBS. He is the recipient of a Young Psychologist award, a Guggenheim Fellowship, a citation from *Parents' Choice* magazine, and a career contribution award from the Massachusetts Psychological Association. Dr. Cottle is married to Kay Mikkelsen Cottle, a high school teacher. They live in Brookline, Massachusetts, and have three adult children and three grandchildren.

Other Books by

Thomas J. Cottle

———— ⚜ ————

For more information, go to www.thomascottle.com